LEARNING TO READ

Solving Problems in the Teaching of Literacy

Cathy Collins Block, *Series Editor*

Engaging Young Readers:
Promoting Achievement and Motivation
Edited by Linda Baker, Mariam Jean Dreher, and John T. Guthrie

Word Journeys:
Assessment-Guided Phonics, Spelling, and Vocabulary Instruction
Kathy Ganske

Learning to Read:
Lessons from Exemplary First-Grade Classrooms
*Michael Pressley, Richard L. Allington, Ruth Wharton-McDonald,
Cathy Collins Block, and Lesley Mandel Morrow*

LEARNING TO READ
Lessons from Exemplary
First-Grade Classrooms

Michael Pressley
Richard L. Allington
Ruth Wharton-McDonald
Cathy Collins Block
Lesley Mandel Morrow

THE GUILFORD PRESS
New York   London

KH

Printed in the United States of America

This book is printed on acid-free paper.

Last digit is print number: 9 8 7 6 5 4 3

Library of Congress Cataloging-in-Publication Data

Learning to read : lessons from exemplary first-grade classrooms / Michael Pressley . . . [et al.].
       p.   cm. — (Solving problems in the teaching of literacy)
    Includes index.
    ISBN 1-57230-648-3 (hard) — ISBN 1-57230-649-1 (pbk.)
       1. Reading (Primary) — Case studies. 2. First grade (Education) — Case studies. I. Pressley, Michael. II. Series.
    LB1525 .L36 2001
    372.4—dc21   2001018802

10/25/04

About the Authors

Michael Pressley, PhD, is the Notre Dame Chair in Catholic Education and Professor of Psychology at the University of Notre Dame. He is an expert in comprehension processing and in primary-level reading education, which is related to his career-long research on children's learning. He has published about 250 articles, chapters, and books. His most recent research involves exploration of how literacy can be motivated in classrooms.

Richard L. Allington, PhD, is the Irving and Rose Fien Professor of Education at the University of Florida, where he continues the study of exemplary elementary teaching.

Ruth Wharton-McDonald, PhD, is currently Assistant Professor in the Department of Education at the University of New Hampshire. Dr. Wharton-McDonald's research interests focus on the school literacy experiences of young children. She has collaborated with several of the other authors in this book on studies of exemplary teachers and their students. She is currently involved in a study of first graders' perspectives on schooling.

Cathy Collins Block, PhD, has served on the graduate faculty of Texas Christian University since 1977. She has taught at Southern Illinois University–Carbondale, served as Research Assistant at the

Wisconsin Research and Development Center for Cognitive Development, and taught kindergarten through high school in private and public schools. Dr. Block has directed and served as principal investigator of six nationally funded research projects and is presently serving on or has served on the board of directors for a number of organizations, including the National Center for Research and Training for Learning Disabilities and the National Reading Conference.

Lesley Mandel Morrow, PhD, is Professor and Chair of the Department of Learning and Teaching at the Graduate School of Education at Rutgers University, where she is coordinator of the PhD program in Literacy. She began her career as a classroom teacher and later became a reading specialist. Her area of research deals with early literacy development with an emphasis on physical and social contexts to motivate reading. Dr. Morrow has more than 200 publications to her credit. Her articles have appeared in journals such as *Reading Research Quarterly, Journal of Educational Psychology,* and *The Reading Teacher.* Her most recent books are *Literacy Development in the Early Years: Helping Children Read and Write* (2001, 4th edition) and *The Literacy Center: Contexts for Reading and Writing.* She received the Rutgers University awards for research, teaching, and service and the International Reading Association's Outstanding Teacher Educator or Reading Award from Fordham University. She also served as an elected member of the International Reading Association.

Preface

This book is about something that happened to every one of its readers. It is about first grade. Thus, one reason it makes sense to write a book about first grade is because of its universality. A book about first grade especially makes sense, however, because there has been so much debate about what first grade should be like, with special attention in recent years to the impact of first grade on literacy achievement.

Much of the discussion about first grade has been accusatory, with policymakers and parents sometimes blaming Johnny's and Janey's failures to learn how to read on what goes on in first grade. This book does not continue in that tradition. It is not about what is wrong with first grade. Rather, this book is about what first grade is like when it is done well. It is intended to inform elementary teachers who are now teaching grade 1 or who may teach it in the future. Even so, we expect that elementary school administrators, school board members, and parents will find much in the volume that can be helpful in informing them about what grade 1 is like when it is excellent.

To accomplish our purposes, we developed three types of chapters. The first part of the book provides a history of grade-1 literacy instructional practices, as well as a review of important research contributing to our understanding of contemporary grade-1 literacy instruction. Some of the most important findings in this first section are fleshed out in the second part, which is a set of five case studies of exemplary grade-1 teachers. These case studies illustrate well the nature of first grade when student engagement and achievement are high. The third part of the book considers the implications of the research summarized in the volume, particularly with respect to the preparation of first-grade teachers in the future.

What emerges from this volume is an envisionment of first grade that is different from all the currently popular models, different from all the rather extreme conceptions of the nature of first grade. For example, good first grades include most of the elements of whole-language approaches to primary-level literacy—including good literature and much student writing. But good first grades comprise much more, including substantial, systematic skills instruction. Unlike the first-grade experiences favored by some advocates of skills instruction, however, it is not all skills instruction in good first grades. Rather, skills are learned and practiced as children grapple with good literature and compose their first stories. What emerges from this volume is an envisionment of first grade at its best.

Also emerging from this volume is a description of the first-grade experience as being very complicated, with many components articulated in the creation of classroom wholes that are much more than the sums of the parts. There is no quick fix that follows from what is reported in this volume. Rather, what follows from the analyses presented here is that the great first-grade teacher must have a commanding knowledge of classroom management; sound-, letter-, and word-level skills; children's literature; a variety of approaches to pedagogy (e.g., direct instruction, scaffolding, writers' workshop); and academic motivation. The excellent first-grade teacher combines these components every day, with expertise as impressive as that of a circus juggler riding a unicycle on a high wire without a net below. This book is about complex instruction.

Much of the work summarized and featured in this volume was supported by the U.S. Department of Education through its Office of Educational Research and Improvement (OERI). Some of the work was sponsored by the National Reading Research Center, headquartered at the Universities of Maryland and Georgia from 1992 until 1997. The more recent work was supported by Grant No. R305A60005 to the National Research Center on English Learning and Achievement. The Center is headquartered at the University at Albany, State University of New York, and the University of Wisconsin–Madison.

The researchers are very grateful to the participating schools and teachers across the country that have been involved in this work, and the coauthors of the volume are especially happy that a few of the very best teachers we have studied are featured in the case studies part of this book. What was frustrating to us in composing this volume, however, was that it became quite apparent that there are no words to describe well the excellent teaching we have been privileged to study in these teachers' classrooms. We hope that the words we have been able to pen about these classrooms will create in you, the reader, an image of what first grade should be like for all children. We also hope that this envisionment is the start of activities that will result in an increasing number of first grades being like the excellent first grades that are the focus of this book.

Contents

Part I

First Grade: History and Contemporary Practice

The first four chapters provide an overview of what is known about grade 1, especially in regard to literacy instruction, both as it is now and how learning to read has been conceived in the past. A historical perspective is important, for much of what is now grade-1 reading instruction is very different from what was experienced by many readers of this volume when they were 6. Within any historical era, including the present, there has always been variability between classrooms, with some first grades teaching reading one way and others another way. It is contended in the chapters that follow that such variability can provide important clues about the nature of excellent grade-1 instruction, especially when some types of instruction produce greater engagement and achievement than others. In fact, most of this first part and the parts that follow are dedicated to detailing first-grade instruction that seems to work especially well.

1

A Brief History of First-Grade Reading Instruction

This is a book about a common phenomenon in modern life: the teaching of reading in first grade. Except for children who are schooled at home, just about everyone experiences first grade. Moreover, an important goal in every first-grade classroom is to get children reading. This is such an important goal that it is impossible to walk into a first-grade classroom on any morning of the school year and not be immersed in literacy development experiences. And it has been that way for as long as there has been first grade (Smith, 1986).

This first chapter is about what everyone who studies first-grade reading knows about first-grade reading instruction. This is to set the stage to present our recent work on first-grade reading, for the conclusions we offer about first-grade reading based on our recent research contrast somewhat with what was known about beginning reading instruction before we began the work summarized in this book. Indeed, the effective beginning reading instruction now being offered is very different from the traditional instruction offered as beginning reading lessons in the past three millennia—that is, at any time in the history of the teaching of reading.

A LONG HISTORY OF BEGINNING READING INSTRUCTION

With the invention of the alphabet by the Phoenicians and its adaptations by the Greeks and Romans came the task of teaching people how to read. For most of the 3,000-year history of reading, reading instruction began with letter-level skills, the students typically learning the letters and their names, acquiring letter–sound associations next, followed by learning how to read syllables, and then progressively more complex words (Mathews, 1966; Smith, 1986). There is definitely nothing new about a skills-first approach to reading instruction.

It is only in the past century and a half that beginning with something other than letters was tried. In the mid-19th century, the word method was offered as an alternative in North America (Mathews, 1966; Smith, 1986), with students taught some sight words before they received any instruction on the component letters. The argument was made then that reading whole words was more natural than learning letter sounds and blending them, consistent with the position that the child always experiences objects and events in the world as wholes before there is any analytical understanding of objects or events (e.g., a cow is understood as a whole cow long before it is understood as a number of interacting biological systems). There is definitely nothing new about the argument that focusing beginning literacy instruction on wholes is more natural than focusing it on letter- and sound-level parts.

Before the 20th century, all claims about reading instruction were based on philosophical commitments rather than scientific analyses. It was only at the beginning of the 20th century that scientific analyses of reading and beginning reading instruction began to appear as part of the earliest efforts in experimental psychology (Smith, 1986). In general, scientific analyses in the early 20th century favored skills-first approaches over holistic approaches. Thus, scientific analyses favoring skills-first are nothing new. Even though the early scientific work on beginning reading was not wholly supportive of whole-word approaches, whole-word instruction thrived for most of the 20th century.

Although educators have been aware for centuries that some students learn to read with more difficulty than others, the scientific approaches to measurement developed in the 20th century permitted more exacting specification of reading difficulties. The concept of learning disabilities (i.e., some students have very specific learning deficiencies) is an invention of the later 20th century, yet the concept of dyslexia is about a century old. All who study beginning literacy development have recognized, over their entire lives, the existence of students who are very hard to teach to read—students with dyslexia.

For centuries, beginning reading instruction has also been about more than beginning reading. Religious and ethical instruction has often been prominent in beginning reading, with the earliest reading instructional materials filled with religious ideas. For example, young readers used to learn how to read using a wooden paddle-shaped hornbook. The most important material on the hornbook was laid out in the shape of a cross, and some hornbooks also included the Lord's Prayer and the Creed. Postcolonial-era materials in the United States were filled with readings designed to inspire patriotism and devotion to the new nation (Smith, 1986; Venezky, 1986). Since the mid-19th century, reading materials have often included subject matter appropriate to scientific, cultural, and literary content that elementary students were expected to learn. Thus, current reading materials that connect to other aspects of the curriculum are nothing new, although the new content-rich reading materials contrast decidedly with the beginning reading materials experienced by the authors of this book when they were going through school.

In summary, beginning reading instruction is an ancient art, being informed by science only in the 20th century. Like most artists, however, those interested in beginning reading have not always been persuaded by scientific analyses of reading, even when such analyses certainly could be informative. Reading instructionalists have often been more persuaded by philosophy, including the arguments about the naturalism of whole-word approaches that informed the reading instruction that the authors of this book experienced as first graders a few decades ago.

FIRST-GRADE READING INSTRUCTION AT MIDCENTURY: HOW WE REMEMBER IT

The authors of this book experienced a form of reading instruction that has been elevated to heroic status in some nostalgic accounts of education (Kismaric & Heiferman, 1996) and condemned as the reason for "Why Johnny Can't Read" by others (Flesch, 1955, 1981).

All of the authors of this book went through grade 1 in the late 1940s or in the 1950s, except for Ruth Wharton-McDonald, who experienced the same type of instruction in the early 1970s. We have memories of Dick and Jane, the brother and sister featured in the most popular first-grade reading series of that era, published by Scott Foresman. We remember experiencing the preprimers when we entered first grade, which were books filled with pictures, intended to stimulate picture comprehension skills. They also included exercises aimed at stimulating visual discrimination capacities. And, of course, they provided an opportunity to learn some basic print concepts, such as how to hold a book and that books proceeded from front to back and left to right. The preprimers were followed by primers, including several short paperback readers; then came the first hardbound book that was ever presented to us in school, *Fun with Dick and Jane*. Not all children of that era experienced Dick and Jane, but 80% of American kids did. Those who did not were immersed in similar worlds, reading about life in Alice and Jerry's neighborhood, Ned and Nancy's world, or Susan and Tom's adventures. Every American child growing up at midcentury had an opportunity to read about a dominant, all-American boy and his pretty, bright-eyed, second-banana sister (Staiger, 1958).

Like others, we experienced classes with three reading groups, dubbed, for example, the Rockets, the Jets, and the Racers. Reading group meetings often began with a lesson on the new words that would be in the story of the day. Consistent with the Scott Foresman reading philosophy, the emphasis was on whole words rather than phonics, with phonics not taught at all until about 50 sight words had been introduced in the program. Even then, this analytic phonics was a backup strategy, with look–say the predominant method of developing word recognition skills in students experiencing the Dick-and-Jane approach. After we repetitively read the words from the board as a group, we would preview the story, usually by looking at the pictures, at least on the first few pages of the story. This was an important part of reading group because so much of the story was told by the pictures, and Scott Foresman's series (like its competitors) emphasized that an understanding of the story included understanding the actions and feelings of the characters as presented in the illustrations. We remember vividly how our teachers urged us to think about what the characters in the Dick-and-Jane stories were doing and what they might be thinking. Our first-grade classrooms were filled with artifacts, including Halloween, Christmas, and Valentine's Day cards from the brother and sister, that made it easy to imagine that Dick and Jane were real children. The illustrations in the stories were very lifelike, at least to young, white, middle-class students, and very memorable, easily stimulating our imaginations to believe that somewhere life might really be like it was in the Dick-and-Jane stories.

As charming as the pictures and stories were, the center of the Dick-and-Jane approach was the high-frequency sight words, with a few hundred introduced in each of the first three grades, summing to about 1,700 words by the end of grade 3. Consistent with behavioral psychology, which was prominent during that time, the sight words were repeated many times, with the assumption that children's recognition of them would improve and become more automatic with each successive repetition. This became known as a controlled vocabulary approach.

Following the introduction of sight words and the picture preview came the main part of the small-group lesson, round-robin reading, with each member of the group getting a chance to read some small part of the story. This provided the teacher with a daily opportunity to monitor how reading development was progressing, with reading development defined as oral reading skill. We still remember who struggled with round-robin reading and who did not. We also came to understand that being in the Rockets group in grade 1 predicted success in the later grades, whereas the Racers would struggle to keep up throughout the grade school years until they ended up losing the race by being assigned to the lower tracks in junior and senior high school. That is, we knew from the experiences of childhood what researchers such as Connie Juel (1988) would document years later, that reading difficulties in grade 1 predict reading difficulties in subsequent years.

The reading group often concluded with a seat work assignment from the *Think-and-Do* book. The directions for each *Think-and-Do* workbook page were printed on the side, and the most visible evidence of the teacher's great reading skill was that she could read those directions, which were printed in very tiny print, with great ease. Students who did not pay careful attention to the directions when they were covered at the end of the reading group lesson could be in big trouble, for there was no cooperative learning in those days. Every student returned to her or his desk and worked alone on the *Think-and-Do* book assignments.

Behaviorism flourished in American classrooms at that time. Sticker charts were common. Thus, when a *Think-and-Do* page was completed absolutely correctly, the teacher would prominently mark a "100" on the top of the page with a red pencil and award a sticker to the student, who could then place it on the sticker chart that was publicly displayed in the classroom. The same children who shone during round-robin reading had their names on charts overflowing with stickers. Another lesson we soon learned was that no matter how reading was measured, the same kids always did well and the same kids always fared poorly.

Literacy development really seemed to be centered on the teacher during that era, with the series designed to give the teacher a large role in the process. The teacher's edition provided a great deal of guidance about how to present each lesson, including how vocabulary should be covered, what aspects of the pictures should be pointed out to the students, and what questions about character actions should be asked. The centrality of the teacher in the learning process was reinforced by the practice of not permitting a Dick-and-Jane reading book to go home until the entire book was completed. At that point, members of the reading group could take the book home for one night and were urged to read to Mom and Dad to show them how much they had learned. Teachers seemed to frown on much more involvement by parents, especially in respect to reading with children from the Dick-and-Jane reader. One of us recalled a classmate getting in trouble because his parents had obtained a set of readers and was permitting him to read ahead at home. The teacher scolded the youngster for ruining a story for everyone else in the class by telling other members of the reading group how it ended. The teacher admonished the child not to read any more stories from the reader at home. Reading Dick and Jane was an at-school thing, something done during reading group rather than at any other time, something done under the direction of the teacher, who acted on prompts in the teacher's edition.

One of us (Michael Pressley) recalled a harsh lesson learned in connection with the *Think-and-Do* books. When a first-grade reader was completed, so was the *Think-and-Do* book that accompanied it. One member of the reading group asked what would happen to the completed *Think-and-Do* books. The teacher explained that she would burn them. This was a first lesson that there was not much value in doing workbook work.

None of us could remember ever writing our own stories in first grade. Composing was just not something that first-grade children did during the late 1940s and 1950s. In those days, first-grade writing meant learning to print. Just as the behaviorists convinced teachers of the benefits of dispensing stickers, they also convinced them that printing skills largely involved the development of motor habits, and thus there was lots of repetitive practice in printing letters (Thornton, 1996). The *Think-and-Do* books were largely aimed at developing the eyes, by including many visual discrimination exercises, which presumably improved visual processing of whole words; writing instruction was more penmanship than composition and was aimed at developing the motor control required to write words. First grade in the 1940s and 1950s was much about the development of very basic skills and habits.

None of the authors of this book could remember anyone in the class ever looking at the Dick-and-Jane readers when there was free-choice reading. Although classroom libraries were not nearly as extensive as they are today, that was where we looked for something to read when there were free moments. That is not to say that the content of the Dick-and-Jane readers was not meaty. In fact, the stories were intended to teach many great lessons of life, consistent with a long history of American reading instruction aimed at developing the moralities and sensibilities of children (Smith, 1986). Kismaric and Heiferman (1996) offered the following list of life lessons conveyed by the Dick-and-Jane stories: Respect your parents, help your siblings, cooperate, families have fun when they work together, play is valuable, use your imagination, don't complain, be kind to animals, help others, be enthusiastic, take chances, be considerate, share what you have, amuse yourself, be like your parents, be curious, work hard at your job, mind your manners, be creative, all people are equal, be self-assured, express what you feel, appreciate nature, be proud of your accomplishments, behave in the car and on the bus, work and play well with others, the older you are the more you should do, take school seriously, cleverness is rewarded, clean up after yourself, follow directions and rules, ask permission when you're in doubt, watch out for the safety of others, accept other people's limitations, be nice to people, encourage others, keep your sense of humor, and reading is good. If we do not remember every one of these life lessons, none of the authors of this book had any trouble recalling that our first-grade reading lessons were filled with messages about how to be better human beings. Years later, all of us were a little surprised to learn that the Dick-and-Jane approach was so very controversial, but one of the things that every reading researcher knows is that the Dick-and-Jane whole-word method set off a firestorm of debate.

WHY JOHNNY CAN'T READ

In 1955, Rudolf Flesch wrote a book about beginning reading that made the bestseller list. *Why Johnny Can't Read and What You Can Do about It* was a well-written, unapologetic attack on the whole-word method, which Flesch blamed for what he perceived to be a national epidemic of reading failure at the time. The book was exceptionally pro-phonics, reviewing the research literature comparing phonics and whole-word instruction, with Flesch concluding that phonics won in every comparison. The book included 86 pages of material that parents could use to teach their children to read with phonics and thus do what Dick and Jane, and the schools hosting Dick and Jane, were not doing. The book was exceptionally disrespectful of teachers, reading specialists, and curriculum developers associated with the basal reader publishers. Even so, the book got a lot of attention then and still does, for it remains in print and can be found in most of the large chain bookstores.

THE GREAT DEBATE CONTINUES

Jeanne Chall's (1967) classic book, *Learning to Read: The Great Debate*, went far in finishing off whole-word, look–say approaches, such as those used in the Dick-and-Jane reading series. In this book, Chall reviewed a great deal of work conducted throughout the 20th century related to beginning reading instruction. Chall made a strong case for synthetic phonics instruction, which involves teaching children letter–sound associations as well as teaching them to blend the sounds of letters to pronounce words. In particular, she made the case that synthetic phonics instruction was more effective than whole-word, or look–say, approaches to beginning reading. Synthetic phonics won out over look–say in respect to a number of measures, including word recognition and oral reading. To be certain, there were advantages to look–say, including better comprehension and vocabulary during first grade. Moreover, look–say first graders tended to read faster than students receiving synthetic phonics instruction, but it was at the price of accuracy.

Advocates of look–say could point to the fact that their approach did include phonics instruction, but it was a different type of phonics than presented by the synthetic approach. Students reading Dick and Jane first learned words as sight words, with analysis of those words into their component sounds performed after each sight word was learned as a whole. This approach was dubbed "intrinsic phonics" by Chall, although it is also sometimes referred to as analytic phonics. The problem for advocates of intrinsic phonics was that it did not fare very well in comparison with synthetic phonics, particularly because students receiving synthetic phonics were able to recognize more words than those taught by the look–say method. One of the most important conclusions emerging from the Chall (1967) analysis was that even though synthetic phonics produced superior achievement with children across the achievement spectrum, its advantage for students with lower academic achievement was especially pronounced.

The publication of Chall's book was a landmark event, offering a synthesis of a great deal of the research produced until that point. After its appearance in 1967, there would be no more editions of Dick and Jane. Scott Foresman's final edition of that series was published in 1965, and its sales ended in 1970. If Chall's synthesis was not *the* nail in the coffin for look–say, as defined by Dick-and-Jane-type books, it was one of the nails, with another one also appearing in print in 1967, the published report of a study that very much influenced Chall's thinking as she composed her book, a study in which she had participated as a contributor.

THE FIRST-GRADE STUDIES

The First-Grade Studies were a valiant attempt to settle once and for all which method of beginning reading instruction worked best (Graves & Dykstra, 1997). This series of large-scale comparisons was conceived in the early 1960s, with the goal of the U.S. Department of Education to fund a number of coordinated investigations aimed at understanding beginning reading methods. Guy Bond, a professor at the University of Minnesota, was selected as the coordinator, with 27 studies funded as part of the research program. The individual investigations occurred at different sites, with the common denominator being that all of the studies focused on approaches to beginning reading. A diversity of methods and problems were studied, as reflected in the titles of the separate investigations (see Table 1.1). Even so, the coordination of the projects permitted some comparability across projects and sites.

A variety of analyses were conducted within and across studies, with 15 studies in particular used to construct comparisons of the efficacy of the most visible approaches to beginning reading of the day: basals, basal plus phonics, the initial teaching alphabet (i.e., an approach based on an altered alphabet, with one distinct letter for each of the 44 sounds of English), the linguistic approach (i.e., an approach emphasizing meaning and syntactic structures), the language experience approach (i.e., an approach that included a great deal of student composition of stories through dictation, with reading instruction based on teacher transcriptions of students' compositions), and a combined phonics and linguistic approach.

Coming to conclusions by summarizing across studies carried out in so many different settings and for so many particular purposes was challenging. However, it was aided by the agreement of all the investigators to collect certain measures and to record these data in particular formats (i.e., in the particular fields of two computer cards, with one pair of cards for each student in the study shipped to the University of Minnesota for analyses). There was also an agreement to use a common control approach, conventional basal instruction, although this admittedly varied from site to site because not every school used Dick and Jane, inasmuch as competitors had penetrated 20% of the market. Even so, there was enough commonality across the basal series for the collaborators in the First-Grade Studies to believe they had a common benchmark.

The First-Grade Studies proved anything but straightforward to interpret, although there were some strong interpretations of the studies offered in the marketplace of ideas (Pearson, 1997). The conclusion that had perhaps the greatest impact was that the basal approach was not very powerful relative to its alternatives, and a variety of analyses in the First-Grade Studies supported alternatives to the basal. For example, much was made of the finding that the basal plus phonics produced superior reading achievement as compared

TABLE 1.1. Titles of the Funded First-Grade Studies

1. An Evaluation of Three Approaches to Teaching Reading in First Grade
2. A Study in Depth of First-Grade Reading
3. Comparison of the Basal and the Coordinated Language-Experience Approaches in First-Grade Reading
4. First-Grade Reading Instruction Using Diacritical Marking System, Initial Teaching Alphabet, and Basal Reading System
5. A Study of the Relative Effectiveness of Three Methods of Teaching Reading in Grade One
6. Comparing Reading Approaches in First-Grade Teaching with Disadvantaged Children (the CRAFT Project)
7. An Attempt to Secure Additional Evidence Concerning Factors Affecting Learning to Read
8. Effects of an Intensive In-Service Program on Teachers' Classroom Behavior and Pupils' Reading Achievement
9. A Comparison Between the Effect of Intensive Oral–Aural Spanish Language Instruction and Intensive Oral–Aural English Language Instruction on the Reading Readiness of Spanish-Speaking School Beginners in Grade One
10. A Comparative Study of Two First-Grade Language Arts Programs
11. An Experimental Study of the Group versus One-to-One Instructional Relationship in First-Grade Basal Reading Programs
12. Evaluation of Level Designed Visual–Auditory and Related Writing Methods of Reading Instruction in Grade One
13. A Comparative Study of Reading Achievement under Three Types of Reading Systems at the First-Grade Level
14. First-Grade Reading Using Modified Co-Basal versus the Initial Teaching Alphabet
15. A Study of Approaches to First-Grade English Reading Instruction for Children from Spanish-Speaking Homes
16. A Study of Two Methods of Reading Supervision
17. Reading Achievement in Relation to Growth in Perception of Word Elements in Three Types of Beginning Reading Instruction
18. Evaluation of Three Methods of Teaching First-Grade Reading to Children Likely to Have Difficulty with Reading
19. The Effects of Different Approaches of Initial Instruction on the Reading Achievement of a Selected Group of First-Grade Children
20. The Effects of Four Programs of Reading Instruction with Varying Emphasis on the Regularity of Grapheme–Phoneme Correspondences and the Relation of Language Structure to Meaning on Achievement in First-Grade Reading
21. Comparison of Reading Achievement of First-Grade Children Taught by a Linguistic Approach and a Basal Reader Approach
22. Effect of First-Grade Instruction Using Basal Readers, Modified Linguistic Materials, and Linguistic Readers
23. A Study of a Longitudinal First-Grade Reading Readiness Program
24. Individualized Reading versus a Basal Reader Program at First-Grade Level in Rural Communities
25. Effectiveness of a Language Arts and Basic Reader Approach to First-Grade Reading
26. A Comparison of the Effectiveness of Three Different Basal Reading Systems on the Reading Achievements of First-Grade Children
27. Reading Achievements of First-Grade Boys versus First-Grade Girls Using Two Approaches: A Linguistic Approach and a Basal Reader Approach with Boys' and Girls' Groups Separately

with the basal alone. This superiority occurred on standardized reading measures, and particularly on word recognition measures. This conclusion certainly contributed to the downfall of the sight word basal in the American school, partly because it resonated so well with the rantings of Rudolf Flesch (1955), but also because Chall (1967) interpreted the First-Grade Studies by emphasizing that phonics was a superior approach to the whole-word approach. However, phonics superiority was not the interpretation favored by the authors of the First-Grade Studies (Bond & Dykstra, 1967) or many other interpreters of the investigations (Pearson, 1997).

A conclusion emerging from the First-Grade Studies that also attracted a great deal of attention was that other aspects of educational settings mattered a great deal. That is, the impact of particular programs varied greatly across research sites and projects. One version of this conclusion was that the teacher mattered more than the particular reading program. Such conclusions went far in discouraging much additional work aimed at discovering the one best method of beginning reading instruction. Although, as we discuss later in this chapter, there has been a renaissance of interest in searching for best methods in recent years, there were few studies comparing alternative beginning reading methods during the two decades following the First-Grade Studies.

In summary, the most famous set of investigations of first-grade reading methods ever conducted did not produce a definitive answer to the question, "What is the best method for teaching beginning reading?" The knowledge of this failure is ingrained in the thinking of virtually everyone who has been interested in first-grade reading instruction in the latter part of the 20th century. The First-Grade Studies certainly contributed to the ultimate downfall of the Dick-and-Jane basal, for this set of studies captured a great deal of attention in the educational community. After they appeared, it was hard to defend the adoption of the same old basals in revised form, for if the First-Grade Studies accomplished nothing else, they discredited the Dick-and-Jane approach.

The result in the early 1970s was a rather eclectic reading materials marketplace, with new series appearing that were not Dick and Jane but which retained many of the pedagogical techniques in the old basals. Granted, the stories in these books were more diverse and the controlling of vocabulary was not always as stringent, but they appeared to be more different than they actually were. However, because the First-Grade Studies provided evidence that alternatives to the dominant whole-word approach often produced superior achievement, this was an era of some experimentation in beginning reading instruction. In addition, because of the First-Grade Studies, a series of new research efforts were funded. These new projects often produced new curriculum materials. For instance, it was out of such projects that the *Wisconsin Design for Reading* (WDR), a skills-mastery management system, was developed. Although there were other similar systems, WDR was popular as an attempt to monitor student skill development in beginning reading. The basic framework was a pretest–teach–posttest model. The WDR could be used with virtually any basal reader series to track student development of reading subskills. This was not so much an instructional system as a management system. The emphasis on frequent skills testing and the prominent role assigned to practice worksheets produced very skills-oriented lessons. Likewise, the Sullivan Programmed Readers, the Miami Linguistic Readers, the Economy analytic phonics readers, the Merrill Linguistic Readers, the direct instruction materials marketed as DISTAR, and Individually Prescribed Instruction were touted as research-based reading programs, all with an emphasis on word-level skills development. The classroom emphasis on skills work in isolation, in both reading and writing, led to the criticism that reading and writing activities were largely absent from elementary classrooms (Allington, 1977; Graves, 1978). In addition, this array of new curriculum materials threatened the dominance of the established textbook publishers as never before.

Even so, published reading series would rebound through the 1980s and continue to be prominent in elementary language arts instruction into the 1990s (Canney, 1993; Strickland & Walmsley, 1993). An important alternative approach to beginning reading instruction, however—one that recommended throwing out the basals altogether—began to emerge during the 1970s, gathered momentum in the 1980s, and became predominant in the 1990s.

WHOLE LANGUAGE

Frank Smith's writings, beginning with his 1971 book, *Understanding Reading*, were important in stimulating the development of beginning reading instruction oriented toward making meaning construction the center of such instruction, rather than letter- and sound-level processes (as the phonics enthusiasts would have it) or word-level processes (as the look–say programs advocated). Smith argued that teaching children to sound out words did not make sense, for mature readers did not sound out words, but routinely recognized them without sounding them out. Smith also argued that semantic context cues were very important in word recognition. That is, as readers read a passage, they constructed an understanding of the passage's meaning, with this understanding helping them to recognize words not previously encountered in print. Thus, when a young reader reading "The Three Billy Goats Gruff" encountered the word "bridge" for the first time, the understanding of the story was important in helping the reader decide that the word was "bridge" rather than "bride" or "birds." Of course, the Dick-and-Jane look–say approach also encouraged use of context clues in word recognition, but Smith was going much further. For example, Dick and Jane admitted some teaching of analytic phonics after a sight vocabulary had been acquired. Smith was adamant that the teaching of phonics probably interfered with learning to read rather than facilitated it (e.g., Smith, 1979, p. 138).

Frank Smith was joined by others, including Kenneth Goodman (e.g., 1986), in arguing that learning to read was largely about learning to predict words based on the meaning cues in text, as well as on the reader's prior knowledge. Hence, he described reading as a "psycholinguistic guessing game" (e.g., Goodman, 1996, Chap. 7). Like Smith before him, Goodman adamantly opposed isolating attention on letters and sounds, believing that it oriented readers away from the meaning of text and attention to higher-order language structure (e.g., syntactical structures) and that both meaning and syntactical cues were critical in effective word recognition (e.g., Goodman, 1993).

Although neither Smith nor Goodman actually developed comprehensive descriptions of what they thought beginning reading instruction might look like, Don Holdaway (1979) did. His book, *The Foundations of Literacy,* provided the sort of details (e.g., shared reading as an alternative to isolated vocabulary teaching; predictable, patterned texts as an alternative to vocabulary control in creating early reading materials) needed to begin to reshape first-grade reading instruction from a part-to-whole pedagogy toward a whole-to-part pedagogy that differed substantially from the whole-word pedagogy and beginning reading materials. Likewise, Hansen (1987) offered the reading/writing workshop approach that deeply integrated the processes of learning to read and write and was, in some respects, an extension of the process writing movement popularized by the Bay Area Writing Project.

The writings of Smith, Goodman, Holdaway, and Hansen inspired the development of a set of beginning reading practices that were very different from the Dick-and-Jane approach or phonics approaches (Bergeron, 1990). At the heart of whole-language instruction was the reading of real children's literature, specifically, trade books. Such stories differed from Dick and Jane in more than just content. Most critically, there was anything but controlled vocabulary in children's trade books. At the earliest levels of beginning reading materials, there was an emphasis on attempting to control the difficulty of the stories through the use of "predictable texts." The new texts were not typically authentic children's trade books, but little books specifically written to foster early reading growth. However, traditional forms of vocabulary control—restricting the number of new sight words introduced and providing for the frequent repetition of those words or restricting the new words to vowel rules or patterns already taught—were largely ignored in these new materials (Cunningham, 1989). The emphasis was on creating beginning reading texts that used more natural language patterns while still offering a manageable beginning reading curriculum. Thus, a new feature in the beginning reading curriculum was these predictable texts—texts that attempted to simplify learning to read through a focus on predictable language use, repetition of key phrases, and, often, the use of rhyming patterns. These new curriculum plans also included a much greater emphasis on independent reading and rereading of the new texts, and on children's selecting the books they read.

Constructing an understanding of what was read was emphasized in the whole-language philosophy. A key instructional practice for accomplishing this goal was to emphasize thinking about meaning in order to recognize words in a story. Thus, when a child encountered an unknown word, she or he was urged to think about the story and to look at the pictures, to think about what word would make sense. Letter- and word-level cues (e.g., word shape) were definitely played down, although whole-language teachers and theorists often pointed out that they emphasized the use of multiple cues for word recognition, including semantic, syntactic, and letter/sound-level cues (Adams, 1998). Yet important letter- and sound-level strategies, such as sounding out a word by blending its component sounds, typically were downplayed or ignored in classroom instruction.

Teachers in whole-language classrooms also emphasized children's writing, largely in response to the books and stories read by the children. Writing in whole-language classrooms emphasized conveying meaning, rather than mechanics. For example, children were encouraged to invent spellings, with the transition to conventional spelling occurring over the primary years and being developed as part of writing rather than with traditional spelling lists and tests. Of course, this approach to spelling was consistent with the general whole-language position, that skills are best developed in the context of reading and writing rather than with decontextualized activities, such as with workbooks and worksheets.

Cooperative learning was prominent in whole-language classrooms, with students reading together (e.g., partner reading) and writing together (e.g., reading each other's stories, making suggestions for revision). Thematic units were common in whole-language classrooms, with literacy instruction connected to science and social studies. That is, one of the most attractive features of whole-language classrooms was the emphasis on connections—between students and between ideas.

Such instructional interpretations of the whole-language approach really caught on, perhaps because so many teachers found the skill-and-drill emphasis of the 1970s frightfully uncompelling. Whole-language became the predominant approach to beginning literacy education in the United States by the 1990s. For example, it was endorsed as the way to teach beginning reading in the 1987 frameworks defining acceptable instruction by the State of California. Because California is a large basal reader adoption state, the 1987 frameworks fueled the development of literature-based basal reader series for the nation. The book companies began putting together anthologies filled with real literature. The stories were not written especially for the basal, as during the Dick-and-Jane era, but rather were reproductions of stories previously published as children's books or parts of children's books (e.g., one chapter from a multichapter book). When Texas, another large basal adoption state, followed with a literature-based requirement for basal reader series in 1993, each of the major textbook publishers created and marketed new "whole-language" basal readers. Thus, beginning reading materials were now almost universally organized around design principles that were very different from those that had dominated throughout the century (Hoffman & McCarthy, 1995).

But the very idea of a basal reader series contradicted many of the principles of the major whole-language theorists (Goodman, Shannon, Freeman, & Murphy, 1988). Some, in fact, saw a "whole-language basal" as an oxymoron. Nonetheless, key features of the new basals—anthologies of natural-language predictable texts, integrated reading and writing lessons, class sets of award-winning children's books—were obviously influenced by the whole-language movement.

The whole-language approach fueled the growth in publication of children's books, as well as the meteoric increases in the marketing of children's books in the late 1980s, continuing into the 1990s. Barnes and Noble and Borders have become supermarkets for children's books. Amazon.com provides unprecedented access to every children's title in print. American society has changed in ways that are consistent with the current educational efforts emphasizing the reading of children's books. Although Captain Kangaroo often read to his 1950s audiences, shows like *Reading Rainbow* and *Shining Time Station* are entirely focused on familiarizing children with wonderful books that they could read. And, of course, these television efforts directed at increasing awareness of children's literature are complemented by shows such as *Ghost Writer,* which is aimed to increase children's interest in and understanding of writing.

Despite the fact that beginning reading instruction focusing on the reading of real books makes intuitive sense and meshes with forces in the culture encouraging children to read literature, this shift in instruction—the "whole-language approach"—has met with much criticism from the media. Some of it seems justified to us, but not all of it. Moreover, even some of the justified criticism appears to go too far. Just as whole-language instruction evolved, so did criticisms of this approach. To appreciate these evolutions, it is helpful to think about the criticisms appearing in the 1980s versus those appearing in the 1990s.

CRITICISMS OF BEGINNING READING EDUCATION IN THE EARLY 1980S

In his second book, *Why Johnny Still Can't Read: A New Look at the Scandal of Our Schools*, Flesch (1981) made clear that the new directions in reading education stimulated by Frank Smith and Kenneth Goodman were no good in his view (see Chapter 2 in that book). Flesch believed that Smith and Goodman were simply making small advances away from the whole-word tradition, so small that, in fact, they were continuing in the whole-word tradition of teaching beginning reading. Thus, Flesch's second book reiterated and expanded his previous attack on the whole-word method, targeting especially the educator community concerned with reading. The book included chapters aimed at themes that were becoming and did become prominent conceptual justifications for the whole-language approach—for example, that no one method of beginning reading instruction is best, a phonics emphasis is problematic because English is not a wholly phonetic language, and word calling isn't reading. Although Flesch's second book did not capture as much attention as the first *Johnny* book, its presence made obvious to many Americans that all still was not rosy in beginning reading education, despite the purging of Dick and Jane from the marketplace more than a decade earlier.

The alarm bell was sounded again in 1983 with the government publication of *A Nation at Risk* (ANR; National Commission of Educational Excellence, 1983). This report made the case that there was increasing mediocrity in American education and increasing reason for concern about the quality of the graduates of American education. This general report was followed a year later by one much more focused on reading instruction, *Becoming a Nation of Readers* (BNR; Commission on Reading, 1984). The tone of BNR was not as pessimistic as ANR, and the Commission on Reading concluded that much could be done to improve reading instruction in America. Its specific recommendations (see Table 1.2) drew from a number of traditions. There was much in the report critical of the prevailing skill-and-drill practices and supportive of whole-language practices, including an emphasis on better-quality texts, improving comprehension, enhancing independent reading, and extended writing. Even so, whole-language advocates found plenty to criticize in the document, including the Commission's implicit acceptance of basal reader series as a fact of classroom life and the endorsement of the teaching of phonics to beginning readers.

By 1984 the federal government had completed four waves of assessment of reading as part of the National Assessment of Educational Progress (1985). The good news was that reading in elementary school (i.e., as measured at age 9) was better in the 1983–1984 assessment as compared with assessments in the early 1970s. The

TABLE 1.2. Commission on Reading's 1984 Recommendations for Elementary Reading Instruction

Parents have an obligation to support their children's growth as readers.

Kindergarten programs should emphasize oral language and writing as well as the beginning steps in reading.

Phonics instruction improves children's ability to identify words.

Reading primers should be interesting, comprehensible and instructive.

Teachers need to teach comprehension strategies.

Workbook and skill sheet tasks take too much of the time allotted for reading.

A reading lesson should stress understanding and appreciating the content of the selection.

Both oral and silent reading are important for the beginner.

Priority should be given to independent reading.

Students should do more extended writing.

bad news was that improvement seemed to have leveled off in the 1980s following a surge in the 1970s. This leveling off caused concern because the 1983–1984 assessment provided a great deal of evidence that there was plenty of room for improvement in the reading of American elementary students.

In short, there was much dissatisfaction being expressed about beginning reading in the early 1980s. In part, this reflected the general concern about education at this time. Even well-informed observers, such as the members of the National Commission on Reading, noted many faults in elementary reading instruction and offered a number of recommendations based on the research of the day. The suggestions in BNR ranged from increasing skills instruction, particularly comprehension strategies instruction, to increasing the proportion of the school day spent on truly literate tasks (i.e., real reading and writing rather than completing workbooks and worksheets). The data from the National Assessment of Educational Progress were interpreted by many as indicating a need for more effective reading instruction in the elementary grades.

CRITICISMS OF BEGINNING READING EDUCATION IN THE LATE 1980s AND 1990s

In the two decades following the First-Grade Studies, there was very little research involving direct comparisons of alternative approaches to beginning reading instruction. By the end of the 1980s, however, studies comparing the whole-language approach with alternatives were appearing, with enough work in this tradition to permit Stahl and Miller (1989) to put together a review article of studies comparing whole-language and closely related approaches with basal approaches, with respect to standard measures of reading achievement (i.e., standardized test data). Although Stahl and Miller concluded that whole-language approaches were effective in promoting prereading competencies at the kindergarten level (a finding later supported by Sacks and Mergendoller, 1997), the outcomes at the end of grade 1 were more mixed, with most horse races between basals and whole-language resulting in a dead heat. Nonetheless, Stahl and Miller also reported that whole-language tended to be less effective than basal approaches with weaker, at-risk first-grade readers.

The publication of Stahl and Miller's (1989) review stimulated the publication of criticisms of the whole-language approach. There was much less attention paid when researchers documented the benefits of whole-language instruction, partly, because the benefits were typically obtained on measures other than standardized tests (e.g., Dahl, Scharer, & Larson, 1999; Dahl & Freppon, 1995; Eldredge, Reutzel, & Hollingsworth, 1996; McIntyre & Freppon, 1994; Purcell-Gates, McIntyre, & Freppon, 1995; Traw, 1996). Even so, there was quite a bit of evidence generated by very good researchers documenting the benefits of the whole-language approach.

Attending whole-language classrooms proved consistently to increase children's understanding of the nature of reading and writing, as well as increase their tendencies to engage in "literate" activities (Freppon, 1991; Graham & Harris, 1994; Morrow, 1990, 1991; Morrow, O'Connor, & Smith, 1990; Neuman & Roskos, 1990, 1992; Purcell-Gates et al., 1995; Rosenhouse et al., 1997; Rowe, 1989). For example, book sharing between teachers and students increased students' comprehension of stories, including their drawing inferences when hearing stories (Cochran-Smith, 1984; Reutzel, Hollingsworth, & Eldredge, 1994). Extensive exposure to literature, as occurred in whole-language classrooms, increased world knowledge—for example, as reflected by a larger vocabulary (Elley, 1989; Robbins & Ehri, 1994; Rosenhouse, Feitelson, Kita, & Goldstein, 1997).

In a particularly visible study comparing whole-language classrooms with skills-oriented classrooms, Dahl and Freppon (1995) documented a cascade of differences favoring the whole-language students, including the following: Whole-language students responded to literature in a more sophisticated fashion than students in skills-oriented classrooms; for example, they more certainly related a current story to other stories read. Whole-language students coped more and better when confronting difficulties in reading than did students in skills-oriented classrooms. The whole-language students were more likely to see themselves as readers and writers than did the students in skills-oriented classrooms. The whole-language students were more often engaged in reading and writing when observed than were the students in skills-oriented classrooms. Consistent with the emphasis on the use of multiple cues during word recognition, the students in the whole-language classrooms did rely more on contextual clues when encountering an unknown word, as compared with the skills-oriented students, who more often attempted to sound out unfamiliar words.

Despite these benefits of whole-language instruction, there were increasing criticisms of the approach, stimulated in part by a book by Marilyn Jager Adams (1990), *Beginning to Read*, which summarized the research base supporting skills instruction in beginning reading instruction. The book made a strong case for phonics instruction based on the data available at that time, but it also made a very strong case for skills instruction even before children were ready for phonics. Adams summarized elegantly the case that an essential prereading skill is the awareness that words are composed of sounds blended together (i.e., phonemic awareness). She also reviewed the evidence that such skill could be developed in prereaders, and when it was, the risk of later reading failure was reduced. Adams's book captured a great deal of attention in the early 1990s and was frequently cited in critiques of the whole-language approach to beginning reading.

In the late 1980s and early 1990s the whole-language approach also suffered from a number of demonstrations that direct, intensive phonics instruction helps many struggling beginning readers with word recognition (e.g., Alexander, Anderson, Heilman, Voeller, & Torgesen, 1991; Foorman, Francis, Novy, & Liberman, 1991; Lovett, Ransby, Hardwick, Johns, & Donaldson, 1989; Lovett et al., 1994; Manis, Custodio, & Szeszulski, 1993; Olson, Wise, Johnson, & Ring, 1997; Torgesen & Burgess, 1997; Torgesen et al., 1996;

Vellutino et al., 1996). To be certain, the value of effective instruction in decoding as a remedial approach for some struggling beginning readers had been known for some time (e.g., Abt Associates, 1977). The more recent work, as well as Adams's (1990) *Beginning to Read*, however, especially captured the attention of some outspoken policy-makers, such as California's Bill Honig (1998), and well-placed federal officials, such as the National Institute on Child Health and Human Development's (NICHD) G. Reid Lyon (e.g., Fletcher & Lyon, 1998), who advocated prominently that recent research on beginning reading skills made obvious the need for much skills instruction in primary-level classrooms. The adversarial nature of advocates such as Honig and Lyon comes through in the title of the book in which the just-cited position papers were published, *What's Gone Wrong in America's Classrooms* (Evers, 1998), which was put out by the conservative Hoover Institution. For those familiar with Rudolf Flesch's (1955, 1981) earlier books, both the themes and the tone of the Hoover Institution volume are familiar.

The final administration of the National Assessment of Educational Progress (NAEP) in the 20th century (1998) may leave historians of the future wondering about this acrimony. The 1998 NAEP student performances in reading recorded all-time high achievements at all grade levels, with the average fourth grader's achievement having improved about a half grade level since 1990. The fourth graders taking this administration of the NAEP would have been in first grade in 1994, just about the time when each of the major textbook publishers first offered the literature-based, integrated basal reader series (the whole-language series). But although achievement was improved, the NAEP results pointed still to substantial discrepancies in achievement between more- and less-advantaged children and to disappointing student performances on higher-order comprehension tasks. It seems as though the instructional shifts fostered by the whole-language movement (literature-based integrated reading and writing instruction) had begun, perhaps, to produce small, incremental improvements in student literacy development.

Nonetheless, the debate on the nature of beginning reading instruction continued to flourish (Allington & Woodside-Jiron, 1999; Fletcher & Lyon, 1998; Pressley & Allington, 1999). The debate over whole-language versus skills instruction was particularly intense in the early 1990s and exceptionally acrimonious. Many termed it a war (e.g., Smith, 1994). As this war was raging, however, something of an intermediate position was emerging: that extensive and systematic skills instruction could occur in first-grade classrooms featuring the reading of literature and extensive student writing. Moreover, this argument for balancing skills instruction and whole-language components came from a who's who of reading instructional researchers, including Courtney Cazden (1992), Lisa Delpit (1986), Gerald Duffy (1991), Charles Fisher and Elfrieda Hiebert (1990), and Mary McCaslin (1989). In addition, there was increasing appreciation that the most respected and respectable of the scholars documenting the need for skills instruction argued that such instruction should be accompanied by immersion in literature and composing, with Marilyn Adams (1990) and Jeanne Chall (1967/1983) both making such a case. A recent National Research Council panel, which argued in its final report, *Preventing Reading Difficulties in Young Children* (Snow, Burns, & Griffin, 1998), that the scientific literature favored skills instruction in beginning reading, also made the case that such instruction should occur in the context of extensive reading of real literature and writing.

Thus, in the 1990s, a reading war was culminating, one in which advocates of whole-language and skills instruction battled. At the same time, a number of prominent reading researchers could see a middle ground, which they referred to as a balanced approach to literacy instruction. In this book we describe that middle ground in detail, because it was just such a middle ground that we found while studying documentably outstanding beginning reading teachers, whose work is discussed in some detail in the chapters that follow.

SUMMARY

Beginning reading education has a 3,000-year history. For most of that history, alphabet skills were taught before children experienced real words and texts. In the past two centuries, however, alternative models of beginning reading instruction have been debated, most notably, skills-first versus whole-word approaches, and, more recently, skills-first (i.e., phonics-first) versus whole-language approaches. The scientific study of beginning reading is now about a century old. Although skills-first approaches generally seem to win in experimental horse races between skills-first and more holistic approaches, the more holistic approaches have generally prevailed in 20th-century instruction and a growing number of students have attained increasingly sophisticated levels of reading achievement. But the literacy demands of modern society have also increased at a dizzying pace as the core economic activity has shifted from manufacturing to information processing.

First-grade reading instruction is important. Perhaps that is why it has been an arena of such emotional debate for such a long period. As experienced first-grade researchers, we live with this history and the debate. In living with it, we are also impressed by how first grade seems to be reduced to a trivial experience when it is conceived of as a debate between skills-first and more holistic instruction. In contrast, whenever we have been in first-grade classrooms, they seemed to us to be very complex places. Long before we conducted the studies summarized in this book, such complexity suggested to us that excellent first-grade instruction may not be due to just a skills-first or a more holistic orientation. Hence, we entered this investigation open to the possibility that there might be a number of ways in which excellent first-grade instruction differed from more typical first-grade instruction. That hypothesis was supported with the relevant evidence summarized later in this book.

REFERENCES

Abt Associates. (1977). *Education as experimentation: A planned variation model: Vol. IV-B. Effects of follow through models.* Cambridge, MA: Abt Books.

Adams, M. J. (1990). *Beginning to read.* Cambridge, MA: Harvard University Press.

Adams, M. J. (1998). The three-cueing system. In J. Osborne & F. Lehr (Eds.), *Literacy for all: Issues in teaching and learning* (pp. 73–99). New York: Guilford Press.

Alexander, A., Anderson, H., Heilman, P. C., Voeller, K. S., & Torgesen, J. K. (1991). Phonological awareness training and remediation of analytic decoding deficits in a group of severe dyslexics. *Annals of Dyslexia, 41,* 193–206.

Allington, R. L. (1977). If they don't read much, how they ever gonna get good? *Journal of Reading, 21,* 57–61.

Allington, R. L., & Woodside-Jiron, H. (1999). The politics of literacy teaching: How "research" shaped educational policy. *Educational Researcher, 28*(8), 4–13.

Bergeron, B. S. (1990). What does the term whole language mean? Constructing a. definition from the literature. *Journal of Reading Behavior, 22,* 301–330.

Bond, G. L., & Dykstra, R. (1967). The cooperative research program in first-grade reading instruction. *Reading Research Quarterly, 2,* 1–142.

Canney, G. (1993). Teachers' preferences for reading materials. *Reading Improvement, 30,* 238–245.

Cazden, C. (1992). *Whole language plus: Essays on literacy in the United States and New Zealand.* New York: Teachers College Press.

Chall, J. (1967). *Learning to read: The great debate.* New York: McGraw-Hill.

Chall, J. S. (1983). *Learning to read: The great debate* (updated edition). New York: McGraw-Hill.

Cochran-Smith, M. (1984). *The making of a reader.* Norwood, NJ: Ablex.

Commission on Reading. (1984). *Becoming a nation of readers.* Champaign–Urbana: University of Illinois, Center for the Study of Reading.

Cunningham, P. (1989). Will this experiment work? *California Reader, 23,* 3–7.

Dahl, K. L., & Freppon, P. A. (1995). A comparison of inner-city children's interpretations of reading and writing instruction in the early grades in skills-based and whole language classrooms. *Reading Research Quarterly, 30,* 50–74.

Dahl, K. L., Scharer, P. L., & Lawson, L. L. (1999). Phonics instruction and student achievement in whole language first-grade classrooms. *Reading Research Quarterly, 34,* 312–341.

Delpit, L. D. (1986). Skills and other dilemmas of a progressive black educator. *Harvard Educational Review, 56,* 379–385.

Duffy, G. G. (1991). What counts in teacher education? Dilemmas in educating empowered teachers. In J. Zutell & S. McCormick (Eds.), *Learner factors/ teacher factors: Issues in literacy research and instruction: Fortieth yearbook of the National Reading Conference* (pp. 1–18). Chicago: National Reading Conference.

Eldredge, J. L., Reutzel, D. R., & Hollingsworth, P. M. (1996). Comparing the effectiveness of two oral reading practices: Round-robin reading and shared book experience. *Journal of Literacy Research, 28,* 201–226.

Elley, W. B. (1989). Vocabulary acquisition from listening to stories. *Reading Research Quarterly, 24,* 174–187.

Evers, W. M. (1998). *What's gone wrong in America's classrooms.* Stanford, CA: Hoover Institution Press.

Fisher, C. W., & Hiebert, E. H. (1990). Characteristics of tasks in two approaches to literacy instruction. *Elementary School Journal, 91,* 3–18.

Flesch, R. (1955). *Why Johnny can't read—And what you can do about it.* New York: Harper & Row.

Flesch, R. (1981). *Why Johnny still can't read: A new look at the scandal of our schools.* New York: Harper Colophon.

Fletcher, J. M., & Lyon, G. R. (1998). Reading: A research-based approach. In W. M. Evers (Ed.), *What's gone wrong in America's classrooms* (pp. 49–90). Stanford, CA: Hoover Institution Press.

Foorman, B., Francis, D., Novy, D., & Liberman, D. (1991). How letter–sound instruction mediates progress in first-grade reading and spelling. *Journal of Educational Psychology, 83,* 456–469.

Freppon, P. A. (1991). Children's concepts of the nature and purpose of reading in different instructional settings. *Journal of Reading Behavior, 23,* 139–163.

Goodman, K. S. (1986). *What's whole in whole language?* Richmond Hill, Ontario: Scholastic. (Distributed in the United States by Heinemann.)

Goodman, K. S. (1993). *Phonics facts.* Portsmouth, NH: Heinemann.

Goodman, K. S. (1996). *On reading.* Portsmouth, NH: Heinemann.

Goodman, K. S., Shannon, P., Freeman, Y., & Murphy, S. (1988). *Report card on basal readers.* Katonah, NY: Richard Owen.

Graham, S., & Harris, K. R. (1994). The effects of whole language on children's writing: A review of literature. *Educational Psychologist, 29,* 187–192.

Graves, D. H. (1978). *Balance the basics: Let them write.* New York: Ford Foundation.

Graves, M. F., & Dykstra, R. (1997). Contextualizing the first-grade studies: What is the best way to teach children to read? *Reading Research Quarterly, 32,* 342–344.

Hansen, J. (1987). *When writers read.* Portsmouth, NH: Heinemann.

Hoffman, J., & McCarthy, S. (1995). The new basals: How are they different? *Reading Teacher, 49,* 72–75.

Holdaway, D. (1979). *The foundations of literacy.* Sydney, Australia: Ashton-Scholastic.

Honig, B. (1998). Preventing failure in early reading programs: A summary of research and instructional best practice. In W. M. Evers (Ed.), *What's gone wrong in America's classrooms* (pp. 91–116). Stanford, CA: Hoover Institution Press.

Juel, C. (1988). Learning to read and write: A longitudinal study of 54 children from first through fourth grades. *Journal of Educational Psychology, 80,* 417–447.

Kismaric, C., & Heiferman, M. (1996). *Growing up with Dick and Jane: Learning and living the American dream.* San Francisco: HarperCollins.

Lovett, M. W., Borden, S. L., DeLuca, T., Lacerenza, L., Benson, N. J., & Brackstone, D. (1994). Treating the core deficits of developmental dyslexia: Evidence of transfer of learning after phonologically and strategy-based reading training programs. *Developmental Psychology, 30,* 805–822.

Lovett, M. W., Ransby, M. J., Hardwick, N., Johns, M. S., & Donaldson, S. A. (1989). Can dyslexia be treated?: Treatment-specific and generalized treatment effects in dyslexic children's response to remediation. *Brain and Language, 37,* 90–121.

Manis, F. R., Custodio, R., & Szeszulski, P. A. (1993). Development of phonological and orthographic skill: A 2-year longitudinal study of dyslexic children. *Journal of Experimental Child Psychology, 56,* 64–86.

Mathews, M. M. (1966). *Teaching to read: Historically considered.* Chicago: University of Chicago Press.

McCaslin, M. M. (1989). Whole language: Theory, instruction, and future implementation. *Elementary School Journal, 90,* 223–229.

McIntyre, E., & Freppon, P. A. (1994). A comparison of children's development of alphabetic knowledge in a skills-based and a whole language classroom. *Research in the Teaching of English, 28*(4), 391–417.

Morrow, L. M. (1990). Preparing the classroom environment to promote literacy during play. *Early Childhood Research Quarterly, 5,* 537–554.

Morrow, L. M. (1991). Relationships among physical designs of play centers, teachers' emphasis on literacy in play, and children's literacy behaviors during play. In J. Zutell & S. McCormick (Eds.), *Fortieth yearbook of the National Reading Conference: Learner factors/teacher factors: Issues in literacy research and instruction* (pp. 127–140). Chicago: National Reading Conference.

Morrow, L. M., O'Connor, E. M., & Smith, J. K. (1990). Effects of a story reading program on the literacy development of at-risk kindergarten children. *Journal of Reading Behavior, 22,* 255–275.

National Assessment of Educational Progress. (1985). *The reading report card.* Washington, DC: U.S. Department of Education.

National Commission of Educational Excellence. (1983). *A nation at risk: The imperative for educational reform.* Washington, DC: U.S. Department of Education.

Neuman, S. B., & Roskos, K. (1990). The influence of literacy-enriched play settings on preschoolers' engagement with written language. In J. Zutell & S. McCormick (Eds.), *Literacy theory and research: Analyses from multiple paradigms* (pp. 179–188). Chicago: National Reading Conference.

Neuman, S. B., & Roskos, K. (1992). Literacy objects as cultural tools: Effects on children's literacy behaviors in play. *Reading Research Quarterly, 27,* 203–225.

Olson, R. K., Wise, B., Johnson, M., & Ring, J. (1997). The etiology and remediation of phonologically based word recognition and spelling disabilities: Are phonological deficits the "hole" story? In B. Blachman (Ed.), *Foundations of reading acquisition* (pp. 305–326). Mahwah, NJ: Erlbaum.

Pearson, P. D. (1997). The First-Grade Studies: A personal reflection. *Reading Research Quarterly, 32,* 428–432.

Pressley, M., & Allington, R. L. (1999). What should educational research be the research of? *Issues in education: Contributions from educational psychology, 5,* 1–35.

Purcell-Gates, V., McIntyre, E., & Freppon, P. (1995). Learning written storybook language in school. *American Educational Research Journal, 32,* 659–685.

Reutzel, D. R., Hollingsworth, P. M., & Eldredge, J. L. (1994). Oral reading instruction: The impact on student reading development. *Reading Research Quarterly, 29,* 40–59.

Robbins, C., & Ehri, L. C. (1994). Reading storybooks to kindergartners helps them learn new vocabulary words. *Journal of Educational Psychology, 86,* 54–64.

Rosenhouse, J., Feitelson, D., Kita, B., & Goldstein, Z. (1997). Interactive reading aloud to Israeli first graders: Its contribution to literacy development. *Reading Research Quarterly, 32,* 168–183.

Routman, R. (1994). *Invitations: Changing as teachers and learners K–12.* Portsmouth, NH: Heinemann.

Rowe, D. W. (1989). Author/audience interaction in the preschool: The role of social interaction in literacy lessons. *Journal of Reading Behavior: A Journal of Literacy, 21,* 311–349.

Sacks, C. H., & Mergendoller, J. R. (1997). The relationship between teachers' theoretical orientation toward reading and student outcomes in kindergarten children with different initial reading abilities. *American Educational Research Journal, 34,* 721–740.

Smith, C. B. (Moderator) (1994). *Whole language: The debate.* Bloomington, IN: EDINFO Press.

Smith, F. (1971). *Understanding reading.* Hillsdale, NJ: Erlbaum.

Smith, F. (1979). *Reading without nonsense.* New York: Teachers College Press.

Smith, N. B. (1986). *American reading instruction.* Newark, DE: International Reading Association.

Snow, C. E., Burns, M. S., & Griffin, P. (Eds.). (1998). *Preventing reading difficulties in young children.* Washington, DC: National Academy Press.

Stahl, S. A., & Miller, P. D. (1989). Whole language and language experience approaches for beginning reading: A quantitative research synthesis. *Review of Educational Research, 59,* 87–116.

Staiger, R. C. (1958). How are basal readers used? *Elementary English, 35,* 46–49.

Strickland, D. S., & Walmsley, S. A. (1993). *School book clubs and literacy development: A descriptive study.* Final report to the M. R. Robinson Foundation.

Thornton, T. P. (1996). *Handwriting in America: A cultural history.* New Haven: Yale University Press.

Torgesen, J. K., & Burgess, S. R. (1997). Consistency of reading-related phonological processes throughout early childhood. In J. Metsala & L. Ehri (Eds.), *Word recognition in beginning literacy* (pp. 161–188). Mahwah, NJ: Erlbaum.

Torgesen, J. K., Wagner, R. K., Rashotte, C. A., Alexander, A., Lindamood, P. C., Rose, E., & Conway, T. (1996). *Prevention and remediation of phonologically based reading disabilities.* Paper presented at the Spectrum of Developmental Disabilities XVIII: Dyslexia. Baltimore, MD: Johns Hopkins Medical Institutions.

Traw, R. (1996). Large scale assessment of skills in a whole language curriculum: Two districts' experiences. *Journal of Educational Research, 89,* 323–340.

Vellutino, F. R., Scanlon, D. M., Sipay, E. R., Small, S. G., Pratt, A., Chen, R., & Denckla, M. B. (1996). Cognitive profiles of difficult-to-remediate and readily remediated poor readers: Early intervention as a vehicle for distinguishing between cognitive and experiential deficits as a basic cause of specific reading disability. *Journal of Educational Psychology, 88*, 601–638.

Venezky, R. L. (1986). Steps toward a modern history of American reading instruction. In E. E. Rothkopf (Ed.), *Review of research in education, 13* (pp. 129–167). Washington, DC: American Educational Research Association.

2

Surveying Nominated-Effective
First-Grade Teachers
about Their Instruction

A visitor walking into a first-grade classroom anywhere in the nation may find it to be somewhat overwhelming. So many little folks and so few adults! And those little folks will be learning to read and write this year (and learning the basics of mathematics, science, social studies, health, and so on). In these classrooms there may be a small group of children reading with the teacher. A classroom aide or parent volunteer may be reading with other children. It is not unusual to see lots of different books being read at any one moment, and it is clear that the first graders in many classrooms are anything but on the same page. Their world is filled with a great many books that they can select to read, with lots of reading in the classroom and, often, several books going home for the evening to be read to or with parents.

The artifacts in the classroom often include bulletin boards dedicated to recent themes in science or social studies, themes relating to books the children have read, and displays featuring the covers of relevant titles. There may be a book cart in the room, from the library, filled with titles relating to content that will be covered in the coming weeks. The teacher's desk may have piles of order slips for book clubs, used by the students and their parents to build home libraries. Sometimes a television will be on, as some children catch the latest episode of *Reading Rainbow* or watch a tape relating to a title they have read previously.

Some students will be at their desks, writing. The writers will include students working on first drafts, others revising, and some proudly displaying their most recent publications. Writing, typically, is individualized. Even if the members of the class are all writing in response to a story that was read, each child crafts, drafts, and revises his or her own very personalized response.

The classroom artifacts often include letter–sound cards and various prompts reminding children about how to recognize words. Often, there is a word wall (Cunningham & Allington, 1998) that contains frequently encountered words and word family words that children use in decoding and editing their writing. Pocket charts often contain the sentences in a recently read story. Some pocket charts are dedicated to word play and exploration, permitting students to manipulate first letters and common rhymes—for example, a chart dedicated to "-ay" words, with student constructions of the words "day," "pay," "stay," "lay," and "play." There may also be story maps or character webs drawn on chart paper, reflecting support for a retelling of a story or a discussion of a character from a recently read book.

It takes no time for the visitor to a first-grade classroom to come to the conclusion that a great deal goes on in such a place. Moreover, if the visitor drops by a few times, it is clear that every day is different, with students continuously slipping into new and more challenging books, writing longer and more complicated narratives and journal entries. Indeed, if the visitor stays for an entire morning, the flow of activity will prove to be truly complex, with some students heading out for special instruction, some receiving more attention from the teacher and aides than others, some completing many tasks, and others needing assistance to complete any tasks.

When we reflected on the first grades we had visited, we were struck that they seemed much more complex places than was implied in much of the literature on beginning reading instruction. Even in classrooms in which skills instruction was emphasized, there was a lot more going on than drilling on skills, with many literature and writing experiences typical. When visiting classrooms headed by teachers claiming commitment to whole-language instruction, we often noted a great deal of skills instruction. Neither the extremist writing about skills instruction nor the extremist dedicated to whole-language educational theories seemed to describe the classrooms we visited.

We wanted to capture the complexity of first-grade literacy instruction, especially excellent first-grade literacy instruction. None of the methodologies commonly encountered in studying first-grade literacy instruction seemed likely to lead to as complete an understanding as we desired. In particular, experiments (or quasi-experiments) in which a number of classrooms using one method of instruction were compared with a number of classrooms using another method of instruction, seemed to focus too much on a very few outcome measures and to be minimally informative about the richness of the instruction being studied. Ethnographies of a few classrooms seemed better matched to capturing the typical complexity, but such methodologies permitted study of only a very few classrooms. Yet we wanted to make something of a national statement, which seemed to require information from a number of classes across the nation. Unfortunately, we did not then have the resources to do ethnographies in a number of classrooms, especially classrooms distributed throughout the nation. We decided on a methodology not much used to study first grade (or to study any elementary grade, actually). We surveyed first-grade teachers across the nation about their literacy instruction, although in doing so, we departed in many ways from traditional survey methodology, erring on the side of getting as much information as we could from the participating teachers.

A SURVEY OF FIRST-GRADE TEACHERS BELIEVED TO BE EFFECTIVE BY THEIR ADMINISTRATORS

When Pressley, Rankin, and Yokoi (1996) designed their survey study of first-grade teachers, they were aware that very good teachers are quite conscious of the decisions they make. They are reflective practitioners (Schön, 1983). We believed that they, like experts in many fields, would have detailed knowledge of the instructional practices (Chi, Glaser, & Farr, 1988; Ericsson & Smith, 1991; Hoffmann, 1992) that stimulated the literacy development of their students. Moreover, we knew that professionals typically can talk about what they do when they are questioned about it, especially if the questions are well focused (Diaper, 1989; Meyer & Booker, 1991; Scott, Clayton, & Gibson, 1991).

Methods

The first challenge was to identify a sample of very good first-grade teachers. To do so, we wrote to 50 reading supervisors across the nation who were members of the International Reading Association. We asked each of them to nominate the one first-grade teacher in their district who was most effective in educating a large proportion of his or her students to be readers and writers. The supervisors were left to their own devices to decide whom to nominate. In general, the supervisors nominated teachers whom they had observed directly and who had excellent reputations with administrators, other teachers, and/or parents as being effective in stimulating literacy development. The 50 letters to supervisors yielded 34 teachers from across the nation who completed all phases of the study.

In the first phase of the investigation, each nominated teacher was asked to list 10 instructional practices that were essential in his or her literacy instruction. More than 300 different practices were mentioned by the teachers who responded in the first phase. In the second phase of the study, the teachers responded to a more focused questionnaire. This questionnaire contained one question for each of the 300 practices cited in the first phase of the study, in order to determine just how prevalent the various practices were. The diversity of practices mentioned in the first phase necessitated diverse types of questions in the second phase. For example, the various concepts of print that teachers claimed to target in the first phase were tapped in this second-phase question:

Which of the following concepts of print do you teach?
_____ None
_____ Directionality of print
_____ Concept of a letter
_____ Concept of a word
_____ Punctuation
_____ Parts of a book
_____ Sounds that are associated with print

Teachers were asked to indicate the frequency with which they engaged in a number of instructional practices, providing a response on a scale ranging from 0 = never to 7 = several times a day. For example, they responded to the following questions on such a scale:

Do you use "big books"?

After a story, do you ask students comprehension questions?

The participants also estimated their use of some instructional practices, as illustrated by these examples:

What percentage of the material read by your students is outstanding children's literature?

... written at a "controlled" reading level?

... written to provide practice in phonetic elements and/or patterns?

... high-interest, low-vocabulary material?

In short, during the second phase of the study, a number of types of questions were used to tap the many instructional practices mentioned in the responses from the first phase of the study.

Findings

The overarching finding in the study was that the first-grade teachers reported doing many different things to support and encourage the literacy development of their students. Thus, the impression of classrooms, mentioned in the introduction to this chapter, as being filled with literate experiences was confirmed in the study. Each of the participating teachers indicated that his or her classroom was filled with print, most reporting chart stories and poems and the posting of word lists and labels. All of them reported in-class libraries. Students read aloud a great deal in these classes; they also read silently every day. Moreover, the teachers said they read daily to their students; many claimed to tell stories to their students and to play audiotaped and videotaped stories in their classes. Most of the teachers reported using themes and attempting to connect their literacy instruction to content-area instruction.

Most of the teachers also reported that their students were writers. Students were portrayed as writing stories, responding to literature read in class, and journaling several times a week. Writing in these classrooms involved planning, drafting, and revising, with most teachers reporting that at least some of student writing was eventually "published," for example, in the class storybook. Most teachers also reported displaying student work.

Just as there were many whole-language components in the instruction reported by the teachers (i.e., literature experiences and writing), a great deal of skills instruction was also reported. The teachers reported daily teaching of phonics and related skills, such as the alphabetic principle (i.e., that sounds in words are encoded by the letters in the words) and the teaching of letter–sound associations, a finding also reported by Morrow and Tracey (1997) and Baumann, Hoffman, Moon, and Duffy-Hester (1998). The teachers reported explicit teaching of vocabulary, comprehension strategies, and critical thinking skills. Consistent with whole-language principles, however, the teachers reported that for the most part, skills were taught in the context of real reading and writing, although most teachers also claimed at least some decontextualized skills instruction.

The teachers emphasized that they worked hard to make literacy and literacy instruction motivating. They reported working to make their classroom a risk-free environment for students, providing positive feedback to students, conveying the importance of reading and writing in life to them, setting an exciting and interesting mood for reading and writing, encouraging an "I can read, I can write" attitude, accepting where the child is at present and working toward improvement from that point, conveying the goals of the lessons and explaining why each lesson is important to each student, encouraging students to find and read materials they like, encouraging personal interpretations of texts, and encouraging student ownership of writing (e.g., by allowing them to select their own topics for writing).

Discussion

The teachers in this study reported being extremely eclectic in their literacy instruction. They favored whole-language principles, 97% reporting their instruction to at least somewhat reflect whole-language tenets. They also reported offering frequent skills instruction, both in the context of actual reading and writing and in lessons in which the skills were isolated and presented in a decontextualized situation. Their responses did not seem to be consistent with any of the more extreme perspectives that have been offered in the literacy debates of the 20th century. They certainly did not contend for skills-first instruction, nor was there anything in their responses consistent with a whole-word approach. Their version of whole-language instruction was tempered by much attention to skills instruction, although it was found that the more committed the teacher was to the whole-language approach, the less skills instruction he or she reported.

The decisions made by these teachers made a great deal of sense, however. The instructional practices they endorsed were defensible, based on what is known from research:

- Placing children in environments filled with books, as these teachers reported doing, stimulates students to do things that are connected with literacy (Guice, Allington, Johnston, Baker, & Michelson, 1996; Morrow, 1990, 1991; Neuman & Roskos, 1990, 1992).
- The focus on good literature in these classes made sense, inasmuch as reading such literature encourages students' independent reading of literature and improves their attitudes toward reading (Guthrie & Anderson, 1999; Morrow, 1992; Morrow, O'Connor, & Smith, 1990). Experience with excellent literature also improves children's understanding of language in ways that positively affect oral communication, comprehension, and writing (Feitelson, Kita, & Goldstein, 1986; Morrow, 1992; Purcell-Gates, McIntyre, & Freppon, 1995). For example, experiences with literature expand children's vocabulary (e.g., Elley, 1989; Robbins & Ehri, 1994).
- Letter- and sound-level instruction makes sense because such teaching does increase word recognition skills (Adams, 1990) and other word-related skills, such as spelling (Ball & Blachman, 1991; Lie, 1991; Nelson, 1990; Tangel & Blachman, 1992; Uhry & Shepherd, 1993). That these teachers reported modeling and explaining these skills makes very good sense because, according to research, such modeling and explaining does translate into improved student competence with such skills (Duffy et al., 1986, 1987; Duffy, Roehler, & Herrmann, 1988).
- These teachers reported teaching their students to plan, draft, and revise as part of writing instruction, which is consistent with approaches to writing instruction documented to improve the writing achievement of elementary-level students (Harris & Graham, 1996).
- Given that primary-level classrooms differ greatly in how much and how well they motivate children to do things connected with literacy (Turner, 1993), it was striking how committed these teachers were to doing their best to motivate literacy.

In summary, the teachers did not seem to teach according to any of the extreme positions described in the traditional first-grade literacy instruction literature. Rather, they seemed to combine and blend a number of elements of instruction that have been validated in recent years by researchers, contrary to the perception that primary-grade teaching is not typically informed by research.

In addition to including many effective components in their literacy instruction, it is notable that the teachers reported little or no use of some traditional approaches to beginning literacy teaching that have been reported to produce potentially negative effects on achievement. Thus, the teachers did not report using grouping by achievement, a practice that when used inflexibly seems to undermine the literacy achievement of many students (e.g., Allington, 1984; Juel, 1990; Slavin, 1987). Likewise, these teachers did not report relying on whole-class basal reader lessons but, instead, reported using a mixture of large- and small-group instructional plans as well as side-by-side reading and writing opportunities (Knapp, 1995). Instead of round-robin reading, which was so common when the authors of this book were in school, these teachers reported flexible use of grouping and variety in the kinds of reading done by students (Eldredge, Reutzel, & Hollingsworth, 1996; Freppon, 1991; Hoffman, 1987; Reutzel, Hollingsworth, & Eldredge, 1994).

These teachers seemed committed to balancing a number of components, some more consistent with whole-language instruction and some more consistent with skills instruction. Although such balancing was advocated by a number of first-grade researchers earlier (e.g., Adams, 1990; Cazden, 1992; Delpit, 1986; Duffy, 1991; Fisher & Hiebert, 1990; McCaslin, 1989; Pressley, 1994; Stahl, McKenna, & Pagnucco, 1994), Pressley, Rankin, and Yokoi (1996) really put some flesh on the balancing model, with their teacher reports raising the possibility that the balance approach was extremely complicated. Based on the findings of Pressley, Rankin, and Yokoi (1996), effective curricular balance can be thought of as juggling hundreds of balls in the air, each carefully coordinated with the other—the particular balance of the "balls" varying from child to child and from situation to situation during the school day.

A SURVEY OF PRIMARY-LEVEL
SPECIAL EDUCATION TEACHERS

Among the most interesting and surprising findings in the survey of nominated-effective first-grade teachers were their reports about teaching struggling beginning readers. Basically, they said that instruction for struggling readers did not differ qualitatively from instruction for their other students. Certainly, skills instruction was more extensive and intensive than with typically achieving students, but struggling readers were also immersed in literature and writing experiences.

This finding was intriguing enough to prompt Rankin-Erickson and Pressley (2000) to follow up. Specifically, the follow-up surveyed primary-level teachers who were especially concerned with struggling readers, that is, primary-level special education teachers who were considered by their administrators to be very effective in stimulating literacy development. The methodology in the study was quite similar to the methodology in the Pressley, Rankin, and Yokoi (1996) investigation, with an open-ended question (What are the essential elements in your literacy instruction?) followed by a detailed questionnaire asking teachers about each of the instructional practices mentioned in the open-ended responses.

Just as in the survey of nominated-effective primary-level teachers, the nominated-effective primary-level special educators mentioned hundreds of specific elements of instruction in their responses to the open-ended question. The second questionnaire tapped 436 instructional practices, using a variety of question types, as in the Pressley, Rankin, and Yokoi (1996) study.

The most interesting, overarching conclusion of the study was that the instruction reported by the nominated-effective primary-level special educators was not much different from the instruction reported by the nominated-effective first-grade teachers. The special educators indicated a great deal of skills instruction in their lessons, but they also reported extensive literature and writing experiences. In general, the explicitness and completeness of skills instruction was reported as increasing with the severity of the student's difficulty in learning to read. Although some skills instruction was portrayed as decontextualized, most skills instruction was reported as occurring in the context of real reading and writing. These teachers were emphatic that whole-language instruction and skills instruction were not contradictory but, rather, complementary approaches in their instruction of students who were struggling beginning readers. They reported providing education to students in special education that was not much different from the instruction provided to other students. It is true that the special education students received the more intensive sound-, letter-, and word-level skills instruction they needed, but they also received the rich mix of literacy experiences that excellent first-grade teachers reported providing to average and above-average students.

A CAUTIONARY NOTE

We must also note that not all first-grade classrooms offer instruction like that described here. The beginning reading instruction described here is the instruction of teachers nominated as effective in developing beginning reading and writing proficiencies in their students. Although examples of exemplary first-grade classrooms can be located in virtually every community across the nation, the research suggests that far too many first-grade classrooms do not look much like the effective learning environments portrayed in the survey data. Instead, in some classrooms one can still observe whole-class lessons dominating the day, as all children are virtually dragged, ready or not, through the same story selections and skill lessons with little regard for their actual instructional needs. Unfortunately, in some schools this is a result of a misguided administrative mandate. In others it is a result of limited professional development opportunities, producing teachers who know no better than to replicate failed past practices. In a few places, classrooms are actually staffed with adults who have no teaching credentials and who know no better than to teach as they were taught.

In some classrooms, there has been no replacing of round-robin oral reading with more effective shared reading approaches. In these classrooms students still copy from the board rather than compose original sentences. Here students memorize abstract phonics rules in isolation and spend large parts of the school day working alone on low-level worksheets and workbook pages. In these classrooms, teachers are mandated to follow scripted lesson plans prepared by district officials or commercial publishers. These teachers teach materials. They attend less to the instructional needs of individual students than do the effective teachers reported here. In these classrooms student obedience is nurtured, not student self-regulation. It is truly unfortunate that all of these ineffective classroom environments seem more common in schools that serve larger numbers of children from lower-income families (Allington, Guice,

Michelson, Baker, & Li, 1996; Knapp, 1995; Hoffman et al., 1998).

DISCUSSION

First-grade teachers who are considered very effective by their superiors in promoting student literacy report that their instruction is quite complex. They are neither wedded to a whole-language perspective that eschews skills instruction altogether or admits skills instruction only in the context of reading and writing, nor are they wedded to a traditional skills-first perspective that emphasizes the necessity of lots of decontextualized skill activity until initial decoding development has been achieved. Rather, they report blending practices derived from both whole-language and direct skills instruction perspectives.

One reaction to this survey when it was first reported was that it had to be distorting first-grade instruction: First-grade teaching just could not be as complex as suggested by the survey responses. If the surveys are to be believed, first-grade instruction involves a blending of skills teaching, literature, and writing experiences, all of these coordinated with one another. That is, the skills instruction is driven, at least in part, by the needs of the students as they tackle stories and write about their worlds. But these teachers also seem to have a general framework for the development of reading and writing skills, which they use to guide lesson planning as well. The literature the children experience increases in complexity as their skills improve, and the demands made on writing also increase as skills increase. Although the teachers reported that they provided qualitatively similar instruction to students regardless of achievement level, they also reported that they adjusted the specific skills and stories and writing experiences to the competencies of their students. Indeed, the survey responses suggested a great deal of tailoring of instruction, so that individual students were receiving instruction consistent with their needs and interests.

If the survey responses are to be believed, excellent first-grade reading instruction today is not anything like the reading instruction reviewed in the opening chapter of this book, nor anything like the first-grade teaching envisioned by many policymakers and researchers. Not one of the surveyed teachers said that he or she was a skills-first teacher. Not one claimed to use the whole-word approach.

Basals were never reported as the driving force behind the instructional program. Instead, what was reported was often quite consistent with a balanced and research-based view of beginning literacy instruction.

As we reflected on what was reported by the teachers, we also noted what was not mentioned by them. Despite the fact that there are many publishers of reading instruction materials, we were struck that there was little mention of commercially published reading instructional materials by the nominated-effective first-grade teachers. (There was more mention of use of basal materials by the special education teachers.) These effective first-grade teachers seemed to focus on children's needs more than on commercial scope and sequence plans and teacher's guides in their instructional planning and delivery. The published materials that were mentioned by the nominated-effective first-grade teachers were more typically the trade books that define the contemporary primary-level literature canon. Whether we agree with the moral lessons in the old Dick-and-Jane-style readers, we like the idea that reading instruction has often gone hand in hand with character instruction. We were disappointed that the survey responses did not contain even a hint of character education as part of literacy development. In short, although published reading instruction programs and moral education drove literacy development in the past, these dimensions were not reported as the focus of teaching by the nominated-effective teachers surveyed by Pressley, Rankin, and Yokoi (1996) and Rankin-Erickson and Pressley (2000). At the same time, these teachers reported working to foster student independence, responsibility, cooperation, and self-regulation as they designed their instructional programs. Choosing appropriate books, working alone and with others, and editing and revising of writing all seem to reflect personal qualities that should be widely heralded.

The obvious concern in interpreting survey responses is that they are somewhat removed from the actual teaching. In general, social scientists of all sorts are suspicious of self-report data, giving much more credence to actual observations. Although these survey data offered an intriguing possibility—that effective first-grade reading instruction is a complex blending of key features of both direct skills instruction models and whole-language learning frameworks, there had to be more direct evidence of such balancing of instructional components if anyone was to be convinced that the balance hypothesis was on target. The rest of this book reports such observational data. As it turned out, the surveys did provide a good preview of what researchers would see when they spent time in first-grade classrooms where literacy instruction was going well and proving to be effective. This was true even when the first-grade classrooms were filled with children from low-income families. But unlike the survey data, the classroom observations were filled with specifics and with poignant and powerful examples of how complex excellent first-grade teaching actually is.

REFERENCES

Adams, M. J. (1990). *Beginning to read.* Cambridge, MA: Harvard University Press.

Allington, R. L. (1984). Content coverage and contextual reading in reading groups. *Journal of Reading Behavior, 16,* 85–96.

Allington, R. L., Guice, S., Michelson, N., Baker, K., & Li, S. (1996). Literature-based curriculum in high-poverty schools. In M. Graves, P. van den Broek, & B. Taylor (Eds.), *The first R: Every child's right to read* (pp. 73–96). New York: Teachers College Press.

Ball, E. W., & Blachman, B. A. (1991). Does phoneme awareness training in kindergarten make a difference in early word recognition and developmental spelling? *Reading Research Quarterly, 26,* 49–66.

Baumann, J. F., Hoffman, J. V., Moon, J., & Duffy-Hester, A. (1998). Where are teachers' voices in the phonics/whole language debate? Results from a survey of U.S. elementary teachers. *Reading Teacher, 50,* 636–651.

Cazden, C. (1992). *Whole language plus: Essays on literacy in the United States and New Zealand.* New York: Teachers College Press.

Chi, M. T. H., Glaser, R., & Farr, M. J. (Eds.). (1988). *The nature of expertise.* Hillsdale, NJ: Erlbaum.

Cunningham, P. M., & Allington, R. L. (1998). *Classrooms that work: They can all read and write.* New York: Addison-Wesley.

Delpit, L. D. (1986). Skills and other dilemmas of a progressive black educator. *Harvard Educational Review, 56,* 379–385.

Diaper, D. (Ed.). (1989). *Knowledge elicitation: Principles, techniques, and applications.* New York: Wiley.

Duffy, G. G. (1991). What counts in teacher education? Dilemmas in educating empowered teachers. In J. Zutell & S. McCormick (Eds.), *Fortieth yearbook of the National Reading Conference: Learner factors/teacher factors: Issues in literacy research and instruction* (pp. 1–18). Chicago: National Reading Conference.

Duffy, G. G., Roehler, L., & Herrmann, G. (1988). Modeling mental processes helps poor readers become strategic readers. *Reading Teacher, 41,* 762–767.

Duffy, G. G., Roehler, L. R., Meloth, M., Vavrus, L., Book, C., Putnam, J., &

Wesselman, R. (1986). The relationship between explicit verbal explanation during reading skill instruction and student awareness and achievement: A study of reading teacher effects. *Reading Research Quarterly, 21,* 237–252.

Duffy, G. G., Roehler, L. R., Sivan, E., Rackliffe, G., Book, C., Meloth, M., Vavrus, L., Wesselman, R., Putnam, J., & Bassiri, D. (1987). Effects of explaining the reasoning associated with using reading strategies. *Reading Research Quarterly, 22,* 347–368.

Eldredge, J. L., Reutzel, D. R., & Hollingsworth, P. M. (1996). Comparing the effectiveness of two oral reading practices: Round-robin reading and the shared book experience. *Journal of Literacy Research, 28,* 201–225.

Elley, W. B. (1989). Vocabulary acquisition from listening to stories. *Reading Research Quarterly, 24,* 174–187.

Ericsson, K. A., & Smith, J. (Eds.). (1991). *Toward a general theory of expertise.* Cambridge, UK: Cambridge University Press.

Feitelson, D., Kita, B., & Goldstein, Z. (1986). Effects of listening to series stories on first graders' comprehension and use of language. *Research in the Teaching of English, 20,* 339–356.

Fisher, C. W., & Hiebert, E.H. (1990). Characteristics of tasks in two approaches to literacy instruction. *Elementary School Journal, 91,* 3–18.

Freppon, P. A. (1991). Children's concepts of the nature and purpose of reading in different instructional settings. *Journal of Reading Behavior, 23,* 139–163.

Guice, S., Allington, R.L., Johnston, P., Baker, K., & Michelson, N. (1996). Access?: Books, children, and literature-based curriculum in schools. *The New Advocate, 9,* 197–207.

Guthrie, J. T., & Anderson, E. (1999). Engagement in reading: Processes of motivated, strategic, knowledgeable, social readers. In J. T. Guthrie & D. Alvermann (Eds.), *Engaged reading: Processes, practices, and policy implications* (pp. 17–45). New York: Teachers College Press.

Harris, K. R., & Graham, S. (1996). *Making the writing process work: Strategies for composition and self-regulation.* Cambridge, MA: Brookline Books.

Hoffman, J. V. (1987). Rethinking the role of oral reading in basal instruction. *Elementary School Journal, 87,* 367–373.

Hoffman, J. V., McCarthy, S. J., Elliott, B., Bayles, D., Price, D., Ferree, A., & Abbott, J. (1998). The literature-based basals in first-grade classrooms: Savior, satan, or same-old, same-old? *Reading Research Quarterly, 33,* 168–197.

Hoffmann, R. R. (1992). *The psychology of expertise: Cognitive research and empirical AI.* New York: Springer-Verlag.

Juel, C. (1990). Effects of reading group assignment on reading development in first and second grade. *Journal of Reading Behavior, 22,* 233–254.

Knapp, M.S. (1995). *Teaching for meaning in high-poverty classrooms.* New York: Teachers College Press.

Lie, A. (1991). Effects of a training program for stimulating skills in word analysis in first-grade children. *Reading Research Quarterly, 26,* 234–250.

McCaslin, M. M. (1989). Whole language, theory, instruction, and future implementation. *Elementary School Journal, 90,* 223–229.

Meyer, M., & Booker, J. (1991). *Eliciting and analyzing expert judgement: A practical tour.* London: Academic Press.

Morrow, L. M. (1990). Preparing the classroom environment to promote literacy during play. *Early Childhood Research Quarterly, 5,* 537–554.

Morrow, L. M. (1991). Relationships among physical designs of play centers, teachers' emphasis on literacy in play, and children's literacy behaviors during play. In J. Zutell & S. McCormick (Eds.), *Fortieth yearbook of the National Reading Conference: Learner factors/teacher factors: Issues in literacy research and instruction* (pp. 127–140). Chicago: National Reading Conference.

Morrow, L. M. (1992). The impact of a literature-based program on literacy achievement, use of literature, and attitudes of children from minority backgrounds. *Reading Research Quarterly, 27,* 251–275.

Morrow, L. M., O'Connor, E. M., & Smith, J. K. (1990). Effects of a story reading program on the literacy development of at-risk kindergarten children. *Journal of Reading Behavior, 22,* 255–275.

Morrow, L. M., & Tracey, D. H. (1997). Strategies used for phonics instruction in early childhood classrooms. *Reading Teacher, 50,* 644–653.

Nelson, L. (1990). The influence of phonics instruction on spelling progress. In J. Zutell & S. McCormick (Eds.), *Literacy theory and research: Analyses from multiple paradigms* (pp. 241–247). Chicago: National Reading Conference.

Neuman, S. B., & Roskos, K. (1990). The influence of literacy-enriched play settings on preschoolers' engagement with written language. In J. Zutell & S. McCormick (Eds.), *Literacy theory and research: Analyses from multiple paradigms* (pp. 179–188). Chicago: National Reading Conference.

Neuman, S. B., & Roskos, K. (1992). Literacy objects as cultural tools: Effects on children's literacy behaviors in play. *Reading Research Quarterly, 27,* 203–225.

Pressley, M. (1994). Commentary on the ERIC whole language debate. In C. B. Smith (Moderator), *Whole language: The debate* (pp. 155–178). Bloomington, IN: ERIC/REC.

Pressley, M., Rankin, J. L., & Yokoi, L. (1996). A survey of the instructional practices of primary teachers nominated as effective in promoting literacy. *Elementary School Journal, 96,* 363–384.

Purcell-Gates, V., McIntyre, E., & Freppon, P. (1995). Learning written storybook language in school. *American Educational Research Journal, 32,* 659–685.

Rankin-Erickson, J. L., & Pressley, M. (2000). A survey of the instructional practices of special education teachers nominated as effective teachers of literacy. *Learning Disabilities Research and Practice, 15,* 206–225.

Reutzel, D. R., Hollingsworth, P. M., & Eldredge, J. L. (1994). Oral reading instruction: The development of student reading development. *Reading Research Quarterly, 29,* 40–59.

Robbins, C., & Ehri, L. C. (1994). Reading storybooks to kindergartners helps them learn new vocabulary words. *Journal of Educational Psychology*, *86*, 54–64.

Schön, D. A. (1983). *The reflective practitioner: How professionals think in action*. London: Temple Smith.

Scott, A. C., Clayton, J. E., & Gibson, E. L. (1991). *A practical guide to knowledge acquisition*. Reading, MA: Addison-Wesley.

Slavin, R. E. (1987). Grouping for instruction in the elementary school. *Educational Psychologist*, *22*, 109–128.

Stahl, S. A., McKenna, M. C., & Pagnucco, J. R. (1994). The effects of whole language instruction: An update and reappraisal. *Educational Psychologist*, *29*, 175–185.

Tangel, D. M., & Blachman, B. A. (1992). Effect of phoneme awareness instruction on kindergarten children's invented spelling. *Journal of Reading Behavior*, *24*, 233–261.

Turner, J. C. (1993). Situated motivation in literacy instruction. *Reading Research Quarterly*, *28*, 288–290.

Uhry, J. K., & Shepherd, M. J. (1993). Segmentation/spelling instruction as part of a first-grade reading program: Effects on several measures of reading. *Reading Research Quarterly*, *28*, 218–233.

3

———

The Nature of First-Grade Instruction
That Promotes Literacy Achievement

The planning of a study is always informed by previous research. Often, this means building incrementally on what has been done before. For example, in the past few years there have been many studies reported on the development of phonemic awareness skills in kindergarten and first-grade children. New studies on this topic have often been slight variations on previous studies—for example, investigations of training that is slightly different from training investigated previously. In contrast, however, there was much less research that we could look to for guidance in deciding how to study the nature of excellent beginning reading instruction.

Yet there was some work that we found inspirational and informative as we designed our study. For example, the work of Ruddell (e.g., 1997) on the characteristics of influential literacy teachers is an essential reading in starting a project on effective teaching. Ruddell studied teachers who were nominated by former students, teaching peers, and administrators as outstanding in their effectiveness as teachers. As a validation of sorts, Ruddell observed that better students were likely to have had more influential teachers than less successful students. Ruddell relied heavily on interviews of both students and teachers, although there were also some observations of teaching.

Ruddell concluded that influential teachers use powerful instructional strategies, including careful monitoring of students and provision of feedback about progress in literacy. Influential teachers possessed in-depth knowledge of reading and writing processes, as well as extensive knowledge of the content covered in elementary schools, complemented by extensive knowledge about how to teach reading, writing, and elementary content. Influential teachers did much to motivate learning in their students but did not rely on external, tangible rewards to do so. Influential teachers had personal characteristics that affected their teaching, including high energy, warmth, flexibility, and sensitivity to students. They were enthusiastic about reading, writing, and content learning. Influential teachers were concerned about their students. They did much to make learning personally relevant to students and tried to make learning a discovery experience. For example, Ruddell and his associates observed that influential teachers were especially likely to engage in meaning negotiation with their students, with students and teacher together asking questions about the texts being read and constructing alternative interpretive possibilities.

Researchers interested in the effects of culture on literacy development have been especially sensitive to classroom processes, drawing conclusions about instruction that works with minority students based on extensive observations in classrooms. For example, based on years of work at Hawaii's Kamehameha School, Au (1998) concluded that beginning reading instruction that works with Hawaiian children has the following characteristics: There is attention to letter- and word-level processes but also to higher-order literacy competencies, including reading comprehension and the writing process. Phonics instruction is embedded in a broad curriculum that includes extensive reading and frequent writing that permit the use of skills being learned through classroom instruction. Au observed much guided reading and discussion of literature in effective Kamehameha classrooms.

Others interested in minority children have similarly come to the conclusion that effective and desirable instruction with minority children is highly meaningful, focusing more on comprehension, composition, and immersion in important cultural and world knowledge. Luis Moll (e.g., 1998), who has studied the teaching of Hispanic American students, and Gloria Ladson-Billings (e.g., 1994), who has documented teachers who were successful with African American students are two such investigators. Both Moll and Ladson-Billings described how teachers made connections between classroom learning and the cultures and communities of their students, emphasizing that education at its best is a cooperative enterprise rather than a competitive one.

One of the most extensive analyses of effective teaching in elementary classrooms was offered by Michael S. Knapp and Associates (1995), who observed 140 elementary-level classrooms, each for at least one school year. The most important finding of Knapp and Associates was that achievement was higher in classrooms in which there was much teaching for meaning. That is, with respect to literacy, achievement was higher to the extent that reading instruction emphasized comprehension and the teaching of comprehension strategies, and to the extent that writing emphasized composition (i.e., the writing of stories and expositories). In contrast, achievement was less impressive when teachers emphasized letter- and word-level skills during reading and writing instruction. The most effective teachers in the Knapp and Associates study were able to cover the lower-order skills within the context of higher-order instruction (i.e., as students tackled challenging texts and wrote multiple-paragraph passages).

Although Ruddell (1997), Au (1998), Moll (1998), Ladson-Billings (1994), and Knapp and Associates (1995) offered converging data in support of elementary-level literacy instruction that goes well beyond letter- and word-level skills, none of these studies chose as a focus beginning reading instruction in first grade. We saw this as an important omission, given the emphasis on first grade in recent years by the many constituencies interested in beginning literacy. This book reports work that explicitly informs about grade 1, and, in particular, first-grade classrooms in which children make good progress in becoming readers and writers. Granted, there have been entire books written on what should happen in whole-language first grades as well as in first grades attempting to be rich in direct instruction of basic skills. We found lots of teacher's manuals available, detailing publishers' envisionments of what first-grade classrooms, driven by their products, should look like. Even so, we found nothing like an observational study focusing on first-grade classrooms per se, a study undertaken to represent excellent first-grade teaching as completely as possible and attempting to do so in an agenda-free manner (i.e., not written by an advocate for a major literacy development perspective, such as whole-language or direct instruction).

We came to this investigation with some previous experience in sizing up elementary-level classrooms with respect to literacy instruction. Pressley et al. (1992) had carried out a series of observational studies that detailed how comprehension instruction occurs in elementary classrooms dedicated to a strategies-instructional approach. That work mostly involved observations of classrooms, but was complemented by interviews of teachers who were observed and of others who were not observed. Those data were analyzed to produce a theory grounded in data (Strauss & Corbin, 1990).

In the investigations presented in this chapter, we chose to follow Pressley et al.'s (1992) approach with respect to data collection and analyses. In both of the studies summarized here, analyses of individual classrooms were carried out, based on observation and interview data to produce a grounded theory. Then, there were analyses across the conclusions about individual classrooms in order to generate more general conclusions.

OBSERVING FIRST-GRADE CLASSES IN UPSTATE NEW YORK

Most research involves convenience samples—that is, the individuals studied usually live and work near the researchers. So it was in the first study reported here, which was a doctoral dissertation by Ruth Wharton-McDonald when she was a student at the State University of New York at Albany. Administrators and reading specialists in a number of upstate New York school districts were asked to nominate a first-grade teacher in their district, specifically one whose teaching was considered exemplary in promoting literacy, as well as another teacher in the district who was considered more typical of the district (i.e., very solid in promoting academic achievement but not as outstanding as the teacher who was nominated as exemplary). Those making the nominations were asked to consider a variety of factors, including their own observations of the teachers, teacher enthusiasm, reading and writing achievement of students, student enthusiasm for reading, whether they would want their child in the teacher's first grade, whether the teacher reached a wide range of abilities, and positive feedback from parents. When the study began, the research team had 10 teachers in the sample, 5 who were nominated as outstanding in promoting their students' literacy and 5 who were nominated as more typical of their districts.

Several observers made multiple visits to the 10 first-grade class-rooms. These observers then coded their data for each classroom with respect to categories of events occurring in the classroom (e.g., morning meeting, one-to-one sessions with teachers). Each of these events was described in detail. Visits to a classroom continued until the observers were confident that they were coming to no new insights about what was going on in the classroom, although there was an additional constraint that observations be spread across the entire school year. (We established this requirement because it seemed possible, a priori, that the nature of first-grade literacy instruction might change as the first graders became more competent in reading and writing.)

The teachers were interviewed, with the interviews very much informed by the observations. That is, questions were design to clarify what the observers had seen during the classroom visits, and each interview was tailored to what had been observed in each teacher's own classroom. The questions posed to the teacher included the following:

What kinds of things do you ask parents to do in your class-room?
Can you tell which kids read at home with their parents?
Are all of the students' parents literate?
Do the students help each other?
Do you consider yourself a whole-language teacher?
When you were conducting a reading group, it seemed as though you were doing some on-line assessment of the kids. What were you doing?
How do you know which kids are going to need more literature? Phonics?
When do you think students do the weekly homework assign-ments?
Do all the kids take books home?
How often do they write in their journals?
What kinds of grades do you give in first grade?

For every teacher/classroom studied, a model of the teacher's instruction was constructed. A penultimate version of the model was given to the teacher for review and then adjusted, based on feedback from the teacher. (The only adjustments made, however, were very minor, for all of the teachers agreed that the researcher-constructed models were fair and complete representations of their literacy instruction.) These models were intended to be comprehensive with respect to what happened in the observed classrooms during literacy instruction.

For example, one teacher's model included sections on the teacher's philosophy, the areas of reading emphasized, the use of grouping in the class, materials read and used in the class, frequently observed activities, teaching strategies, process writing instruction, students' written products, student engagement, general classroom atmosphere, seating arrangement, other adults in the classroom, home–school connections, and the reading levels of students in the class. Each of these sections of a model included a number of indicators. Thus, for one teacher, the process writing section included information about writing instruction to the whole class, the use of story webs during writing, the effect of talking with partners as part of process writing, how writing and drawing were integrated, teacher monitoring and feedback during the writing process, and how teacher scaffolding supported student writing. In short, by the end of the observations and interviews it was possible to put together detailed summaries of the teaching in each first-grade classroom that was observed. (Chapters 5 through 9 are based on the ultimate summaries of teaching for five of the most effective teachers identified in this study and in the second study addressed in this chapter.)

As part of the observations, the researchers explicitly looked for indicators of literacy achievement in classrooms. The reason was that the researchers did not want to accept the school district's appraisals of teachers as exemplary or more typical without corroboration. Three indications of achievement characterized classrooms with high literacy achievement as compared with those with less achievement:

1. By the end of the study, it was clear that reading achievement was better in some classrooms than others. That is, in some classrooms most students were reading books at or above grade level by the end of first grade, whereas in other classrooms there were many students who were reading books well below grade level.

2. By the end of the year, in some classrooms writing was more advanced than in other classrooms. Thus, in some classrooms, most students were writing more than one-page stories, with the stories reasonably coherent; punctuation, capitalization, and spelling were

often quite good in some classrooms. In contrast, in other classrooms the stories were much shorter on average (e.g., perhaps two or three lines long), with less evidence that students understood and used punctuation, capitalization, and spelling conventions.

3. In some classrooms student engagement was much more consistent than in other classrooms. Most striking, in classrooms with high reading achievement, there was also high writing achievement. Moreover, in the classes with high reading and writing achievement, most students seemed to be working productively on literacy tasks most of the time.

During the course of the study, one teacher, who had been nominated by her administrator as outstanding in promoting student achievement, dropped out because of personal reasons unrelated to the study, leaving a total of nine teachers who were observed over the course of the year and interviewed. Of these nine, three were notable for promoting reading achievement, writing achievement, and engagement; two of the three were originally nominated as outstanding teachers and one was originally nominated as more typical of his district. Three teachers were notable as being not as successful as the others in getting their children to read and write and to be engaged in literacy activities. The remaining three were in a middle category with respect to their success in promoting literacy and engagement in their students.

As it turned out, in addition to the differences in achievement, there were some striking differences in the teaching in classrooms with high achievement on average, especially relative to the classrooms with low achievement on average. Those differences are discussed later in this section, but first we consider the similarities across the classrooms that were studied by Wharton-McDonald, Pressley, and Hampston (1998).

Commonalities across Classrooms

Despite the differences in literacy achievement that were observed, it was obvious to the observers over the course of the study that there were marked similarities across the first-grade classrooms. When a formal cross-case analysis was made of the nine case studies of teaching, many similarities across classrooms emerged, including the following:

- There was a mix of direct skills instruction and more authentic reading and writing in all classrooms.
- All classrooms included process writing instruction, with students planning before they wrote, drafting, and revising.
- Eight of the nine classrooms included a spelling program.
- In seven of the nine classrooms the desks were arranged in small clusters so that students could work together on reading and writing.
- All teachers used small grouping for instruction to some extent, but all teachers also had students doing independent reading and writing some of the time.
- In eight of the nine classrooms, there was abundant positive reinforcement, with students consistently being praised for their literacy efforts and achievements.
- All of the teachers cared for their students; their dedication to help them grow and achieve was obvious during the observations.
- All of the teachers realized that parents play an important role in the literacy development of students.

In summary, there was a remarkable sameness across the first-grade classes that were observed, despite the fact that some of the classes served economically disadvantaged children and others were in affluent districts. This situation differed dramatically from that found in upper-elementary-grade classrooms in the same districts (Pressley, Wharton-McDonald, Mistretta, & Echevarria, 1998), with every fourth and fifth grade seeming to have a different orientation and different schedule of events. For instance, we could walk into any one of the first-grade classrooms on any day and expect to see a morning meeting, followed by reading of outstanding literature, and students writing as part of their literacy-oriented morning. Despite these striking similarities, however, there were also some very great differences between the classes in which literacy achievement seemed high relative to other classes in the study.

Instructional Practices Distinguishing First-Grade Classes with High Achievement

The three classes in which reading and writing achievement seemed especially positive were also the classes in which the students seemed most motivated to achieve, for engagement was very high in these classes. In fact, in these classes, 90% of the time when observers looked around and estimated the percentage of students who were on task, 90% of the students were on task. The high-achieving classrooms were busy classrooms, abuzz with reading and writing activity. A cross-case analysis of these classrooms, and then a cross-case comparison of high-achieving classrooms relative to lower-achieving classrooms, resulted in the identification of a number of features distinguishing the classrooms with high achievement from those with less achievement.

Instructional Balance

Although all teachers combined skills instruction with reading of literature and writing, the teachers with the highest-achieving students seemed to integrate skills instruction with holistic activities better than the teachers of classes with lower levels of achievement. During the interviews, the teachers with high-achieving students were emphatic that neither an exclusive skills orientation nor an exclusive whole-language approach would fit their students well. Given the predominance of the whole-language model in upstate New York, we were struck with these teachers' openness about their skills instruction, with two of the three even using basal materials to develop phonics skills in students. What was also striking during every visit was how many skill-oriented mini-lessons occurred, with these teachers seeming to monitor their students carefully to detect who needed a mini-lesson and when they needed it (e.g., a mini-lesson on the sound "h" makes as a student struggled to spell the word "heart"). Despite the frequency of such mini-lessons, these classes never seemed like skills-driven classrooms, however, for the students were immersed in the reading of excellent children's trade books and in the writing of real stories and essays.

In contrast to the teachers with the highest-achieving classes, the other teachers who were observed did not integrate skills instruction and holistic experiences nearly as well. Rather, there seemed to be times in these classrooms that were set aside for skills teaching and times set aside for reading and writing. For example, in classes with lower achievement, spelling lessons were observed, but there was no connection to spelling made later during writing (i.e., invented spellings in compositions were accepted, even for words covered in spelling lessons). The connectedness between skills learning and application in the highest-achieving classrooms was not as apparent in the other classrooms observed in this investigation.

Instructional Density

There was always a great deal going on in the classrooms with the highest achievement, and, in particular, there was a lot of instruction. Moreover, the instruction was typically aimed at achieving multiple goals. For example, in one class the teacher taught about the long-"o" sound as she encouraged a student's vocabulary acquisition and conceptual development. This mini-lesson occurred as students were generating a list of words with the long-"o" sound as represented by the "oa" combination (see Chapter 6, p. 121).

Such mini-lessons happened all day in the classrooms with the highest-achieving students. Even mundane events, such as filling a stapler, were transformed into lessons in the classrooms with the highest achievement (e.g., the teacher asking students to name the color of the stapler, which was "silver," a new vocabulary word for them). Classroom routines, such as dismissal, were transformed into instruction in the high-achieving classrooms (e.g., students were required to spell words to get into the dismissal line). In contrast, instruction was not nearly as much an every-minute thing in first-grade classes with lower achievement.

Scaffolding

Many of the mini-lessons in the high-achieving classes involved scaffolding. That is, the teacher provided just enough support to enable a student to begin to make progress on a task but not so much as to be doing the task for the student. Scaffolding required that the teacher monitor students carefully and consistently. It also required that the teacher thoroughly understand the tasks students were attempting (e.g., having a complete knowledge of phonics in order to scaffold students' sounding out words). Consider, for example, this mini-lesson, as a student struggled to spell "duck":

TEACHER: D-u . . . What's at the end?

STUDENT: I don't know.

TEACHER: (*Writes "duk" on the board.*) Does that look right?

STUDENT: No

TEACHER: No. What's missing?

STUDENT: (*No response.*)

TEACHER: How do you spell "back"?

STUDENT: B-a-c-k.

TEACHER: So how are you going to spell "duck"?

STUDENT: D-u-c-k.

TEACHER: Good. (*Writes "duck" on the board.*)

Scaffolding was everywhere in the high-achieving classrooms and much more prominent in the high-achieving classes as compared with the low-achieving classes.

Encouragement of Self-Regulation

Good readers can read and write on their own—and do so. In the high-achieving classrooms, students were strongly encouraged to do things on their own as much as possible. As children were taught word attack, spelling, and comprehension strategies, they were also taught to use the strategies whenever they were appropriate. When students in the high-achieving classes did self-regulate, teachers often noted their self-regulation and reinforced it. Thus, after a boy named Kevin self-corrected himself during reading, his teacher remarked, "When Kevin made a mistake, what did he do? . . . Yes, he went back over it. It is okay to make mistakes." Teachers with high-achieving students consistently encouraged them to monitor how well they were doing and to make corrections as necessary.

Integration of Reading and Writing

In the high-achieving classrooms, there was thorough integration of reading and writing. Consistently, students were asked to respond to what they read by writing. Moreover, students in the high-achieving classes did a great deal of reading of their own writing, especially their rough drafts, as part of revising. Writing assignments often involved research, which required students to find materials in the library (and other places), which were read. Then the students wrote about the topic by incorporating ideas from the materials that were found in the library. Such projects permitted an integration of reading, writing, and content learning, with cross-curricular connections very prominent in the high-achieving classrooms.

High Expectations

Teachers with high-achieving classes had high expectations, believing that their students could learn, that they could be readers and writers. Moreover, the effective teachers communicated a "can-do" attitude to their students. Their expectations included high standards for behavior, with students knowing very well how they were to act in class. Indeed, all of the students in the high-achieving classes were well behaved most of the time.

Good Classroom Management

Management was impressive in classrooms where there was high achievement. The teachers had a set of routines to take care of the tasks that occurred every day, with morning meetings, movement to special classes, and dismissals all occurring efficiently. It was obvious in these classrooms that much planning had been done in advance of the school day. Yet, at the same time, these teachers seemed to be able to accommodate flexibly the moment-by-moment needs of their students, many of which were unpredictable (e.g., providing mini-lessons to small groups of students when it became apparent that there was a need). Time was well managed in these classrooms, with the daily calendar posted and teachers sticking to it throughout the day. Finally, the teachers with high-achieving students did a very good job of managing the other adults who entered their classrooms. Visitors to the class did not disrupt the class; the talents of adults, such as aides, were well used. In contrast, there were many disruptions in the classrooms in which achievement was lower, with outside adults drawing the teacher's attention from the class and aides often not knowing what to do.

Summary

The classrooms with high achievement in the Wharton-McDonald et al. (1998) study seem almost too good to be true. Although these classrooms were similar in many ways to other first-grade classes in the study, they were distinguished by the consistent engagement of students in reading, writing, and content learning. Teachers in the high-achieving classrooms were always coaching students, providing lots of assistance that permitted students to make academic progress. As helpful as these teachers were, they also encouraged students to do things on their own as much as possible (i.e., they encouraged self-regulation), consistent with their generally high expectations of their students. Even though the students did work on their own much of the time, these classrooms were filled with cooperative students, with little off-taskedness and much positive reinforcement.

OBSERVING FIRST-GRADE CLASSES IN NEW YORK, NEW JERSEY, TEXAS, WISCONSIN, AND CALIFORNIA

This section describes a study (Pressley et al., 2001) that followed up on the research of Wharton-McDonald et al. (1998), generating additional evidence to support the general conclusions reached in that investigation. Whereas the Wharton-McDonald et al. (1998) study was carried out in one geographic region of the United States, the follow-up was a national study. Faculty at the University at Albany had a wonderful opportunity in the mid-1990s, receiving a major grant from the U.S. Department of Education to host the Center for English Learning and Achievement (CELA). As part of that Center, it was proposed to carry out a study much like that of Wharton-McDonald et al. (1998), this time sampling from five states rather than just upstate New York. The University at Albany team was fortunate in being able to persuade some very able first-grade senior researchers to join them in this effort, including, most prominently, Lesley Mandel Morrow of Rutgers in New Jersey and Cathy Collins Block of Texas Christian University. The goal was to generate conclusions about excellent first-grade instruction that would not be tied only to New York state. We believe we succeeded in doing that; our efforts and the results of those efforts are summarized in this section (Pressley et al., 2001).

In each of five states, school administrators were asked to nominate first-grade teachers who were regarded as very effective in promoting literacy in their students, as well as teachers who were more typical in stimulating literacy development. As in the study by Wharton-McDonald et al. (1998), the administrators were left to their own devices to nominate teachers, with their selections depending on a variety of indicators ranging from test scores to parental perceptions of teacher effectiveness. In the end, eight teachers in New York were included in the study, six in New Jersey, eight in Texas, four in Wisconsin, and four in California. All of the teachers who were nominated, as being either very effective or more typical, were observed repeatedly over the course of the 1996–1997 school year and interviewed about their teaching in late 1997.

As in the Wharton-McDonald et al. (1998) study, rather than simply accepting the school administrators' evaluations of who was very effective versus more typical, the researchers who observed the teachers made their own judgments about teacher effectiveness based on what students were reading at the end of the year, the quality of student writing, and the extent of student engagement. That the researchers' judgments were valid received some support from an analysis of standardized test data that were collected in the study. A standardized reading test (Terra Nova) was administered to six students in 29 of the 30 classes in the study (i.e., two students considered to be high achievers by the teacher, two considered to be average, and two believed to be low achievers by the teacher). In the 30th class, only five students were tested (two high, two average, and one low). The analyses discussed in the rest of this section involved the very best teacher at each of the five sites, in comparison with the least effective teacher in each of the five sites. That is, the most effective teacher and the least effective teacher at each state site, as defined by observed achievement and engagement, were compared. Most critically, at all locales, reading test scores were descriptively better in the most effective, as compared with the least effective, classroom. The descriptive differences favoring the students in the five most effective classrooms are apparent in the data summarized in Table 3.1, which reports the comparison of student performances on the end-of-year standardized testing. Although the descriptive differences favored the students of the most effective-for-locale teachers at all achievement levels, it was the word analysis performances of the children in the most effective-for-locale classrooms that differed statistically from the performances of children in the least-effective-for-locale classrooms.

However, the differences in end-of-year achievement were most striking for the low-achieving students, as summarized in Table 3.2. The descriptive data for the standardized test performances illustrate

TABLE 3.1. Mean Terra Nova Scores for Students Taught by Most Effective and Least Effective Teachers (Collapsing across All Five Sites)

Subtest score	Most effective		Least effective	
	Mean	SD	Mean	SD
Passage reading	57.63	24.98	48.00	23.02
Vocabulary	55.17	22.36	48.41	18.83
Reading composite	55.87	24.63	48.07	21.55
Language	55.13	28.24	48.28	23.85
Word analysis*	57.80	20.75	43.76	15.09

Note. Means based on student of $n = 30$ for 5 most effective teachers and $n = 29$ for 5 least effective teachers, with 6 students (2 high, 2 average, 2 low) provided by each of the classrooms, except for one least effective classroom, which provided only one low reader.

*Difference significant, $p < .01$; all other differences, $p > .05$.

the clear differences in the performances of the lower-achieving students in the two types of classrooms. That is, the primary impact of the most effective teachers was observed in the dramatically improved performances of their lower-achieving students.

At each of the five sites, there were teachers who definitely produced higher achievement than other teachers at their site, as defined by test scores, the level of the books their students were reading by the end of the school year, and the length, coherence, and mechanical expertness of the students' writing. The teachers

TABLE 3.2. Mean Terra Nova Scores for Low-Achieving Students Taught by Most Effective and Least Effective Teachers (Collapsing across All Five Sites)

Subtest score	Most effective		Least effective	
	Mean	SD	Mean	SD
Passage reading*	51.50	22.30	28.78	16.66
Vocabulary	41.20	18.93	31.00	14.49
Reading composite	45.40	19.57	28.55	15.69
Language	42.70	30.43	30.89	19.09
Word analysis*	53.30	24.27	35.00	10.39

Note. Means based on student $n = 10$ for 5 most effective teachers and $n = 9$ for 5 least effective, with 2 provided by each of the classrooms, except for one least effective classroom, which provided only 1 low reader.

*Difference significant, $p < .05$; all other differences, $p > .05$.

who produced the highest achievement at their sites also had students who were more engaged in literacy than students in other
classrooms studied at the sites, with productive reading and writing
seeming to occur with 90% of their students more than 90% of
the time. In the classrooms of the five most effective teachers, most
students were reading at least at end-first-grade level by May, writing often involved several pages of coherent text, and students typically were busy reading and writing even when the teacher was not
looking over their shoulders. In contrast, in the five least effective
classrooms, there were high proportions of children who were not
at end-first-grade level by May. Typically, they wrote less than a
half page, with less coherence than students in the best classrooms
and less impressive mechanics. The least effective classrooms were
characterized by low student engagement and high proportions of
students typically off task.

Much was learned about these teachers because a great amount
of time was spent in their classrooms, with field notes taken during
every visit. The observers worked with the field notes to identify
comprehensively the elements of instruction for each teacher, in the
end constructing a portrait of each teacher's teaching, as had been
done in the Wharton-McDonald et al. (1998) study.

Commonalities across the Most Effective Classrooms

Especially striking was the degree of sameness in the most effective
classrooms, regardless of the state and regardless of the school setting (e.g., in the schools of most effective teachers, the status of their
populations ranged from socioeconomically advantaged to extremely
disadvantaged). Thus, we feature here a cross-case analysis that captured, in particular, the similarities across the most effective classrooms.

Skills Explicitly Taught

There was much teaching in the classrooms of the most effective
teachers, most of it occurring in the context of authentic literacy
tasks (i.e., real reading, writing of stories). Students were taught a
variety of word recognition, vocabulary-building, spelling, composition, and comprehension skills. When students experienced difficulties during reading and writing, there were mini-lessons (i.e., teach-

ing was opportunistic and driven by the needs of students). It was not unusual to see 10 or 20 skills taught explicitly during the course of an hour of instruction and activity.

Literature Emphasis

Literature featured prominently in the most effective classrooms, some read by the teacher and some by students. There were bins and bins of books and many nooks and crannies in the room set up to promote reading and literature experiences (e.g., an author-of-the-month table, a reading corner, a books-on-tape listening center). Teachers modeled skills for students and scaffolded the students' use of skills (i.e., by providing assistance when students experienced difficulties in using a skill).

Much Reading and Writing

There was much reading in the most effective classrooms, including buddy reading, choral reading, sustained silent reading, reading homework (i.e., books sent home to be read to parents), and one-to-one reading with the teacher. Similarly, there was much writing; writing was a daily activity.

Matching of Tasks to Student Competence

Teacher expectations of students were realistic; students were assigned tasks that were somewhat challenging but not overwhelming. The teacher monitored student progress carefully in order to make realistic assignments and demands, providing teaching as needed when students had problems in making progress (i.e., keeping frustration to a minimum).

Self-Regulation Encouraged

The teacher modeled self-regulation and encouraged students to self-regulate (i.e., to do tasks on their own as much as possible). As part of the instruction to encourage self-regulation, the teacher made certain that students knew what they were to do, taught them to check and reflect on their work, and taught them how to make wise choices (e.g., teaching them how to select books that would challenge them but not be too difficult).

Connections across the Curriculum

Students had opportunities to practice the skills they were learning across the entire school day (e.g., reading and writing about social studies and science themes). The vocabulary taught was driven by what the student read in the content areas, with the content-area instruction often driven by thematic units.

Positive, Reinforcing, Cooperative Environment

The observers were struck by the caring atmosphere in the most effective teachers' classrooms, with positive reinforcement and encouragement prominently occurring in the classrooms where achievement was highest. Cooperative learning translated into a consistent cooperative outlook in the classroom. Students learned that appropriate risk taking is okay; there was a can-do attitude in the classrooms headed by the most effective teachers.

Excellent Classroom Management

In the most effective classrooms, there were clear rules and expectations, as well as efficient routines. Teacher planning was apparent everywhere, from procedures of the morning meeting to the homework that left with the students. The tasks of the school day were planned so that students spent much more time on academically rich exercises than on assignments that were not mentally expansive (e.g., writing involved mostly writing, with little time devoted to illustrating, in comparison with classrooms characterized by lower achievement, in which writing and story illustration took comparable amounts of student time and effort). As dedicated to planning as the most effective teachers were, they were also flexible, changing plans when it made sense to do so. The most effective teachers also used a variety of grouping structures, ranging from whole groups to small groups to one-on-one instruction, depending on what made sense for particular lessons and the needs of students. Such flexible grouping and regrouping was made easier because the teachers had arranged their rooms physically to support all the types of grouping employed (e.g., the tables were arranged so that there could be multiple small groups, with the rug area used for students to meet as a whole group). Homework served multiple purposes, such as giving a child additional practice or informing parents about their child's progress. The most effective teachers had all kinds of procedures to ensure richness and continuity of instruction. Thus, books that contained great material but were too challenging for students to read on their own were read aloud to students. Students' questions were handled as they came up, but in ways that did not sidetrack the instruction. Discipline was handled quietly and quickly, with the student always back on task in a hurry. The most effective teachers were masterful at marshaling resources for the most at-risk students in such a way that the resources complemented classroom instruction (e.g., Title 1 aides assisted targeted students in the classroom with their regular assignments, rather than having students leave the room for add-on instruction that was not well connected with the regular classroom tasks).

Elements of Instruction Differentiating Most Effective from Least Effective Classrooms

When each pair of teachers (i.e., the most and least effective teachers in New York, the most and least effective teachers in New Jersey, etc.) was considered, there was always more of the following in the most effective classrooms:

- Many more skills were covered during every hour of instruction.
- Word recognition instruction more often involved teaching multiple strategies (i.e., phonics, noting word parts, looking at the whole word, using picture clues, using semantic context information provided earlier in the sentence or story, using syntactic cues).
- There was more explicit teaching of comprehension strategies (e.g., making predictions, mental imagery, summarizing, looking for elements of grammar in a story).
- Students were more likely to be taught to self-regulate.
- Students were taught more to plan, draft, and revise as part of writing.
- There was more extensive scaffolding (i.e., coaching) during writing, for example, with respect to spelling, elaborating on meanings in text.

- There were more printed prompts for the writing process (e.g., a card about what had to be checked as part of revision).
- By the end of the year, there were higher teacher demands that students use writing conventions (e.g., capitalizing, using punctuation marks, spelling of high-frequency words).
- Tasks were more designed so that students spent much time doing academically rich processing (i.e., reading and writing) and relatively little time on nonacademic processing (e.g., illustrating a story).
- The class wrote more big books, which were on display.

In summary, this study provided confirmation of the general conclusions reached by Wharton-McDonald et al. (1998). We close this chapter with a discussion of the nature of first-grade instruction at the end of the 20th century, especially first-grade instruction that is effective in stimulating the literacy development of students; this discussion provides a review of the main findings of Wharton-McDonald et al. (1998) and Pressley et al. (2001).

AMERICAN FIRST-GRADE INSTRUCTION AT THE DAWN OF A NEW MILLENNIUM

The two studies reported here provided a window on an important part of our educational culture. First grade has long been considered a critical experience in the development of children as readers. By immersing ourselves in first-grade classrooms for 2 years, we emerged with a detailed understanding of what such a critical experience is like. Achievement in literacy was much more certain in some first-grade classrooms than in others, and we now better understand how more successful first-grade classrooms differ from those that are less successful.

The grounded theory approach we used in these studies paid off. This approach requires continued observation and interviewing until the investigators have complete understanding of each classroom. By generating a complete case analysis of every classroom, we were in a good position to do cross-case analyses, producing the sets of cross-case conclusions that are the focus of this chapter. These analyses provided a detailed understanding about what grade 1 is like in general at the end of the 20th century in America, and, in particular, what excellent first-grade instruction is.

A visitor to any first-grade classroom in America is likely to see the following: A mix of skills instruction, with reading of real literature and writing of stories and responses to literature. Usually, there is spelling instruction. Small-group instruction is common, as is a physical structuring of the classroom to support small-group work (i.e., students sitting in clusters of four or six). First-grade teachers deeply care about their students and try to connect with their students' homes, recognizing the important role of parents in literacy instruction.

A visitor fortunate enough to walk into a classroom in which student reading and writing achievement is high will discover that the teacher's classroom management is so good that discipline is rarely a problem and that off-task behavior is exceptional, rather than typical. Skills instruction (e.g., word recognition instruction, including phonics and other approaches) is well integrated with reading and writing, and most students are busy with things academic most of the time. Prominent in these academic activities are planning, drafting, and revising as part of writing. The teacher is doing a great amount of scaffolding, noticing which students are struggling and doing what she or he can to help them make progress, but stopping well short of doing tasks for them. Providing "just enough" help so that students can do tasks on their own is consistent with the general encouragement of student self-regulation that occurs in outstanding first-grade classrooms. Moreover, such self-regulation is not just encouraged, but expected, and high expectations are the norm in these classrooms. By the end of the year most students in the class are reading books that end-first-grade students should be reading and are writing coherent stories that are several pages long, with reasonably good use of conventions.

Any first-grade classroom is complex. Excellent first-grade classrooms are very complex. The teacher coordinates the curriculum in response to 20 to 30 students, all of whom have unique developmental trajectories. The excellent teacher uses a variety of materials, tasks, and grouping structures to do so. Monthly, weekly, and daily planning provide a general outline of what will happen in these classrooms. What happens moment to moment, however, typically depends on student needs, with teachers monitoring student progress on tasks and providing scaffolding when they flounder. When students are successful, the excellent first-grade teacher encourages them to take on more challenging reading and more ambitious writing. If what a child is reading today proves to be just too difficult, the excellent first-grade teacher directs the child to books that are less frustrating. The excellent first-grade teacher is teaching mini-lessons all day and making a dozen or more instructional and curriculum decisions every hour.

REFERENCES

Au, K. H. (1998). Constructivist approaches, phonics, and the literacy learning of students of diverse backgrounds. In T. Shanahan & F. V. Rodriguez-Brown (Eds.), *Forty-seventh yearbook of the National Reading Conference* (pp. 1–21). Chicago: National Reading Conference.

Knapp, M. S., & Associates. (1995). *Teaching for meaning in high-poverty classrooms*. New York: Teachers College Press.

Ladson-Billings, G. (1994). *The dreamkeepers: Successful teachers of African-American children*. San Francisco: Jossey-Bass.

Moll, L. C. (1998). Turning to the world: Bilingual schooling, literacy, and the cultural mediation of thinking. In T. Shanahan & F. V. Rodriguez-Brown (Eds.), *Forty-seventh yearbook of the National Reading Conference* (pp. 59–75). Chicago: National Reading Conference.

Pressley, M., El-Dinary, P. B., Gaskins, I., Schuder, T., Bergman, J. L., Almasi, J., & Brown, R. (1992). Beyond direct explanation: Transactional instruction of reading comprehension strategies. *Elementary School Journal, 92,* 511–554.

Pressley, M., Wharton-McDonald, R., Allington, R., Block, C. C., Morrow, L., Tracey, D., Baker, K., Brooks, G., Cronin, J., Nelson, E., & Woo, D. (2001). A study of effective first-grade literacy instruction. *Scientific Studies of Reading, 5,* 35–58.

Pressley, M., Wharton-McDonald, R., Mistretta, J., & Echevarria, M. (1998). The nature of literacy instruction in ten grade-4/5 classrooms in upstate New York. *Scientific Studies of Reading, 2,* 159–191.

Ruddell, R. B. (1997). Researching the influential literacy teacher: Characteristics, beliefs, strategies, and new research directions. In C. K. Kinzer, K. A. Hinchman, & D. J. Leu (Eds.), *Forty-sixth yearbook of the National Reading Conference: Inquiries in literacy theory and practice* (pp. 37–53). Chicago: National Reading Conference.

Strauss, A., & Corbin, J. (1990). *Basics of qualitative research: Grounded theory procedures and research*. Newbury Park, CA: Sage.

Wharton-McDonald, R., Pressley, M., & Hampston, J. M. (1998). Literacy instruction in nine first-grade classrooms: Teacher characteristics and student achievement. *Elementary School Journal, 99,* 101–128.

4

Teaching Writing in First Grade
Instruction, Scaffolds, and Expectations

RUTH WHARTON-MCDONALD

For the literate individual, writing is not an end in itself, but a means for accomplishing something. Researchers and teachers agree that from the earliest levels of schooling, children need frequent opportunities to write (Block, 1997; Graves, 1983, 1994; Hiebert & Raphael, 1998; Pressley, Rankin, & Yokoi, 1996; Wharton-McDonald, Pressley, & Mistretta, 1998). First-grade students in the 1990s did a lot of writing—certainly more than any of us ever did when we were in grade school. According to all of the teachers we interviewed and observed, writing played an important role in their first-grade curricula. Students in nearly all of the classrooms we observed picked up pencils and wrote some form of connected text on a daily basis.

COMMON CHARACTERISTICS OF FIRST-GRADE WRITING INSTRUCTION

The Writing Process

In all classrooms, we observed some form of process writing (Graves, 1983). That is, at some point during the year, students in all first grades were expected to plan, compose a draft, revise and edit it, and produce a final written product. The extent to which teachers taught students how to use those processes, and the frequency with which students were expected to use them, varied widely across classes. Exemplary teachers were much more likely to provide instruction and expect students to use the process approach on a regular basis.

Reading and Writing Connections

Our observations suggested that in the minds of most first-grade teachers, reading and writing were inextricably linked. As one very good teacher put it, "I see writing as an integral part of reading development; I believe they develop together. One developing enables the other to develop." We have elsewhere characterized this relationship—in which reading and writing each contribute to the growth and strength of the other—as dialectical (Pressley, Wharton-McDonald, & Mistretta, 1998). First-grade students wrote in order to strengthen their decoding skills and to extend their understanding of texts; their reading, in turn, offered models for writing and opportunities to apply developing skills. Consistent with our findings in other domains of literacy development, exemplary teachers were much more conscious of the multiple purposes for which they encouraged students to write than were typical teachers (Pressley et al., 2001; Wharton-McDonald et al., 1998). They also facilitated development toward those goals in much more effective ways.

Frequently Observed Forms of Writing

The first-grade students wrote something nearly every day. The contexts for that writing varied across classrooms, but some commonalities were clear. All of the teachers we observed seemed to be familiar, at least in principle, with Don Graves's (1994) recommendation that children have frequent opportunities to write. Graves reports that when they write every day, children (like adults) enter a "constant state of composition," which enables them to maintain momentum in a piece and develop skills as a writer (p. 104). In theory, at least, these students should have been composing with ease.

Two types of writing predominated across the classrooms of the teachers we studied: journals and personal narratives. Other types of texts, produced less frequently, included true narratives (stories), informational texts, reading responses, letters, "how-to" descriptions, word problems, menus and meal orders, memos and announcements, and descriptions of classroom photos. Teachers varied in the extent to which they allowed students to choose the genres and topics for their writing. Because journals and narratives were so pervasive in the writing experiences of first graders, they are described in some detail in the following paragraphs.

Journals

Journals were featured in every classroom we observed. Most students wrote in personal journals at least three times a week, and many wrote every day. In all of the classrooms, teachers emphasized process and content over mechanics in this type of writing; no teacher expected students to edit their journal writing. The most common form of journal was a personal journal in which students described personal experiences and their reactions to events in their worlds. In many classrooms (especially in the exemplary classrooms), students also maintained more specialized journals, including *interactive journals* (in which students communicated with peers or their teacher), *response journals* (for responding to literature), *writers' journals* (for planning and writing more formal pieces), *science journals* (for recording scientific observations and hypotheses), *and home–school journals* (for communicating with parents).

Although journals were ubiquitous in first-grade classrooms, the ways in which they were used varied tremendously from one room to the next. Teachers had different purposes for journals, with the most effective teachers using them for multiple purposes. In general, three primary purposes for student journal writing emerged from interview and observational data:

1. *Student expression and fluency.* Many teachers described offering students an opportunity to get words down on paper without having to worry about spelling, punctuation, or other mechanics. In discussing the role of students' personal journals, one teacher related,

> "My main purpose is for them to write about whatever they want; there's no prewriting. It's a time to get what's going on down. I don't want them to get hung up on the mechanics. I want them to get their thoughts down on paper. . . . To me, the whole point

of [personal] journal writing is fluency, the ability to express your thoughts in words. I feel if you can't get your thoughts into words, there's nothing [on which] to put a capital letter and a period and the quotes."

A number of teachers echoed the words of another exemplary teacher who explained, "I want [my students] to understand that they have wonderful ideas in their heads, and sometimes if you can't express [them], people will never hear your good ideas; so in order to do that, you need to write [them] down in a journal."

2. *A chance to apply learned skills.* Although some teachers did not monitor the writing students did in journals, and none imposed corrections on students' entries, many teachers used students' journal entries diagnostically to monitor the children's understanding and use of the skills they were learning. Some of the typical and all of the exemplary teachers did read students' journal entries on a regular basis, and as they responded to the *content* of students' entries, they also recorded for themselves the extent to which students were incorporating writing conventions and developing phonemic awareness. Areas of strength and weakness were identified, and the exemplary teachers would then reteach specific skills as mini-lessons for children with demonstrated need. Thus, journals were used by some typical and all exemplary teachers to diagnose skill mastery and target instruction to only those students who needed it.

3. *A tool for communication.* A smaller number of teachers described journals as tools for maintaining communication with and among individual students. Student entries in these classrooms (distributed among the typical and exemplary teachers) tended to be predominantly personal narratives, and these teachers always responded to students on a regular basis. One exemplary teacher who used this practice described journals as an opportunity to learn about her students. She characterized their entries as "a window to their world." Other teachers emphasized the social aspects of literacy through shared journaling. Emphasizing communication, one of these teachers expressed a belief that "peer interaction is one of the keys to literacy development. . . . When children write, they are writing for their peers, in my opinion. And this is really clear to me when I have kids write in journals and listen to the conversations that they have about what they're writing."

Narratives

After journal writing, the most common type of text generated in first grade was the personal narrative. And, in fact, many journal entries consisted of narratives as well. Hagerty, Hiebert, and Owens (1989) reported that in classrooms in which teachers believed that children should always choose their own writing topics, children's writing consisted almost *entirely* of personal narratives. Our observations are consistent with that finding. First graders are, developmentally, egocentric little beings (Piaget & Inhelder, 1969). Their worldviews tend to center tightly on themselves. Thus, it is not surprising that the preferred subject and genre of first graders would be stories about themselves and their own lives. The examples in Figure 4.1 are representative of personal narratives written by "average" readers and writers in typical and exemplary classrooms.

Depending in large part on their teachers, children were able to achieve different goals within their narratives. According to Hiebert and Raphael (1998, p. 135), children use personal narratives to "share their inner and social worlds with others, to reflect and explore aspects of these worlds for themselves, and to construct new interpretations of their worlds." We found that, indeed, children with effective teachers did pursue these goals in their writing. In Figure 4.1a, Joey describes a series of significant events in his recent past and makes a generalization about life in his world ("Some days are lucky. Some days are not lucky."). Joey is able to use writing to analyze the circumstances in his world. In contrast, Brian, who has had fewer opportunities to write and no direct writing instruction in first

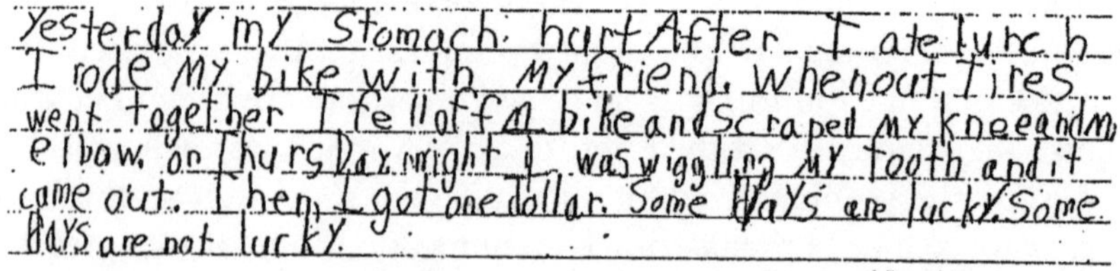
Yesterday my Stomach hurt After I ate lunch I rode My bike with my friend. Whenour Tires went together I fell off a bike and Scraped my kneeandm elbow. on Thursday night I was wiggling my tooth and it came out. Then I got one dollar. Some days are lucky. Some days are not lucky.

FIGURE 4.1a. Personal narrative by an "average" reader/writer in an exemplary first grade: "Yesterday my stomach hurt. After I ate lunch I rode my bike with my friend. When our tires went together I fell off my bike and scraped my knee and my elbow. On Thursday night I was wiggling my tooth and it came out. Then I got one dollar. Some days are lucky. Some days are not lucky."

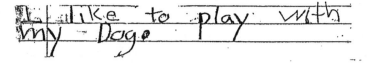

FIGURE 4.1b. Personal narrative by an "average" reader/writer in a typical first grade: "I like to play with my dog."

grade, limits his narrative to a single rote sentence. His other writing samples, when they have not been copied from the blackboard, followed the same pattern: "I like _____." At the time we observed him, Brian was not using writing to help him in any way. For him, writing was a daily exercise to be completed.

CHILDREN'S WRITING IN EXEMPLARY CLASSROOMS

By May of first grade, students in the classrooms with exemplary teachers were constructing full pages—sometimes several pages—of coherent text. They composed in multiple genres, routinely revised their work, and were expected to include conventional spelling, punctuation, and capitalization in their writing (see Table 4.1). Even students who were struggling in reading and writing were consistently able to generate a page of coherent text on a chosen or assigned topic. Figure 4.2 provides representative samples of students' writing in the spring of first grade in classrooms with typical and exemplary teachers. In each pair, it is clear that students in classes with exemplary teachers generated much more interesting, coherent, and understandable text. These students' writing samples scored higher on ratings of both coherency and conventions.

In addition to the individual texts being of a higher quality in classes with exemplary teachers, students in these classes composed in a variety of genres. In part because their teachers were more apt to integrate reading and writing across the content areas, these students were more likely to write different kinds of texts. In addition to personal narratives, which dominated the typical teachers' classrooms, students with exemplary teachers frequently wrote informational texts. In one classroom, for example, students wrote a news release describing the successful hatching of the classroom chicks. In another

TABLE 4.1. Comparison of Representative Writing Products in Exemplary and Typical First Grades

Writing characteristics	Typical first graders	First graders with exemplary teachers
Text length	• Often 2–3 sentences • Rarely longer than a page	• A page or more
Genres	• Personal narratives • Bed-to-bed stories ("First I, then I . . . ") • Repetitive daily journal entries	• Personal narratives • "True" narratives • Reading responses • Letters • Informational text • Science journals • Math journals
Coherency	• Writing is frequently incoherent. • Text most often follows one of two patterns: 1. Predictable and repetitive ("I love my dog. I love my mom. I love my techer"). 2. A series of disconnected sentences ("Today is Monday, March 14, 1995. My dog is name Bade. I play wit anna at my house").	• Writing communicates a coherent idea to an intended audience. • Compositions remain on topic for a page or more, have reasonable beginnings, middles, and endings, and consider the reader.
Conventions	• Left-to-right progression • Spacing between most words • Intermittent use of capitals and periods	• Left-to-right progression • Spacing between words • Consistent and accurate use of capitals, periods • Frequent use of exclamation marks and question marks

class, students explained the steps one needs to take in building a boat. In both these cases, the compositions were closely tied to students' personal experiences, yet they were expository rather than narrative.

In other cases, first-grade students wrote reports about ocean animals or birds in conjunction with units on these topics. The students first did research for the projects, reading informational texts at appropriate reading levels and taking notes to prepare for writing the reports. Report writing demands the integration of information from

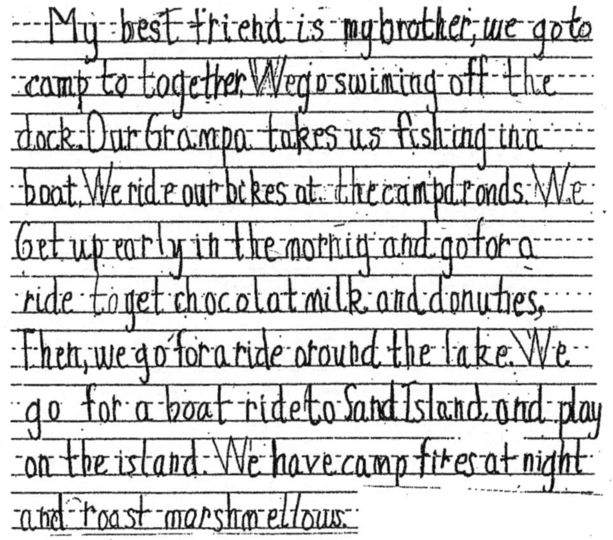

My best friend is my brother, we go to camp to together. We go swiming off the dock. Our Grampa takes us fishing in a boat. We ride our bikes at the campd ronds. We Get up early in the morning and go for a ride to get chocolat milk and donuthes, Then, we go for a ride around the lake. We go for a boat ride to Sand Island and play on the island. We have camp fires at night and roast marshmellous.

FIGURE 4.2a. Spring writing sample from a strong reader/writer in an exemplary first grade: "My best friend is my brother, we go to camp to together. We go swimming off the dock. Our Grampa takes us fishing in a boat. We ride our bikes at the campgrounds. We Get up early in the morning and go for a ride to get chocolate milk and donuts. Then, we go for a ride around the lake. We go for a boat ride to Sand Island and play on the island. We have campfires at night and roast marshmallows."

multiple sources. These students were able to accomplish this with targeted instruction from their teachers.

In addition to informational texts, students with exemplary teachers often wrote what Hiebert and Raphael (1998) term "true" narratives—otherwise known as stories. In contrast to the stories written in classrooms with less effective teachers, these had begin-

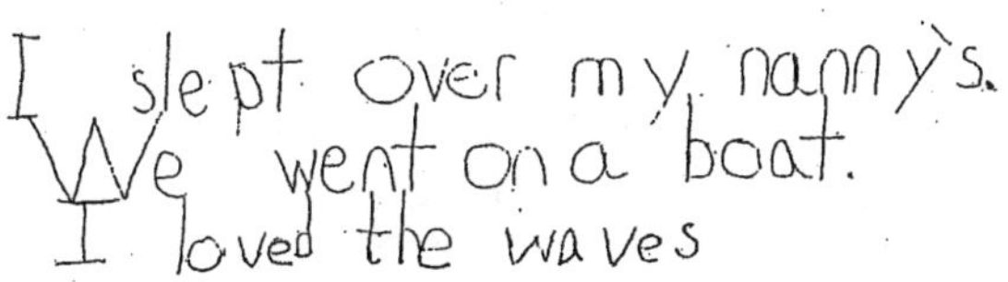

I slept over my nanny's. We went on a boat. I loved the waves

FIGURE 4.2b. Spring writing sample from a strong reader/writer in a typical first grade: "I slept over my nanny's. We went on a boat. I loved the waves."

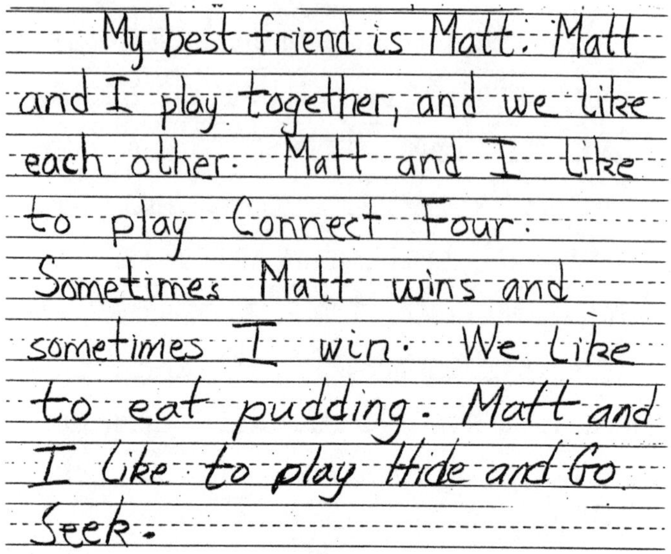

> My best friend is Matt. Matt and I play together, and we like each other. Matt and I like to play Connect Four. Sometimes Matt wins and sometimes I win. We like to eat pudding. Matt and I like to play Hide and Go Seek.

FIGURE 4.2c. Spring writing sample from a struggling reader/writer in an exemplary first grade: "My best friend is Matt. Matt and I play together and we like each other. Matt and I like to play Connect Four. Sometimes Matt wins and sometimes I win. We like to eat pudding. Matt and I like to play Hide and Go Seek."

nings, middles, and ends; they had consistent characters, a plot consistent with practiced story grammar, and they were generally coherent.

In fact, when we rated the approximately 180 writing samples we collected, we had found that the dimension that best differentiated students from exemplary and typical classes was *coherency*. Students with exemplary teachers were much better able to develop a coherent piece of writing—one that stayed on topic for several sentences and either made a point or told a story (or both).

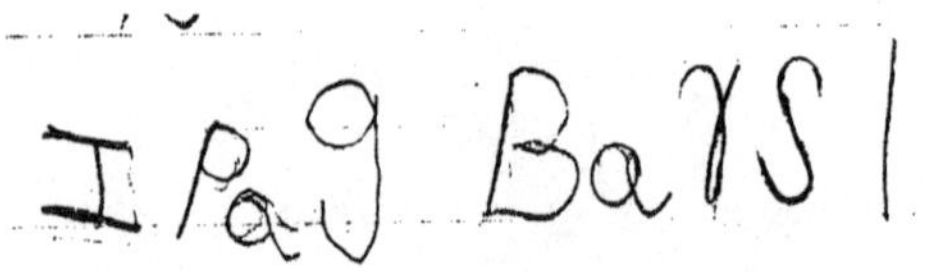

> I Pag Baysl

FIGURE 4.2d. Spring writing sample from a struggling reader/writer in a typical first grade: "I pag Baysl. [I played baseball.]"

INSTRUCTIONAL CHARACTERISTICS
OF EXEMPLARY TEACHERS

In general, the belief among most teachers was that the goals of teaching writing in first grade were to encourage students to enjoy writing, to focus on fluency, and to emphasize phonemic awareness as students moved toward using conventional spellings. What differentiated exemplary teachers from more typical teachers was their (firm) emphasis on using writing for the purpose of communication.

Exemplary teachers helped children use writing to accomplish goals—to communicate in ways that mattered to them. Simply writing words on a page does not constitute communication. An effective early writing program thus addresses the dual foci of communicative intent and writing conventions. The exemplary teachers we studied *taught* students how to write so that the intended readers could understand the message. They provided explicit writing instruction focused on both the message and the medium; they scaffolded students' learning and taught them to monitor their own progress; and they expected students to *use* what they were learning.

Expectations

There was a wide range in what first-grade teachers expected students to be able to accomplish in their writing by the end of the school year. Those with a strong developmental (Gesellian) perspective believed that children should be given opportunities to write, but that they should not be pushed to do anything until they were "ready." A typical teacher explained, "What I expect from children's writing by the end of first grade is that they have made some progress from the beginning of first grade. . . . By the end of first grade, my hope would be that the majority of my class would be . . . writing simple sentences . . . starting to write with lowercase letters. . . . They *may* use periods at the end of sentences." Another typical teacher said, "As far as punctuation's concerned, [I hope] they start with a capital letter and end with a period but . . . many of them don't." Compare this prospect with the expectations of exemplary teachers, which included many sentences on a topic, accurate spelling for high-frequency and phonetically regular words, capitals, periods, and coherency.

A measure that indicated a clear difference between the writers in exemplary and typical classrooms was the accuracy of the students' spelling. Like their more average peers, exemplary teachers encouraged invented spelling during the first few months of school as students were mastering the alphabetic principle. When asked about the role of invented spelling in reading development, one teacher explained, "It slows the [phonemic] process down for them so that they can focus on the sounds." Unlike their peers, however, exemplary teachers continually upped the ante over the course of the year, so that by the spring semester students were expected to use conventional spellings for high-frequency words, words that had been on spelling lists in previous weeks, phonetically regular words, and any words that appeared on classroom walls or in frequently used materials. Thus, it would still be acceptable to use invented spelling for a word like "turtle" or "special" in the spring. But words like "with" (high frequency), "take" (phonetically regular spelling word), or "chick" (in a class studying chicks and filled with books on chicks) must be spelled correctly.

When I asked one exemplary teacher in New York what she expected from her students in writing, she explained:

"My expectation is probably higher than what I might receive, because I don't want to limit [my students] and . . . I want them to work hard. I want them to apply what they know. So I would say, I would like to see complete sentences with a subject and a predicate. I would like to see capital letters and a period at the end . . . I would like to see the capital letter for proper nouns when possible. I would like them to be able to stay on one topic for perhaps four or five sentences. I think they've been *exposed* to much more than that. They've been exposed to paragraphing with a topic sentence and a conclusion (in the form of whole class lessons) . . . some of them will [apply that] and some won't right now."

Writing samples from two of this teacher's students (one struggling, one strong) appear in Figure 4.3. By May, her students were, in fact, writing at least several complete sentences on a topic, with a high proportion of accurate spelling, punctuation, and capitalization.

It was obvious to us that teacher expectations play an unmistakable role in determining what and how students will write by the end of first grade. Yet it is important to keep in mind that high expecta-

In the future
I want to be an
artist and teacher.
I want to be an
artist because I'm good
at drawing, coloring and
painting. I want to be
a teacher because
I'm smart and it looks like
fun. I'm going to colleg
[college]
to larn how to draw things
[learn]
and to teach children
. drawing, painting,
coloring and sculpting.
A teacher would do
math, L.A. and reading.
I will use the money
for the family, house,
taxes and bills, food and
clothes. the end

FIGURE 4.3a. Spring writing sample from a strong reader/writer in an exemplary first grade: "In the future I want to be an artist and teacher. I want to be an artist because I'm good at drawing, coloring and painting. I want to be a teacher because I'm smart and it looks like fun. I'm going to college to learn how to draw things and to teach children drawing, painting, coloring and sculpting. A teacher would do math, L.A. and reading. I will use the money for the family, house, taxes and bills, food and clothes. The end."

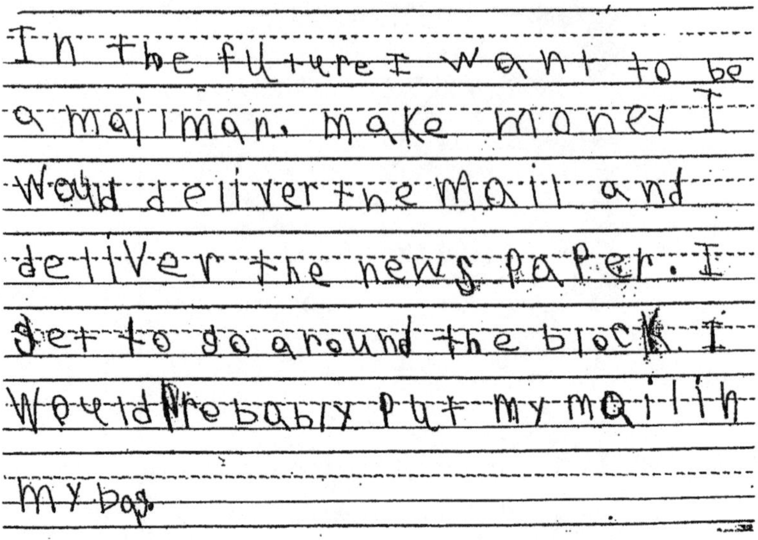

In the future I want to be
a mailman. make money I
would deliver the mail and
deliver the news paper. I
get to go around the block. I
would probably put my mail in
my bag.

FIGURE 4.3b. Spring writing sample from a struggling reader/writer in an exemplary first grade: "In the future I want to be a mailman. Make money. I would deliver the mail and deliver the newspaper. I get to go around the block. I would probably put my mail in my bag."

tions alone are not enough to enable students to write at higher levels. Most students do not come to first grade with an understanding of what it means to construct a coherent piece of text, much less how to construct one. Their mastery of basic writing conventions is rudimentary at best. Children do not acquire these skills just because teachers give them opportunities to write and expect them to produce. Exemplary teachers *taught* their students how to write.

Instruction

Explicit writing instruction in these classrooms typically took the form of a 15-minute group lesson, focused on a particular aspect of writing. Most often this lesson included extensive modeling by the teacher and examples from classroom books. Next, there followed opportunities to use the strategy in composition, during which the teacher provided individualized scaffolding for students who needed it. In the following lesson, an exemplary teacher teaches her students about paragraphs:

TEACHER: Today we're going to be talking about putting a whole idea together. We're going to talk about paragraphs. You've heard me say that before with your writing. What is a paragraph?

STUDENT 1: So you keep it all together.

STUDENT 2: A picture graph.

TEACHER: Teacher: Good for you. You hear the word "graph" in "paragraph." If I take a book—any book—and look at a page . . . (*Picks up a chapter book and opens it for the class.*)

The teacher goes on to show students what a paragraph looks like and explains its function. As she talks, she writes on an easel:

A group of sentences written about the same idea.
To show a paragraph is starting, indent or move in the first sentence.

Next, the teacher explains that they are going to be building a paragraph in the form of a deli sandwich. She asks the students to pick a topic they know a lot about, and someone suggests worms— related to their current science unit. With large pieces of construction paper shaped like the parts of a sandwich, the class proceeds to construct a paragraph "sandwich," using the information they know about worms. After about 10 minutes, they have completed a five-sentence paragraph together (and reviewed what they were learning about earthworms in the process). The teacher rewrites the sentences as an indented paragraph below the sandwich, and the students read it together. Students then select topics on which they are experts and write their own paragraphs, starting with sandwich pieces and ending up with a correctly indented paragraph.

Exemplary teachers made decisions about what to include in their writing lessons, based on two primary sources: The first-grade literacy continuum at the school provided a set of general guidelines for what should be taught by the end of the year. Experience helped effective teachers to know what strategies and skills to introduce when. An equally important source of information for these teachers was the cues they took from the children's writing itself. The exemplary teachers we studied regularly used the writing in students' journals and compositions to determine the skills and strategies they needed to address next (and which ones they needed to review).

Many of the teachers we observed taught children to use basic writing conventions at the level of the sentence: Begin with a capital letter, insert spaces between your words, end with a period. Some expected students to use conventional spelling; some did not. What distinguished exemplary teachers was that the level of their writing instruction went far beyond the level of the sentence to address the structure, content, and message of the entire composition.

Reading and Writing in Multiple Genres

One of the reasons that students in exemplary classrooms could write in multiple genres was that they regularly read (and heard) books from multiple genres. Children like to read and hear traditional narratives, of course. But they also enjoy informational science and social studies books, adventures, autobiographies, historical fiction, joke books, a variety of magazines, and fantasy, among other types of reading. And, like adults, children write using the text structures with which they are familiar. When they read and hear a variety of kinds of texts, students have models that help to guide their own writing. Conversely, if they hear only traditional narratives, they have little to draw on when they are asked to write about whales—even if they know quite a lot about whales. Without models, children are ill prepared to write informational text.

One of the exemplary teachers with whom we worked understood the relationship between exposure to style and the ability to generate a style in this way: "[Students'] reading influences their writing because of the structure of the sentences and the structure of their style in their writing. You can hear when they've been reading a certain author. You can hear the fairy tale. The, 'Hi. I'm Emily Elizabeth' [from the *Clifford the Big Red Dog* series by Norman Bridwell, 1985]. You know, they use their own name, but it's the same structure." This teacher was developing a unit in which she explicitly taught students to monitor the style of particular authors—and then encouraged them to try those styles themselves. By helping students to analyze the writing of Norman Bridwell or Bill Peet or Patricia Reilly Giff, this teacher empowered her students as both readers and writers. They didn't just know Bill Peet as the guy who wrote *Wump World* (1981). They also knew that he loved to use words like

"Kaploof!" and "Kerwham!" when he described action scenes. Students could then choose to borrow from that style in their own descriptive writing.

Also at this higher order of writing development, many teachers described the links between the process of creating for an audience (writing) and that of decoding text to understand a message (reading). As one exemplary teacher put it,

> "I think being able to write helps [students with] reading comprehension . . . because it's a process of how to have a beginning, a middle, and an end. . . . I always start with something they're reading . . . and then you get into *how you get there*. Writing is the message you're trying to give someone else to read. So you have to know how to present it so someone else can decode what you have to say."

Teaching Story Grammar

As part of teaching writing, most of the exemplary teachers we studied taught students the elements of story grammar. They helped students to write coherent pieces by teaching them how to make sure that the composition had a beginning, a middle, and an end. For writing fiction, they taught students to develop characters, settings, conflicts, and solutions. These lessons most often began with some clear examples from children's literature (fairy tales were often used as a starting point). After mapping out the elements in several stories, the teachers followed by composing a story with the class, incorporating the necessary elements. Only after the students had had several opportunities to see how other authors used the grammar to structure their stories would they be expected to use it in their own writing.

Developing Independence and Regulation Strategies

In addition to teaching students the conventions and structures of good writing, exemplary teachers taught students how to regulate themselves as writers. Students learned strategies for choosing a topic, monitoring their progress in a piece, and evaluating completed works and works in progress. Again, much of this was accomplished through teacher modeling. One teacher was observed thinking aloud about how to select her next writing topic: "Let's see. The last thing I wrote was a story about my dog. I usually have the most to write about when I write about something I know a lot about. What else do I know a lot about? I know a lot about my family. I know a lot about fishing because I like to go fishing. . . . Last summer I went fishing in the ocean—they call that 'deep sea fishing'—and I caught shark instead of a fish. Boy, was I surprised! Maybe I'll write about that." After some initial discussion with the students, the teacher created an organizational web on the easel, mapping out the things she wanted to include in her next composition. This was followed by an opportunity for students to do a similar think-aloud exercise of their own.

Writing Conferences

Another way teachers helped students learn to evaluate their writing was through the use of writing conferences. Many of the classrooms we observed included some form of peer conferencing during the writing process. What went on in these conferences differed significantly from one class to the next. The primary difference between peer conferences in the classrooms with exemplary teachers and those in other classrooms was that exemplary teachers *taught* students how to use a conference effectively and thus enabled them to use conferences productively.

When they first introduced the concept of a writing conference, exemplary teachers modeled the process with students. Then students role-played some conferences. The focus in these interactions was on meaning: Did the child's story make sense? Where did the reader get confused? What other information would the reader like to know about the character or topic? The tendency in many of the typical classrooms was for writing conferences to develop a rote pattern in which listeners asked the identical questions of every writer ("How did you choose what to write about?") or gave the same feedback ("I like your picture"), regardless of the piece of writing. In one classroom, I observed a conference among three students who had all written on the topic of bunnies. After each child read his or her story, one of the listeners would ask, "If you had a bunny, what would you name it?" This was the only question asked during the three conferences. Apparently, it was a question the teacher had asked of someone the day before. On this day, however, none of the stories had anything to do with naming a bunny. Clearly, the feedback in a conference such as this has little value to the writer (or to the listener, for that matter).

In contrast to this interaction, the writing conferences we observed in the exemplary classrooms maintained a sense of authenticity. Children were thoughtful about their peers' writing. They sought and received feedback that could actually help to improve their writing. Teachers ensured that this happened by teaching and modeling the process initially, and then continuing to monitor the interactions, intervening when they threatened to go astray, as they did in the preceding example. (In that instance, the teacher was sitting in on the conference and didn't seem to think that there was anything wrong with the way it proceeded.) In classrooms with effective teachers, peer conferences were not just another step in a meandering process. They had purpose and they moved students' writing forward. Moreover, they modeled for individual students the steps they could take themselves prior to the conference. The idea was for the writer to critically evaluate his or her own writing before bringing it to a conference.

Scaffolding

In addition to the direct instruction exemplary teachers provided, there was a great deal of scaffolding that went on in their classrooms. Scaffolding is described elsewhere in detail (see Chapter 3). Don Graves refers to these ongoing, individualized interventions as "nudging" students: "A nudge suggests a slight push in the right direction" (Graves, 1994, p. 93). In the context of writing, teachers did a number of things that helped to nudge individuals and groups of students toward the challenging goals set by their teachers.

Resources

As described earlier, exemplary teachers increasingly expected students to use accurate spelling in their writing. But they did not expect that children would be able to accomplish that entirely on their own. Rather, these teachers made available a range of resources and taught students how to access them. As they wrote, students were encouraged to make use of the information provided by word walls, spelling dictionaries, charts and lists, related books, and peers. Moreover, students were not just permitted to use these resources, they were *ex-pected* to do so.

Group Discussions and Brainstorming

Much of the scaffolding that went on in these classrooms was facilitated by the teacher, but actually provided by peers. A common strategy for developing topics, organizing information, and reviewing skills was to have students meet in groups (often the whole group, sometimes in small groups) to brainstorm ideas. In one classroom, the topic selected by the teacher was "best friends." The students were to compose essays about their best friends. As the students talked about their friends, the teacher wrote categories on a chart: *What is his/her name? What do I like to do with my friend? Places we go? Games we play? What I like best.* Discussions such as these helped to generate ideas, vocabulary, and, often, an organizational structure for a piece.

Graphic Organizers

In the preceding example, the information generated by students was then used to develop a semantic web, with "my best friend" in the middle and the various categories arranged in bubbles around the edges. Exemplary teachers frequently used graphic organizers like this to help students plan their writing or understand the structure of someone else's writing. We collected a variety of charts that teachers used in mapping story grammar with children. These charts were used initially to record the elements of a familiar book (e.g., *Goldilocks and the Three Bears*) and subsequently distributed to the students to help them plan their own stories with well-developed characters, settings, climaxes, and resolutions.

When we commented positively about his students' "best friend" compositions, the aforementioned teacher responded,

> "Yes, they can write a whole page. But if I had just said, 'Go write about your best friend,' they weren't going to write a whole page. . . . There is a lot of preliminary discussion that happens before they go and do that. I mean, we sit down and we make a little web. Best friends. What are some things we know? You fill out several things on the web. Then you can go and write. . . .

But I would never see the kind of successful long-term writing from the number of kids that I do if they didn't have that kind of writing process [see Chapter 6]."

Checklists

As part of their efforts to encourage students to monitor their own performance, exemplary teachers had a collection of checklists and reminders that prompted students to take responsibility for revision and editing. For example, one checklist prompted students to do the following before they could bring a draft to the teacher: Check for capital letters. Check for periods and question marks. Check for spelling. Read it to yourself. Does it make sense? Read it to a friend. These checklists helped students develop independent strategies for improving their writing.

Mini-Lessons and Teacher Conferences

In addition to the planned supports described here, exemplary teachers provided individualized feedback assistance as needed throughout the day. As described elsewhere, these teachers were exceptionally good at monitoring their students' progress and struggles. As a result, they were also very good at intervening with just the right "nudge" to facilitate that progress. Teachers often took aside small groups of students to reteach a strategy or rule. They made sure that students who needed feedback on their writing at multiple stages got it.

Exemplary teachers carefully monitored their students' progress in writing and continually pushed it forward. They set high expectations and then provided the instruction and support that enabled students to meet those expectations.

CONCLUSION

Many teachers believe that students in first grade simply need opportunities to pick up a pencil and put it to paper. They are satisfied when children end the year writing a sentence or two. After all, what can you expect from 7-year-olds? In fact, one of our now exemplary teachers describes her own early expectations of students that way:

"My first year I absolutely did not believe that first graders could write. Period. And any time, in any kind of teacher's manual or in some kind of activity where they said, 'Have your students write such and such,' I'd say, 'They have got to be kidding. Obviously, they don't know anything about first graders, because first graders can't write.' "

Our research indicates that when it comes to writing, first graders will give you what you ask for. If the teacher is satisfied with a single sentence and a picture, then that is exactly what most students will be producing at the end of the year. If, on the other hand, students are taught the attitudes, skills, and strategies of writing—and are expected to apply them—then, in fact, they become writers.

The strategies and approaches that exemplary teachers use to teach writing in their classrooms are not different from the ones they use to teach reading. This is not surprising, inasmuch as exemplary teachers see reading and writing as tightly interwoven processes, each supporting and being supported by the other. Effective teachers provide students with many models of good writing, they teach students how to write effectively to communicate, and they know (as the aforementioned teacher discovered) that with the proper tools and opportunities, first graders *can* write—and write well.

REFERENCES

Block, C. C. (1997). *Teaching the language arts: Expanding thinking through student-centered instruction* (2nd ed.). Boston: Allyn & Bacon.

Bridwell, N. (1985). *Clifford, the big red dog.* New York: Scholastic.

Graves, H. D. (1983). *Writing: Teachers and children at work.* Portsmouth, NH: Heinemann.

Graves, H. D. (1994). *A fresh look at writing.* Portsmouth, NH: Heinemann.

Hagerty, P., Hiebert, E., & Owens, M. (1989). Students' comprehension, writing, and perceptions in two approaches to literacy instruction. In S. McCormick & J. Zutell (Eds.), *Cognitive and social perspectives for literacy research and instruction* (pp. 453–460). Chicago: National Reading Conference.

Hiebert, E. H., & Raphael, T. E. (1998). *Early literacy instruction.* Fort Worth, TX: Harcourt Brace.

Peet, B. (1981). *The wump world.* Boston, MA: Houghton Mifflin.

Piaget, J., & Inhelder, B. (1969). *The psychology of the child.* New York: Basic Books.

Pressley, M., Rankin, J., & Yokoi, L. (1996). A survey of instructional practices of primary teachers nominated as effective in promoting literacy. *Elementary School Journal, 96,* 363–384.

Pressley, M., Wharton-McDonald, R., Allington, R., Block, C., Morrow, L., Tracey, D., Baker, K., Brooks, G., Cronin, J., Nelson, E., & Woo, D. (2001). A study of effective first-grade literacy instruction. *Scientific Studies of Reading, 5,* 35–58.

Pressley, M., Wharton-McDonald, R., & Mistretta, J. (1998). Effective beginning literacy instruction: Dialectical, scaffolded and contextualized. In J. Metsala & L. Ehri (Eds.), *Word recognition in beginning literacy* (pp. 357–373). Mahwah, NJ: Erlbaum.

Wharton-McDonald, R., Pressley, M., & Mistretta, J. (1998). Literacy instruction in nine first-grade classrooms: Teacher characteristics and student achievement. *Elementary School Journal, 99,* 101–128.

Part II

The Case Studies

The conclusions summarized in Chapters 3 and 4 were distilled from case studies of effective first-grade teachers. What has been amazing to us as we have done this research is that the excellent first-grade teachers we have studied do, in fact, have so much in common, regardless of where they teach or the specific characteristics of the children they teach. Over years of observing such teachers, we have marveled at how they do what they do, how they juggle the many facets of grade-1 teaching to construct classrooms that are magnificently orderly and unambiguously effective in advancing children's literacy. We learned much from studying these classrooms, and we believe that you, the reader, will learn much from them as well. Thus, each of Chapters 5 through 9 is a case study of an effective classroom that we studied as part of the program of research summarized in this book. We think you will have little difficulty in spotting the similarities in teaching across these cases, even though each classroom had a unique personality, reflecting a master first-grade teacher's creative orchestration of all that goes on in a first grade that develops readers and writers.

For each case study, a number of observations were made in the classroom over an extended period of time, ranging from several months to the entire school year. Each case study was developed to be revealing about the many activities occurring in exemplary first grades, focusing on the diverse types of reading, writing, and instruc-

tion that fill students' days. There also is attention to management issues, largely because management in these classrooms was so good.
The authors' intent is to provide enough information about these
classrooms that readers can definitely imagine them in the mind's
eye.

5

Barbara Wiesner

Barbara Wiesner, a 27-year veteran of teaching, serves in a Madison, Wisconsin, public school. Although her school is located in one of Madison's more affluent neighborhoods, it has a diverse student body, in part due to bussing of students to the school. Her multigrade (i.e., grades 1 and 2) class is definitely diverse with respect to socioeconomic level, race, and ethnicity. It is also diverse with respect to ability level, with the grade-1 team intentionally making certain that each class contains high-, middle-, and lower-achieving students. Even so, as compared with previous classes, Barb thought that this year's group was composed of mostly average students, with a small percentage of especially strong or weak students.

Barb reported that at the beginning of the year, about a third of the grade-1 students were already reading to some extent. Several were reading at the second- or third-grade level, and others were still emergent readers, knowing no core words. In general, the students arrived at her classroom with a positive attitude about reading and writing, having come from a very strong kindergarten experience in which reading materials and literacy activities were prevalent.

On any given day, Barb is joined in the room by an educational assistant or two, who assist two students with disabilities who are included in the classroom. There are often one or more parent volunteers and, at times, a student teacher.

If there is an enduring image of Barb's classroom, it is one of children engaging productively in reading, writing, and problem solving. Indeed, one of the real hallmarks of Barbara's classroom is that most of the time most of the students are busy doing things that are good for their heads. What is especially striking is that the students consistently know what they are to be doing (or their range of options) and do it. During my visits to Barbara's class I was consistently thinking about how self-regulated the students were. I was also consistently impressed with how fluidly the students interacted with one another, often reading to one another and assisting each other with writing. No one seemed to be marginalized. Indeed, even one little boy who had significant communication impairments participated much like other students in the class, although almost always with the assistance of an aide.

The students' engagement was so complete that they hardly seemed to notice when the recess bell rang; the work simply continued until Barb let the class know it was time to go out. In addition, individual students and groups of students often elected to remain at work rather than take recess.

The self-regulation and engagement that are so apparent in Barb's classroom did not just happen. Barb believes that promoting student self-regulation is very important. From the first days of school in the autumn, Barb encourages self-regulation. The grade-2 students, who were in Barb's grade-1 group the previous year, are paired with grade-1 students to model and help the newcomers to learn classroom routines and expectations. Part of behaving in this class is to do things for oneself—for example, reading with a buddy and then checking off on a record sheet that partner reading was accomplished.

There are clear expectations and ground rules, which the students helped to develop (e.g., "Use quiet voices"). Barb talks a great deal with students about their role and responsibility in making the classroom a peaceful and productive place to learn. Cooperation is expected. These discussions are always respectful of the students and encourage their input to improve the way the classroom works. Thus, when it was a little noisier than usual during a lesson supervised by a student teacher, Barb called the group together to the rug and then lead a soft-spoken discussion of the ground rules, a discussion that emphasized self-regulation. On this occasion she reminded the students, "Each of you will do your own talking in your head about what you are doing." This group discussion worked, and the class was back to business as usual for the rest of the day. In relating this group mini-lesson reminder about following the class rules, I also emphasize that this was the only occasion in my many hours of observation in the class that I observed such a lesson. There simply was not much need for this type of discussion in reaction to student misbehavior, for there was not much student misbehavior or waning of attention to discuss, and certainly not nearly as much as I have witnessed in many other grade-1 classrooms.

One way that Barb encouraged self-regulation was to model it herself. Thus, on one occasion during DEAR (i.e., drop everything and read) time, one of the pupils with disabilities acted out and shouted at his aide. Barb did not miss a beat in her reading, simply remaining engaged while the aide exited with the student. In addition, Barb consistently praised students for their efforts. Indeed, her approach was unambiguously positive; she consistently interacted with students in a good-natured, gentle way, constantly pointing out their accomplishments to them. In doing so, however, she continuously increased demands on students. Thus, it was not unusual at all for Barb to praise a student for excellent reading of a book and in the next instant to be persuading the student that she or he would really enjoy another book, one a little more demanding. On other occasions Barb praised writing ("I really like that you wrote a whole page"), but in the next instant gently demanded better ("But how about writing it over, because I know you can write much more neatly, and I know you'll be prouder of your writing if it is really neat"). When praise was not in order, Barb let students know that too, although always in a friendly, respectful way that made clear the need for greater self-regulation by the student. Thus, a student who attempted to hand in a messy sample of writing was told, "I'm sorry, but that's not good enough. It doesn't take that long. It is part of your responsibility."

In an interview with me, Barb was quite explicit that she felt it important to praise progress made but also to expect the students, even first graders, to do their best and to challenge themselves. She firmly believes that teacher expectations matter a great deal. She was also explicit in her belief that self-regulation was best encouraged by downplaying students' competition with one another and emphasizing student self-improvement. Barb emphasizes the students' own roles in their learning and that it is their efforts that make the difference in how much they learn.

When students made the effort and succeeded, Barb let them know. The air in her classroom was filled with quiet reinforcements to students, such as: "You did very well today, and I'm so proud of you" and "Don't you feel smart, for you did a great job." I do not know how many times I heard, "You did it!"

DAILY SCHEDULE

The day begins with all class members assembled on the rug for the morning meeting. Like morning meetings in many grade-1 classrooms, Barb's meetings included attendance, lunch counts, calendar, student reading of morning messages, and a preview of the day's activities. Much teaching goes on during the morning meeting, however. Thus, when there was some disagreement about what type of weather should be recorded for the day, Barb turned it into a mini-lesson on perspective taking, about how people could differ in their opinions about something. When the students noted the day of the month on February 22, Barb stimulated one student in the group to use concrete manipulatives to represent the number 22 in several different ways and to explain the various representations to the class. There were also more poignant lessons during morning meeting; for example, Barb noted the presence of a child who had been attending school irregularly. "Willy, we miss you when you aren't in school. Will you try to come?" In short, diverse teaching occurred during morning meeting.

After morning meeting, there were typically large blocks of time for language arts activities, such as journaling, spelling, and reading, and after midmorning recess, a large block of time for math. DEAR time tended to occur in the early afternoon, with the rest of the afternoon devoted to special classes and activities (e.g., computers, science, music, gym).

TYPES OF READING

A great deal of reading by both students and the teacher went on in this class. Barb frequently read outstanding literature to the class. Indeed, I never observed Barb read anything to the class that was not a classic piece of literature. Some of the readings were driven by the "Author of the Month"; for example, when Barb read Keiko Kasza's *The Wolf's Chicken Stew* to the class. This reading permitted a writing connection, with Barb discussing how Keiko Kasza wrote about what she knew about, a characteristic of good writers. She described Kasza's writing as being much like the students' extended journal writing over the Christmas holidays. Barb also read excellent poetry to the students, including adults' poems, such as Robert Frost's "Stopping by Woods on a Snowy Evening." Barb did read-alouds for books connected to content areas of the curriculum. For instance, Barb read to the class a book on symmetry, which connected directly to lessons on symmetry during math instruction. One of the purposes of teacher read-alouds, in Barb's view, is to expose students to good literature and a variety of genres that they cannot yet read on their own, but that nonetheless may be quite intriguing to them. Barbara believed that reading aloud to students increases their fluency and comprehension and has a positive influence on their writing as well.

In addition to teacher readings, there were readings of classic children's stories during the daily library storytime, and students in the class often attended such readings. An extensive in-class library of books on tape also afforded students opportunities to hear and re-hear stories. Headset-equipped listening stations were available so that a student could listen to a tape without disturbing other students.

A central reading activity for students, termed "Book-It," was borrowed from the Pizza Hut reading promotion label. Every day students were responsible for selecting a book, which was first read to an adult at school and then taken home to be read to parents. After hearing the child read the book, the parent signed a reading card that was in the plastic bag containing the day's Book-It reading. The student was also responsible for reading each book aloud to two classmates, who also signed the reading card for the student. As part of reading, the student was to identify three new words in the book being read and record them on the same card. Thus, by the time the student read the Book-It book with Barb, she or he would have been through it several times.

Reading of the Book-It books was the centerpiece of side-by-side, one-to-one reading lessons with Barb. Before a student read her or his Book-It book for Barb, she asked the student to recall the story for her, typically with some follow-up questions. This permitted Barb to appraise the student's comprehension and memory of the story. As she listened to the student read, Barb made notes on the student's progress and difficulties. Thus, on one day, she noted for one student that she (1) read slowly, (2) read to periods without halting, and (3) self-corrected. For another student, Barb observed that he (1) read haltingly, (2) did not self-correct, and (3) was not comfortable with problem solving to figure out new words. Barb often gave a mini-lesson, for example, reminding a student about the silent-"e" rule when the child experienced difficulties sounding out a word ending in silent "e." She believes that multiple readings of each Book-It selection promotes fluency and independence. Students hear themselves read well, and, in turn, they are empowered to believe in themselves as readers.

The Book-It activities were supported by a classroom library of books organized by level of difficulty, following the rating system used in Reading Recovery. When the student could read a book successfully with Barb, she helped the student select a new Book-It reading, with that selection informed by her knowledge of how the child had done with the just completed book. If the child seemed to be reading but struggling a bit, another book at the same level of difficulty might be recommended. If the child seemed to have had an easy time with the book just completed, Barb might encourage the student to select a slightly more difficult book.

Consistent with her development of student self-regulation, Barb made recommendations of possible books if needed, but students mostly selected their own books. Thus, the Book-It selections included a variety of genres (i.e., nonfiction, fiction, science, biography, mystery, poetry, math, fairy tale), and Barb encouraged students to select books from all of these categories to read. Barb related in her interview that she thought it was important to encourage and honor student choices. Her view was that if a student found a book to read that was interesting to her or him, that would provide important motivation for reading. Consistent with her orientation to encourage self-regulation, Barb provided students with strategies for making their own choices about whether a book was appropriate in respect to its level of difficulty. She taught them the rule of five, which was to put up a finger for each unfamiliar word in the book (i.e., words they did not know), and if the number exceeded five, the book was probably not a good choice. The students became experts at deciding whether a book was too easy, too hard, or just right. Students also learned how to skim through the pictures of a book and/or read the back cover summary to determine whether the topic was of interest to them.

Self-regulation was encouraged in another way within the context of the Book-It activities. An important part of self-regulation is to have goals and to work toward those goals. Thus, students set reading goals for themselves, indicating how many books they wanted to read during a given month. The number varied from student to student, with Barb encouraging students to set goals for themselves that were challenging yet attainable.

There was a great deal of time provided during the day when students could just read. The amount of opportunity for silent reading generally well exceeded the 15 minutes a day scheduled for DEAR time. Often students read at their worktables, but there also was a reading corner with comfortable pillows. Students read to one another and to others, such as parent volunteers, aides, and other school personnel. Besides the Book-It books, the classroom contained many other books, including a large selection pertaining to science. There was always a collection of books associated with the Author of the Month and whatever science or social studies topic was currently being studied. Students also borrowed books from the school library, and the library served up entire cartfuls of books related to particular themes in the grade-1–2 curriculum. Barb's students definitely had access to a large and varied supply of books to encourage them to become avid readers.

WRITING

Students wrote every day. There was daily journaling, requiring the students to write about their personal experiences. For example, every week there was a student VIP of the week, and students were asked to write in their journal about the VIP. When students were doing research on particular animals, they responded to questions about the animals in their journals. There was journaling related to mathematics also, with students asked to solve a problem each day, recording its solution in their journals. They could use pictures, prose, or a combination of both to do this, with Barb encouraging the students to write. Math problem explanations might be only one or two sentences long, but could be as long as four or five sentences or a half page.

Barbara explained in her interview that at the beginning of the year, journaling was done simply to give students a chance to experience writing without being pressured. As the year progressed, she viewed journaling as an opportunity for students to try the various skills they were acquiring (e.g., learning to write topic sentences).

Sometimes students wrote essays that related to content-area work; for example, at mid-year they wrote essays about animals during the time that a unit on animals was being presented. These essays tended to be three to four sentences long on average, with reasonably good use of conventions (i.e., capitalization, end-of-sentence punctuation) and reasonably good spelling (i.e., correct spelling of most high-frequency words, sensible invented spellings for less familiar words). In fact, one of the strengths of all the writing in Barb's class was the student's appropriate use of conventions and spelling. She encouraged students to use personal and classroom dictionaries and provided a great deal of scaffolding in the use of conventions. For example, journals often included prompts about conventions and spelling, as did rough drafts on which the student had conferred with Barb.

Barb offered explicit teaching of writing to her students. Thus, one day I observed her teach a small group of students how to construct a summary by sharing some good summaries with them, assigning individual students to read then aloud for the group. She talked about why the summaries read were good ones, how a good summary of a story includes information about the characters, the problems they encountered, and tells something about how the story ends. The group discussed how good summaries can stimulate students to form pictures in their minds. They learned that summaries usually had a few sentences, and Barb reminded them about the importance of using appropriate conventions and correct spellings when they wrote summaries. As was typical in Barb's class, this strategy-focused 15-minute lesson was very engaging for students, and all of them were attentive throughout the discussion.

Students were not then left to their own devices to write summaries. Rather, there was support for summary writing—in particular, in the form of a sheet that prompted students to think of the story grammar elements (who, what, where, when, and why) as they summarized the content of a story. The same sheet also served to prompt students to check their writing, asking them to self-evaluate whether every sentence made sense, began with a capital letter, and ended with a punctuation mark. They were also prompted to check on whether names of people and places were capitalized and whether they had done their best to correct spelling. They were reminded as well to have someone else read their writing as part of editing.

That Barb's students used a sheet prompting them to edit and revise was consistent with the general process writing approach in this class, which included the culminating step of publishing student writing in some cases. Thus, Barb published some student stories by word processing them for the students. A particularly impressive effort that I observed was a published big book on birds, containing articles on a number of birds, with each article written by one or two students in the class. Like all authors, the students in this class experienced recognition for their publishing—for example, as when the authors of the bird big book each read their articles from the big book to the class, gathered around the book at the rug.

There were many indications that students internalized the writing processes that were being encouraged. For instance, many students were observed using dictionaries on their own to find correct spellings, and students were also observed monitoring the sensibleness of their writing by saying to themselves, "That doesn't make sense," just before making a revision. In short, Barb's students were writers becoming better writers.

TEACHING OF SKILLS

I observed no decontextualized teaching of skills, but I observed a great deal of teaching of skills, with many indications that skills coverage was systematic. Thus, when a student encountered difficulties with pronouncing a word, Barb reminded the student of pronunciation strategies: (1) sounding the word out; (2) looking for little words in big words; (3) skipping the word, reading to the end of a sentence, and then returning to the word; (4) looking for picture clues (making the point that this strategy works only some of the time); and (5) asking someone else for assistance.

The artifacts that could be observed in the classroom on any given day provided plenty of evidence of attention to skills. There were easel and chart displays relating to skills (e.g., words with double consonants), including charts of the most common spelling patterns in English. From time to time I observed Barb referring to the easel displays and charts—for example, pointing out that "-ope" was representative of the "o-e" spelling pattern rather than the "-op" pattern. Barb often cued students to look carefully at a word to make certain that they recognized its spelling–pronunciation pattern exactly rather than only approximately.

Spelling instruction each week focused on a common spelling–sound pattern (e.g., "-op," "-um," "-up"). Early in the week students would have a homework assignment, which was to generate all of the three-letter, four-letter, and five-letter words they could that included the spelling–sound pattern of the week. The following day the class would generate lists of three-letter, four-letter, and five-letter words that included the sound pattern, referring to their completed homework sheets during this activity. Sometimes there would be another activity, as, for example, when the spelling–sound pattern "-op" was the focus. The students knew the word "hop" and that a rabbit would hop. Thus, they made a rabbit with an "op" on its chest and an open window preceding "op." The rabbit included a pull strip device containing "pl," "ch," "b," "h," "st," "p," and "sh." By playing with this rabbit, students could readily see how easily "hop" could become "plop," "chop," "bop," "stop," "pop," and "shop." There were no spelling tests associated with these exercises for the grade-1 students; the intention was only to stimulate students to see and reflect on how words are organized.

What was so apparent on every single day was that the word-level skills were revisited continuously when students experienced difficulties. Thus, when students found the rhyming words in a poem, they were reminded that the basis of rhyme is usually the occurrence of the same spelling–sound pattern in words. When students experienced difficulties identifying words in texts, Barb and her assistants reminded the students of phonics patterns and rules (e.g., the "-op" pattern, the silent "-e" rule, the similarity in sounds associated with "qu," hard "c," and "k"). The students were also reminded to use their understanding of spelling–sound associations as they wrote in order to generate correct spellings of words. Despite the coverage and cuing of phonics and sounds, there was also much encouragement of the development of sight vocabulary through a variety of activities, ranging from intense sight word drills given to one of the mainstreamed students to games like "Basic Sight Word Bingo."

Skills instruction also included some instruction in and practice of printing. Occasionally, students completed worksheets requiring them to print the letters neatly (e.g., one on capital "E" and lower case "e"). Barbara confided in me that this instruction was in response to parental concerns about handwriting, although that response to parental demands in no way signaled Barb's own lack of concern, for Barbara consistently insisted that students write neatly.

I was struck that Barb knew so much about teaching reading skills—for example, understanding completely the structure of words and how word structure can be used to drive word recognition and spelling. This knowledge base reflected her years of experience, and Barbara explained in her interview that before she came to incorporate so much of the whole-language approach into her teaching, her teaching reflected a more traditional skills-based approach. Barb's teaching was definitely a balancing and integration of whole-language and skills instruction in the best sense of balance, with systematic coverage of important skills and consistent relating of those skills to real reading and writing.

OPPORTUNISTIC TEACHING

As should be apparent by now, Barb and her aides were extremely opportunistic in their teaching, consistently monitoring students as they worked, taking advantage of teachable moments in respect to decoding, spelling, and writing. Opportunistic teaching of vocabulary was also apparent. Thus, when an unknown word was encountered, Barb often provided a definition or asked students to define the word. Sometimes the context would permit extensive discussion, as when Barb defined the term *literally* with reference to Amelia Bedelia's behavior. The students, who had heard and read the Amelia Bedelia stories, could relate many of her literal behaviors. Content-area units permitted much coverage of vocabulary (e.g., there was a list for the "backyard bird" unit) as did the daily routines (e.g., weather words were covered as part of the morning calendar).

ACROSS-CURRICULAR CONNECTIONS

Connection across the curriculum was salient in Barb's classroom. There were thematic units, ranging from shorter ones (e.g., Martin Luther King Jr., which occurred around Dr. King's birthday) to longer ones (e.g., birds). During my interview with Barb, she was quite emphatic that the topics of these units were not important in themselves, that the units were simply vehicles for integrating skills instruction related to reading and writing. There were a few district-mandated units, but for the most part units were selected by Barb or by the grade-1 team at the school.

There was plenty of evidence that the unit themes did result in related reading, with lots of books on the theme units apparent for every ongoing theme during my visits. Moreover, writing was often in response to the readings and ideas covered in the units. Science inspired projects that were theme related, so that there was an entire corner of Barb's room devoted to frog metamorphosis. Art projects related to the themes as well. Besides the planned connections, there were many opportunistic connections, so that when a student was reading a book about Egypt, Barb used the globe to give a mini-lesson on where Egypt is. Another example is that when the concept of symmetry was discussed in math, the students were able to recall what they learned during a unit on animals about creatures that were symmetrical in various ways. During the same discussion of symmetry, the students recalled how they had exploited the property of symmetry during the preceding month in cutting out valentines.

Beyond semantic connections, there were many connections that occurred across time. Skills and ideas introduced earlier in the year, month, or week were revisited when they occurred in a new context. Although Barb prompted students to make connections, they also made many on their own.

If I had a regret about the connectedness of the curriculum, it was that the down-the-hall classes taught by specialist teachers were not connected to what was going on in the class. Typically, the time for "specials" for students corresponded to planning time for teachers, and thus Barb did not usually accompany her class to the specials. When Barb did oversee a special, however, as she did for the computer lab, there was connection between the special and the larger curriculum. The one time I observed the computer lab, the students were word processing stories that were to become part of a big book, so the laboratory experience was related to their ongoing curriculum.

CLASSROOM MANAGEMENT

Barb's classroom involved some whole-group meetings (i.e., for morning meeting, story reading), but for the most part students worked in small groups. Barb and her aides and volunteers spent most of their time working side by side with individual students. Some side-by-side, one-to-one lessons were scheduled, such as Barb's meeting with students to do their Book-It readings. Other side-by-side meetings were more spontaneous, resulting from Barb's noticing a need for a mini-lesson. Other times, Barb provided classic scaffolding in the sense of offering a timely hint, one that allowed the student to make progress. Thus, when looking at a sentence a student had written that did not begin with a capital, Barb remarked, "Something about that . . .," which resulted in the student's then making the needed correction. Barb is very good at giving such hints.

Barb is typically very much aware of what is going on in the class. Thus, the one-to-one Book-It readings occur at a table positioned so that she can look up and see all of the students in the classroom. When students are off task or disruptive, Barb quickly moves to correct the situation, typically in a positive way. Thus, when she spotted a little girl off task, Barb suggested to her that she might read to another student, whose attention also seemed to be waning. The prompt solved two inattention problems at once. But because off-task behaviors were rarely a problem, Barb was able to focus on the student with whom she was working. These side-by-side lessons provided rich information about student development, information that could not be obtained in large-group lessons.

Barb related in her interview how important it is to challenge students appropriately, and this commitment comes through in her management in many different ways. Thus, when another teacher suggested that the students might want to participate in a particular reading incentives program, Barb recognized that it demanded too much reading in too little time and decided not to go with the program. At every visit, I saw Barb monitoring students as to whether they were able to carry out their current reading and writing assignments, and if they were, urging them to try something a little more difficult. Matching classroom demands to student abilities resulted, in part, in more time being spent with the students having the most difficulties. In general, Barb was determined that her students experience success, but that they do so in an environment where they were challenged and learning to take appropriate academic risks.

The aides in Barb's classroom worked closely with her, so the curriculum that mainstreamed students experienced was matched to their abilities but was, as much as possible, similar to the instruction and demands experienced by the regular students. Thus, even some more advanced items, such as use of the computer, were included in the plans of mainstreamed students. In general, the mainstreamed students were much less marginalized in this class than in typical grade-1 classes I have observed, although when an activity was clearly one in which a student could not participate, an aide exited the student with minimal disruption.

As in all well-managed classrooms, there were routines for all frequent events, such as lunch counts and writing folders. There were also clear signals that Barb could give to accomplish certain purposes. If students were slow and noisy getting to the rug, Barb would begin a routine: "If you can hear me, clap hands . . . if you can hear me, snap fingers . . . if you can hear me, hands on hips." In general, by the third "if," students were quiet and getting settled. In addition, materials were arranged in ways that were sensible, permitting ready access. Thus, Barb's many boxes of science books were arranged topically in alphabetical order.

The tasks Barb asked children to perform were designed so that much more time was spent on academic thinking than on other requirements. For instance, when the students made the rabbit with the pull tab for "-op" words, the rabbit was easy to assemble so that relatively little time was spent constructing it. In general, the art that accompanied writing was undemanding, so student time was spent on writing rather than on the art. Moreover, Barbara insisted that the academic portion of tasks be given priority—for example, cuing students to write before illustrating. This was a classroom with high engagement, with engagement in tasks that were worth student effort and thinking.

Barb recognizes the importance of parental participation in the development of student literacy. The Book-It participation and related activities (e.g., reading logs requiring students and parents to record the reading they do together) are intended to stimulate the daily involvement of parents. Barb sees all homework as a means for strengthening the home–school tie. Thus, spelling homework also requires students and parents to work together to generate lists of words consistent with the spelling–sound pattern of the week. In her interview Barb described the communications with home and her goal to make certain that parents understand the curriculum and their role as parents within it. She believed that the parents of her students were comfortable with what was occurring in the class.

JANUARY 22

For a more concrete idea of what happens in Barb's class, consider the day of January 22. At 8:35 A.M., the last students were in the door and Barb asked everyone to come to the rug. The morning meeting began with a quick check of the attendance sticks and the lunch count. Typically, Barb did not have to bother with attendance, but she noticed that some students had forgotten to place their sticks in the attendance can near the door. (Barb monitors everything.) One of the mainstreamed students was then selected to take the attendance to the office that day, accompanied by an aide.

Barbara announced that report cards would be issued later in the day and reminded the students of their responsibility to take good care of the cards. After this announcement, she turned her attention to a little girl who was working on the morning calendar and asked her to explain what she was doing. Because it was foggy outside, the student was not certain whether the day was a rainy day. The class voted on it, using the thumbs up and thumbs down signs, and Barb gave a mini-lesson about how it can sometimes be hard to make clear-cut decisions. As the calendar recording proceeded, Barb had the student represent the date of the month using concrete manipulatives, explaining how she was doing so to the other students in the class. (Students do a lot of explaining in Barb's class.)

Barb explained the journaling activity for the day. Students were to record some news in their journals. In addition, if they had not completed the previous day's journal assignment, which was to write two sentences about the VIP of the week, they were to work on that as well. During journaling, which began at 8:49, Barb met with a number of individual students and scaffolded their writing, prompting them about how they might think of news and providing hints about how they might solve some problems in their writing (e.g., urging students to spell correctly the words they knew, asking them to think hard about whether they knew a word before simply attempting an invented spelling). Throughout the journaling activity, all of the students were engaged most of the time; journaling was wrapped up at 9:17, with students returning to the rug.

At the rug, students took turns reading their journals, with Barb reacting to the readings (e.g., noting that several students had been to the doctor lately, commenting that she would be interested in finding out whether a boy enjoyed the Goosebumps book purchased the night before). Students also responded during journal reading, including the mainstreamed students who were at the rug.

At 9:26 journal reading concluded. Barb then indicated which students would be going to the library to hear an Amelia Bedelia story, mentioning briefly some previous stories the students in the class had read about Amelia Bedelia. The students who remained in the room were asked to begin their math journal work, including, for some, the writing of a story problem.

I followed the students who went to the library, and the self-control so evident in Barb's classroom transferred to the library story time. Her students were raptly attentive while students from other classes were much less so. After watching enough of story time to know what the activity was about, I returned to Barb's class and observed her working one-to-one with students as they did math, most students using concrete manipulatives of some sort as they did so. Again, she was doing a lot of scaffolding, providing hints to students about how they might make progress in their work. As usual, all of the students were engaged most of the time. The writing in the math journals was very good, with several students providing multiple-sentence explanations of problems they had solved and the writing including appropriate capitalization, punctuation, and spelling.

Although I characterized this instruction as one-to-one, it was more than that. I watched in amazement as Barb gave hints to one student and then, as that student started to work, turned to another to offer an apropos hint, only to turn immediately back to the first youngster to remark, "Oh, why don't you write about what you did there?" Barb could really scaffold math, reflecting deep knowledge of mathematics as well as excellent monitoring skills. Her monitoring ability was also apparent when students were distracted; she moved immediately to such children and gently nudged them back on task. But, of course, engagement was not much of a problem, which was obvious when the recess bell rang. Everyone just kept on working. A few minutes into recess, Barb remarked, "I'm so proud of you, you did so very well finding two ways to do the problems." Some students then put their math journals into the finished workbasket and headed outdoors.

Recess concluded at 10:25, and by 10:29 the class was back at the rug. It was snack time, and during snack time students shared reading with one another. There was a discussion of the Amelia Bedelia story, and Barb reacted to some comments by letting students know that they had ideas that might work in their journals. When students completed their snacks, they found their Book-It books and began quiet reading. Barb helped some students select books, and when an adult volunteer arrived, paired a student with the volunteer to give the student an opportunity to read aloud to an adult. Most grade-1 students were reading books that were middle-grade-1 level or more advanced. Again, most students were reading for most of the 15 minutes of quiet reading time. Barb had initiated quiet reading time after recess earlier in the year, after noticing that students often had a difficult time getting settled after recess.

Quiet reading time flowed into a period dedicated to reading Book-It books, with students reading their books on their own or to each other. Barb listened to individual students read their Book-It books, making notes about their strengths and weaknesses as they did so. She also provided mini-lessons both during and after students read their Book-It books for her—for example, she pointed out to a student for whom Spanish was a first language that "s" at the end of an English word means "more than one," explaining how that was different from Spanish. When the student stumbled on a word, Barb asked him to explain what he was doing, and he said that he tried to sound out the word but also looked at the picture. Barb acknowledged that those approaches were good and that the word did start with "st-" and sound like "sticks," which the student had decoded. Barb went on, "That was a good guess, because this new word starts like 'sticks' and looks like 'sticks,' but this is another word for sticks." The little boy responded, "Stilts!" Barb knows elementary reading and her students well enough to provide just the right hints. She believes it is important to acknowledge the skills the child uses (e.g., the student's use of blends and semantic context cues to guess that the word might be "sticks").

As students finished the Book-It reading, some started other activities, such as playing "Basic Sight Word Bingo," going to the listening center to hear an Amelia Bedelia tape as they read along in the book (connecting to the library reading that had occurred earlier in the day), reading poetry charts, or reading other books. As the morning concluded, Barb pointed out that she would listen to a few more children read during DEAR time after lunch.

When the students returned from lunch at 12:15, they went back to work, and DEAR reading lasted for about 20 minutes. As Barb had promised before lunch, she did listen to several more children go through their Book-It books. At 12:42, Barb signaled for the students to come to the rug, and she read a story by the Author of the Month. She previewed the book by talking about why it would be so rich with details. She reminded students that good writers write about what they know, which permits them to put many details in their writing. Barb also talked a little about how the author had studied art when she was young, thinking aloud, "I wonder whether that explains why she does her own illustrations." As Barb read the story, the students were totally absorbed in it, and there were many appropriate responses from students to the story and illustrations each time Barb paused to show a picture from the book.

After 1:00 P.M., the afternoon was consumed with specials, consistent with the general schedule in Barb's class indicating that specials came at the end of the day. At dismissal, everyone had her or his Book-It bag, with more reading ahead in the evening with a parent.

SUMMARY

Barb Wiesner has a class of students who are engaged in a network of connections, largely orchestrated by their teacher. First, there are interpersonal connections, with Barbara working with parents, aides, and volunteers to ensure high-quality literacy instruction at school and at home. She also has her students committed to cooperating and supporting each other in literacy development. In addition, her encouragement of self-regulation results in an orderly classroom environment, with students largely managing themselves and therefore permitting Barbara and other adults in the room more opportunity to work with students on academic matters. There is a very tight network of people cooperating to make sure that Barb's classroom is a place where literacy can thrive. Moreover, all of the adults do so in a way that is respectfully supportive of the students, with the classroom consistently positive as students receive enough support to carry on their work but not so much that they are smothered. That is, Barb, her aides, and volunteers appropriately scaffold learning for the students.

There are also curricular connections, with everything that is happening in reading and writing related to social studies and science. Literacy skills are consistently applied to a variety of texts.

There are appropriate student–curriculum connections as well. Barb engineers the classroom so that all students are doing reading and writing tasks that are challenging to them but not overwhelming. Moreover, the skills part of the curriculum is delivered in a way that is sensible from the perspective of what is known from research. Thus, students are taught to recognize words by using multiple strategies, with the most powerful strategies (i.e., sounding out and looking for parts of words) emphasized. Simultaneously, the whole-language part of the curriculum is also delivered in a way consistent with what makes sense from the perspective of research. Students read real books, books that are largely of their own choosing. They learn to use the processes used by skilled writers, including editing and revising.

Barbara Wiesner's classroom is a very intelligent classroom. How did this come about? Barb told us about her extensive efforts to stay current in education, which include many workshop and institute experiences. She has also had a great deal of experience, both with traditional approaches to the teaching of literacy and with contemporary whole-language approaches. She has definitely thought about her teaching a great deal, coming to a commitment to maintain student motivation in ways that are supported by research—that is, by encouraging students to pursue their interests, matching curricular demands to student abilities and preparedness, and consistently letting students know that they can succeed by exerting appropriate efforts.

In summary, Barb teaches her students the strategies they need to know, perhaps most saliently those needed for word recognition and spelling, but also those required for composition. She does so by providing rich content, so that students' prior knowledge expands as a function of reading and writing. Moreover, her students gain the metacognitive know-how necessary to use the reading and writing strategies they are acquiring by using their skills, albeit with sufficient social support so that they do not falter. All of this occurs in an environment designed to maintain students' motivation to read and write and to believe in themselves as learners. As someone who has argued that student success is most likely attained by developing components of good information-processing capacities—including strategies, world knowledge, metacognition, and motivation—I found Barb Wiesner's classroom to be exceptionally attractive. The consistent student engagement fueled my enthusiasm further, as did the overwhelming evidence that the students were reading a great deal, making progress in reading, and writing well both rhetorically and in respect to mechanics.

REFERENCE

Kaska, K. (1987). *The wolf's chicken stew*. New York: Putnam.

6

Andy Schultheis

RUTH WHARTON-MCDONALD

Andy Schultheis taught in a small rural school district in upstate New York. The elementary school where he taught served students in kindergarten through grade 3. The community was one of primarily blue-collar families, and his students' previous experiences with literacy varied considerably, as did their parents' levels of education. Approximately 12% of the school population received free or reduced-price lunches. Like the populations of most rural districts in the northeast, Andy's students were overwhelmingly Caucasian.

In the year we observed him (1994–1995), Andy's students began first grade with the expected range of early literacy experiences and skills. One child was unable to identify any letters in September; several others were already reading at a first-grade level when the school year began. Most students arrived in Andy's first grade with skills that fell somewhere between the two extremes. All of the students who had attended kindergarten in the district had at least been introduced to the alphabet and its phonetic code. The district's approach to reading and writing in kindergarten was one of fairly structured, skills-based instruction.

The year we observed Andy, he had been teaching for 21 years,

13 of them in first grade. Although he was clearly an experienced teacher, he talked about his experience in the classroom as if it were still fresh, with all the excitement and challenge of a new experience. "I don't feel as though I know [the best way to teach]," he explained. "I've got a lot more to learn [from] other people. And I'm constantly changing. If I see something that somebody has that seems to work well, I try it with my kids."

Like many experienced and expert teachers, Andy refused to be pigeonholed or labeled by the terms of the ongoing debates about teaching reading. Although he believed strongly in the role of oral language in children's literacy development, he firmly denied being a "whole-language" teacher. Nor did he align himself with a "skills-first" approach. Andy's philosophy of early literacy instruction centered on the belief that all students are capable of learning to read when they are offered an approach that makes sense to them and enables them to meet with success. "We need to be able to say that we don't *have* a program that everybody's going to [succeed with], but that we're going to make adjustments and provide a program that is going to best meet the child's needs." It is thus the teacher's responsibility to determine what that approach is for each student.

Consistent with the ever-growing research base in effective literacy instruction (e.g., Adams, 1990; Pressley, 1998; Wharton-McDonald, Pressley, & Mistretta, 1998), Andy knew that his first graders needed word analysis (phonics) skills; they needed frequent and varied access to books; they needed to understand what reading could do for them (reading must serve a purpose in the lives of his 6-year-olds); and they needed opportunities to talk with one another—about books, about spelling patterns, about writing plans, and about their lives. He described each of these components as essential to his literacy program, and he made certain that they were all present in the daily and weekly experiences of his students.

Andy believed strongly that children learn much from their peers, that in the process of collaborating, questioning—even disagreeing with one another—new understandings are created and nurtured. Children in his class therefore had frequent opportunities to interact as a whole class. At different times during the day, students might come together to listen to a story, practice a new spelling pattern, brainstorm ideas for a writing assignment, or use problem solving to address a confusing finding in science.

Andy believed that the oral interactions fostered in whole-class and small-group learning settings benefited students across the achievement continuum. In the group discussions that punctuated the school day, the more successful students were able to share their experiences, explain things to their peers, and make new connections, and the students who struggled with reading and writing had opportunities to express themselves orally, to rehearse skills in a low-stakes setting, and to be exposed to more sophisticated vocabularies, language structures, and experiences. In Andy's classroom, when peers provided models, exposed others to new words, shared ideas, and brought new perspectives, everyone benefited.

DAILY SCHEDULE

The positive, language-rich environment of Andy's classroom was evident from the moment the children arrived in the morning. As they entered the classroom, they greeted Mr. Schultheis and one another enthusiastically, asking about the outcomes of local soccer games, telling about visiting relatives, and sharing books they had brought in from home. When their backpacks and jackets were hung up, they settled quickly into their seats, many children still finishing their conversations as they perused the bins of books at each group of desks. The day always began with independent reading of what Andy called "comfortable books." He described this as a "warm-up" for students who perhaps had not done any reading since they left school the previous afternoon. According to Andy, this reading "exercise" helped students to warm up for the group work that was to follow.

Once the morning logistics had been completed, students gathered on the rug for a whole-class discussion. This began with some connection to the previous day's learning and provided a foundation for what was coming next. The whole-class discussion helped to anchor subsequent activities in a shared vocabulary and understanding of the topic. Thus, this block of time might include a preview of a book students would be reading with a partner, an introduction to new writing topic, and/or a review of a spelling pattern that students would be working with independently or with a partner later.

The rest of the morning was divided into blocks of reading and writing activities, in which students often worked with partners or in small groups. During this time, Andy would meet with small (and occasionally individualized) guided reading groups. These partnerships were fluid and were formed intentionally to address the changing needs of individual students. Thus, on a given day, Andy might sit with three students, reading and discussing *Frog and Toad* (Lobel, 1979), then move on to two children who read from a phonetically regular basal selection, and finish with two others who were reading a book recently completed by some classmates. This reading and writing block was often punctuated by a return trip to the rug to brainstorm additional details for a writing piece or to take a look at the organization and content of students' ideas on a topic, as laid out in semantic webs.

The class took a break in the middle of the morning, during which the students chose independent or group activities in the classroom. The students' most frequent choices included books, puzzles, board games, or a turn at the sand table.

The afternoon in Andy's classroom was typically devoted to math, content area instruction, and specials (music, art, gym). However, because reading and writing were frequently integrated into math and content instruction, these activities often migrated to the morning block. Likewise, a great deal of reading and writing took place in the afternoon as part of math, science, and social studies.

CHARACTERISTICS OF INSTRUCTION

Matching Tasks to Competence

The hallmark of Andy's instruction, an important key to his effectiveness, was the way in which he matched instructional tasks to his students' competencies. In other words, the tasks he provided were in keeping with what has sometimes been called the "porridge principle": They were not too easy (so as to be a waste of time), but not too difficult (so as to be frustrating and result in likely failure). Rather, the tasks Andy expected each child to accomplish were *just right* for that child, providing just the right level of challenge to keep the child engaged and meeting with success. Another way of describing these tasks is to say that the instructional tasks were in each child's zone of proximal development.[1]

---

[1]Vygotsky (1978, pp. 86–87) defined the zone of proximal development as "the distance between the actual developmental level as determined by independent problem solving and the level of potential development as determined through problem solving under adult guidance or in collaboration with more capable peers."

Andy tailored tasks to individual students' competencies in a number of ways. He carefully monitored students' learning; he individualized instructional materials; he varied the size and composition of the groups in which students learned, and incorporated opportunities for students to learn from one another; and he consulted regularly with the specialists children saw outside the classroom to ensure consistent and meaningful experiences for weaker readers.

Andy paid a great deal of attention to the learning of individual students and was thus able to match books with learners. He did not feel bound by any one program, set of books, or approach. Over time, and with the support of colleagues, he had collected a wide range of reading materials in his classroom. He also regularly borrowed materials from colleagues, including the reading specialist. During some reading times—for example, DEAR (i.e., drop everything and read) time—students chose their own books, and at other times (such as when he formed small groups for guided reading), Andy selected materials that offered opportunities to practice skills students were currently working on to ensure success, while pushing them toward new challenges. Thus, for a child struggling with a particular phonetic pattern, Andy might select a phonetically regular reader for guided reading. They (Andy and the student) might read from that book for a day—or two or three—and then move on to a related piece of authentic literature. For three other children working on adding expression to their oral reading, Andy might select a play, in which students took on the parts of the characters. Through his individualizing materials in this way, students were most often in learning situations where they were pushing the limits of their competencies while meeting with frequent success.

As part of this goal, children flowed through multiple types of learning groups throughout the day. Andy's instruction cycled between whole-group, small-group, and independent activities, with clearly understood purposes for each. In a typical day, there might be three or four whole-class lessons on topics ranging from boat building to a particular vowel digraph, two opportunities to work in pairs, a couple of small-group activities, and some independent reading and writing times. Through his flexible groupings, Andy intentionally provided opportunities for students to bootstrap one another's knowledge and understandings. Peers provided models, shared ideas, and exposed others to new vocabulary and perspectives. Consistent with

Vygotsky's (1978) emphasis on learners' social interactions, Andy encouraged students to *talk* about what they were learning.

One day, after the class had previewed a new mini-book[2] and heard it read aloud, Andy explained that they would be reading the book with partners. "When you pick your partner," he explained, "Think about reading together. You'll read one page and your partner will read one page. And if your partner gets stuck, you can help him or her." A while later, when most of the children had finished reading, Andy continued, "With your partner, I want you to find your favorite part of the story and tell your partner what part of the story you liked best. You need to share that with *words*. I want you to talk about it. Tell your partner what you're going to write about. And then I'd like you to write that down. But you need to use words and talk to your partner about what you're going to write about." On this day, as on most days we observed Andy's class, the room was filled with animated conversation—about books.

A couple of students in Andy's class received instruction from the school's reading specialist in sessions apart from the regular classroom. From Andy's perspective, this type of instruction should be given not in place of, but *in addition to*, the literacy instruction he provided in his classroom. He timed his lessons so that children who most needed to participate in classroom literacy activities were present when those activities took place. He also consulted frequently with the reading teacher and other specialists so that students who received instruction from them apart from the classroom experienced a coherent program. He integrated the materials from the resource room into his ongoing activities and modified lessons and materials in consultation with the specialists. Unlike many teachers we observed, Andy never considered the possibility that the literacy development of students receiving special education services was not his responsibility.

Integrated Explicit Skills Instruction

Andy's reading and writing program included a great deal of explicit skills instruction. However, we have almost no record of students

---

[2]A mini-book was a short story photocopied and made into a small book that children read several times in school and then took home to read with parents.

completing phonics worksheets in our field notes. The reason is that students in Andy's class learned and practiced literacy skills in the context of other learning activities. Andy's lessons were always multipurposed. For example, in the following lesson on the "o-a" digraph, Andy gave students semantic clues for the words he wanted them to spell:

ANDY: How about something that Mom puts in the oven—a kind of meat?

STUDENT 1: Meat loaf!

ANDY: I was thinking of something else, but that's a good one, too.

STUDENT 2: Roast beef!

ANDY: Yes. Roast. Put that on your list. (*Students write.*) How about something that comes in a bar?

STUDENT 3: Soap!

ANDY: What happens when you put wood in water?

STUDENTS: Float!

ANDY: Now, I like that word that Amy thought of—What was that?

STUDENTS: Loaf!

ANDY: Put that on your lists. (*Students write.*) How about something that Charlie made in the story we read yesterday [referring to the Tomie dePaola book *Charlie Needs a Cloak*; dePaola, 1973]?

STUDENTS: Cloak.

ANDY: And what's the difference between a coat and a cloak?

Thus, the lesson continued, integrating vocabulary and concept development in an engaging review of the "o-a" digraph. At the end of the lesson, each student had a list of 10 to 12 words, including some from the weekly spelling list as well as several others, that they could add to their spelling notebooks.

Andy followed a scope and sequence he had developed through years of teaching, but did not simply follow it in a linear direction. He regularly cycled back to review, integrate, and expand upon skills he had taught earlier. Early in the year, for example, students had learned the word "ice" as part of a list of long-"i" words. Later, when they were working on long-"u" words, Andy included the

words "ice cube" on the spelling test and expected students to remember the long-"i" spelling. One way Andy built in these rehearsal
opportunities was through weekly dictation sentences. Each week after the children wrote their spelling words, they wrote three sentences that Andy had constructed specifically to emphasize the
week's spelling patterns and review old ones. He considered students'
performance on the sentences a much better indicator of their learning than their spelling of the words dictated in isolation. Better yet
were the spellings students used in their own writing.

Students were expected to use their spelling skills in everything
they wrote. Andy was frequently heard saying, "Not all of the words
are on your spelling list, but you should be able to spell them all correctly." The expectation was that students would apply the strategies
they learned in *all* of their reading and writing. Andy frequently
scaffolded the students' learning through questioning. As he put it,
he tried "to word the question in such a way that they have to think
back to something they know and build on it. [For example, I] try to
force them to do that in spelling. I'll try to force them to think of a
word they already know that has the sound in it." Thus, students not
only received explicit instruction, but had many opportunities to rehearse what they had learned.

As with other kinds of learning, there were frequent opportunities for students to model their understandings for one another. On
one occasion we observed a lesson in which students spent approximately 5 minutes reviewing sight words on flashcards with a partner.
After they had had a couple of runs through their piles—but before
they showed signs of boredom—Andy interrupted: "Stop. Now, put
all of your words down and put them in alphabetical order." When
the students had completed the task, he asked a student, "Why did
you put 'such' before 'surprise'? What helped you make that decision?" This gave the student the opportunity to articulate the strategy she was using, and highlighted it for students who had not yet
mastered its use. As usual, Andy then summarized the rule simply for
the students, reinforcing the student's response in simple and clear
terms.

Skills instruction was not limited to word-level skills, however.
Andy also taught vocabulary and comprehension strategies. Again,
these were not taught as isolated "tricks" to be memorized or used
on a worksheet, but were integrated into the context of engaging activities. Andy never read a story without first previewing the book

with the group. This included attention to the title and picture clues, as well as a discussion of any important vocabulary words the students would encounter. In one case, this included a discussion of the difference between a *relative* and a *friend*. In another, students considered whether leprechauns could be real, and what the world would look like from their perspective if they were real.

Writing Instruction

Andy's students developed semantic webs; they wrote drafts, stories, descriptions, reading responses, science journals, spelling lists, and notes to one another. Students in Andy's classroom wrote every day and throughout the day. According to Andy, writing is "an integral part of [reading development]. It gives [students], I don't know whether the word is 'metacognition.' It gives them the opportunity to tell about what they have learned. And at the same time, as I go around [conferencing with students], I'm monitoring what they're working on *within* their writing. I'm working on *skills*." Andy was careful to add here that the skills he addressed through the writing process were individualized. "If you try to pluck out too much in that process while you're working, then they give up. The first part of writing is getting your writing down. Then we go back and make sure the skills have been incorporated."

By the spring of first grade all of these students routinely wrote a page of text; many wrote more. Moreover, the text was organized, coherent, and the percentage of sentences that were correctly punctuated and capitalized was very high. When I commented to Andy about the high quality of his students' writing relative to that I was observing in other classrooms, his response was typically focused on the process (see Chapter 4 for details). He explained that the type of writing his students generated did not just emerge whole cloth: It was carefully nurtured and supported.

Andy used an adapted form of process writing (Graves, 1983) in his classroom. The process nearly always began with the whole class involved in discussion and brainstorming. As students brainstormed ideas and related vocabulary words, Andy mapped out the information in some form of graphic organizer on an easel. Depending on the topic and the students' familiarity with it, the next step was either for students to discuss their ideas further with a partner and create their own organizer for the topic or to begin writing a draft. Drafts were often shared with partners or small groups or in a conference with Andy, after which the students made revisions and conferred again before writing a final copy.

During these conferences, Andy constantly pushed students to improve. He frequently asked them to read to him what they had written. Then he would ask, "How could we make that sound better?" He used the analogy of a skeleton, asking his students to "fill out" the bones of the story. In all of his conversations with students, the emphasis was on writing pieces that were interesting, coherent, and true to the ideas the students brought to the table.

Although the students were accustomed to the process steps described here, Andy did not always demand the entire process. As he indicated, sometimes children just need to get their ideas out and *write*—without getting bogged down in the steps of revision. In these instances, the students still talked before they wrote. No one in Andy's class ever wrote "cold."

Throughout the year Andy taught students how to manage both the macrostructure (e.g., a story needs a beginning, a middle, and an end) and the microstructure (sentences must be grammatically correct and correctly punctuated) of their writing. Accurate spelling, punctuation, and capitalization were expected—not optional. Students had access to many resources around the room (signs, dictionaries, spelling dictionaries, word lists, peers, Andy) and were encouraged and expected to use them. As a result of his emphasis on the big picture, supported by the details, Andy's students' writing was remarkably coherent and interesting for first grade.

Literacy throughout the Curriculum:
Frequent and Varied Opportunities to Read and Write

It will be clear to the reader by now that students in Andy's classroom had a great many opportunities to read and write during the school day. In fact, there was little time spent in Andy's room that was not connected in some way to literacy goals. From the moment they found their desks in the morning and chose "warm-up" books to read, the children were surrounded by words all day. They were surrounded by words because Andy believed in the power of language to influence children's development. He suggested to parents that the most important (school-related) thing they could do for their children was to take them to the public library and choose high-quality literature to read at home. Rather than the Easy Reader version of "Red Riding Hood," he suggested the original Grimm's. "Kids want to be impressed by what a person says, just as you want them to start adding that kind of [language] to the things that they . . . write. They're not going to do that if they don't hear [models]. You want to get some of those original pieces so that kids can listen to them and really hear how the author intended them to be."

Andy had specific purposes for the different kinds of reading students did. Whole-class lessons provided opportunities for students to "get their juices flowing" as well as a constant flow of models for students who were struggling with a particular skill or lacking information on a topic. Students often read chorally in a group because, as Andy explained, "choral reading [gave] them a . . . better sense of the timing of their reading—the punctuation, the intonation, fluency." He often had students read a passage with different intonations and asked them, "Which sounded better? Which way do you think the author wanted it to sound?"

Similar modeling took place when students read together in pairs. Andy often designated the pairs such that a stronger reader was partnered with a weaker reader. Students were used to helping one another out and could be heard offering hints (/po/ . . . for "potato" or "that's one of our spelling words.") Sometimes students would read a story in pairs and then come back to the group, "so they've had a little practice ahead of time."

When Andy read with individual students or small groups, he engaged in ongoing diagnosis and assessment, enabling him to match materials and tasks to students' ever growing competencies. He tracked this progress in his head, later transferring it to his notes. At the time they were reading, therefore, students never sensed that they were being evaluated. They just relished the opportunity to read with Mr. Schultheis.

In addition to the many opportunities students had to read with peers, there were also many times when they read independently. The class had DEAR time most days, when students chose their own books to read. Students all had independent reading books in their desks. During silent reading times, Andy taught students to "read inside their heads." He sometimes used these opportunities to talk with individual children about what they had read on their own, using these conversations as opportunities to check on comprehension.

Throughout the day, week, and year, students read and wrote to support their learning in the content areas. During a unit on chicks and eggs, the students heard both fiction and nonfiction books on the topic; they wrote stories, hatched chicks, and kept science journals in which they described the process and variables, and reported on the chicks' progress. In the end, when all 12 of their eggs had hatched healthy chicks, the students collaborated on a news story describing their success.

When they were studying plants and gardens, the students read books about potatoes and other vegetables. They read tall tales about vegetables growing out of control, planted a garden, and recorded growth and contrast in their science journals. When all of the plants had grown, they harvested them and ate a salad made from their vegetables. Throughout his instruction, Andy managed to weave reading, writing, and enthusiasm into just about everything in the first-grade curriculum.

Strategies and Self-Regulation

At the end of the year, when I asked him what he considered to be his students' greatest strengths as they left first grade, Andy replied, "Strategies . . . as many strategies as possible." He continued,

"I think that [my students] are comfortable with looking at books and knowing that there are lots of ways of being able to approach . . . a story. It's not just going right away and starting to read the print. But, you know, looking at the whole book, making predictions from just the cover of the book, and the pictures throughout the book, and then using the words to support [a prediction] and knowing that if I'm stuck on a word, I can move ahead and think about it and come back. . . . Listening to what I said, and making sense out of what I'm reading . . . I can look at a word and say, 'Oh, I know a little word inside that word. That word has an ending on it. I know that's like an /f/.' Teaching phonics. *Helping them put it all together* [emphasis added]. Not saying there's one way to solve a problem."

In fact, Andy often suggested to students that they were detectives and that when it came to reading, it was their job to solve the mystery of the words.

Andy provided his students with many strategies to solve those mysteries. Moreover, he taught them to *think* strategically and all the while to monitor the process as it unfolded. Clearly, Andy taught students specific strategies for decoding words. His students knew about "magic 'e' " and the rule about what happens when two vowels go walking. However, despite his explicit instruction, phonics was only one set of strategies available to students. As his earlier response indicates, Andy taught students how to preview a book. They learned to uncover clues hidden in the book's title, its pictures, its author. They learned to make predictions and then return to their predictions later to check for accuracy.

Students in Andy's class did a lot of explaining of the strategies they used in their detective work. They were accustomed to thinking out loud and explaining their decisions, modeling their strategies for one another. Andy frequently asked questions that began, "Why did you make the decision to . . . ?" It was the strategic *process* that Andy was after in these conversations, rather than the answer per se. Thus, no student's explanation was ever labeled "wrong" in these thinking aloud responses. Rather, Andy tried to understand the process the student had used to arrive at even the most puzzling replies.

During a read-aloud story about a potato famine, Andy asked the students what they thought one of the characters was going to find in the soil, on the following page. When one student enthusiastically predicted, "Eggs!" (despite a complete lack of evidence to support such an outcome), Andy asked, "What made you think of that? How did you know that?" As it happened, Easter was approaching, and the student had Easter eggs on his mind. When another student predicted that the character would find potatoes (and he does), Andy asked again, "What were some of the things that helped you know it was a potato?"

Andy's role in these discussions was to clarify and elaborate on students' responses to make them maximally accessible to other students. For example, during an activity in which students were alphabetizing words on individual marker boards, the following interaction took place:

ANDY: I noticed Chandler putting "woman" near the bottom of the board. Why?

CHANDLER: It's near the end of the alphabet.

ANDY: Chandler knows "w" is near the end of the alphabet, so he's already putting it at the bottom of the board. Very good. Why did you put "whale" before "woman"?

CHANDLER: Both start with a "w," but I used the second letter, "h" comes before "o," so "whale" before "woman."

ANDY: That's right. Your group has been learning how to alphabetize using the second letter.

In encouraging students to monitor their own thinking and behavior in these ways, Andy helped students develop the ability to regulate their learning. References to planning (and strategies for doing so) were noted throughout the day. Students were expected to develop a plan before they began an activity—whether that activity was a writing project or a boat they were building. "What's your plan?" was a commonly heard question. I often heard Andy say things like, "We have 10 more minutes to work on our writing before lunch, so plan your time." Then he would set a timer, and students were responsible for reaching a stopping point in the next 10 minutes.

Andy's students also learned to monitor and adjust the noise level in the classroom. When the conversation got too loud, Andy would pose a question such as, "How many people are having trouble hearing their partners read?" Because the noise was hardest for students to control when they worked in small groups, Andy bought a small device from Radio Shack with a visual decibel indicator. He would set the device in the middle of a group at work and show students the acceptable range of decibels. Students thus learned to monitor and adjust their voices to keep the indicator lines within the acceptable range. At other times, Andy described using a videotape of groups at work to generate discussions about on-task and off-task behaviors. Students watched themselves on tape and described what they saw. Then they developed a list of strategies for improving the group's productivity.

Independence was nurtured in many ways in this classroom. Students were surrounded by resources—clues in their detective work—and were expected to use them. Sight words and decoding rules were posted around the room. Students had access to dictionaries, thesauruses, and spelling lists, and used them. Laughing, Andy explained that parent volunteers sometimes thought that kids were "cheating" by looking up words in the dictionary or finding them written on the wall somewhere. He sometimes had to explain that far from being considered cheating, this use of classroom resources was *encouraged*.

Before having a writing conference with the teacher, students were expected to attend to the mechanics and spelling themselves. A sign hanging from the ceiling reminded them to check for the following: Are my letters neat? Did I use a capital at the beginning of my sentences? Did I use a punctuation mark? Only after these preliminary steps had been taken independently would Andy have a final conference with a student. During these conferences, he continued to put the burden of evaluation and improvement on the student. He guided the students as follows: "Look at it, and when you present it to the group, is this what you want people to see? Is this what you want your friends to hear? How will it sound to them?" Thus, students learned to evaluate their work for themselves and gradually took on more of this responsibility as the year progressed.

Motivation

One of the most striking characteristics of Andy's classroom was the positive atmosphere and enthusiasm that predominated. This was clearly a place where kids wanted to be. Moreover, it was clearly a place where Andy wanted to be. His attitude and his interactions with students perpetually communicated his enthusiasm for learning and for children. And Andy's students knew how much he enjoyed them. One afternoon, students were sorting potatoes and describing them in their science journals. Two boys excitedly counted the eyes on their potatoes, wondering which one had the most eyes. When they had finished their writing, one of the boys brought his journal up to Andy for inspection. As Andy read the sentences, Michael looked on impatiently, then beamed when Andy smiled, suppressing a laugh. He had drawn eyeballs to represent the eyes on his potatoes. When he went back to his seat, he commented proudly to his friend, "See? I knew he'd get a chuckle out of that!"

In all of our observations, we do not have a single instance of this teacher getting angry, punishing a student, or even addressing a student in a negative tone. When students' behavior threatened to become disruptive or otherwise problematic, Andy redirected it with a cuing question ("Karl, do you remember the rules about the sand table?") a suggestion ("Rebecca, why don't you read your essay with Jo?"), or, sometimes, just a quiet hand on a shoulder. The success of these gentle interventions was grounded in Andy's relationships with his students and seemed to stem from two parallel sources: his genuine respect for children and his understanding of their individual strengths and needs. Andy knew who among his students would respond to a look, who would understand the message of a hand on a shoulder, and who would need a verbal reminder. Just as he matched instructional strategies to the needs of the individual, he was able to individualize his relationships and behavioral interventions as well.

In addition to his use of positive modeling and reinforcement, there were a number of instructional strategies that contributed to the high level of motivation among Andy's students. First, research suggests that when children experience success on academic tasks that are interesting, meaningful, challenging, and authentic, they are more likely to develop a mastery orientation to learning and to engage in subsequent academic tasks (Ames, 1992; Meece, 1991). Thus, Andy's attention to matching students with tasks and materials and his ability to develop interesting, meaningful tasks resulted in more motivated students.

Second, Andy's instruction fostered—in fact, demanded—collaboration among students. The message to students was that everyone has something important to contribute and that there were lots of ways to solve a problem. There was no reason to compete with one's peers in this class. The research is clear, again, that motivation and achievement are higher in collaborative (rather than competitive) classrooms (e.g., Johnson & Johnson, 1975; Slavin, 1987). Moreover, within this collaborative foundation, Andy's respect for students' input and the many opportunities he provided for participation encouraged students to take risks they might not otherwise take. Because the strategic process was valued as much as the actual product, students did not worry about being "wrong." Even those with the most limited background knowledge or skills had opportunities to participate on an equal footing with their peers.

Third, Andy's curriculum itself was engaging and challenging. He intentionally chose topics and books that had connections not only across the curriculum, but to students' lives. In introducing a mini-book on boats, for example, students spent 10 minutes talking about their own experiences with boats. Then, after reading the book a few times, they developed a semantic web to describe all of the tools and materials they would need to build a boat of their own. (Guess what they did next.) On another occasion, when Andy was introducing the idea of planting their own garden, the children were so excited that they literally jumped up and began hugging one another. These were motivated students. I believe that the motivational nature of Andy's classroom can be summed up by the comment of the class's weakest reader: "Mr. Schultheis, I wish I lived here!"

A DAY IN THE LIFE

One spring day in Andy's classroom, students arrived, arms full of lunchboxes and books, and greeted one another with enthusiasm. Andy situated himself amid the fray, speaking with individual students, reflecting their excitement and interest. Students settled quickly into their seats and selected books from small bins on their desks to read quietly. For the first few minutes of the day, the children read at their desks while Andy completed the lunch count and attendance and spoke with individual students about notes home, parent meetings, sick siblings, and the like. There was a low-level hum in the room as students selected books, read silently and aloud, and shared comments about the books they were reading. Most children selected picture books; a few read from basal readers; several were engaged in chapter books.

Once the morning logistics were completed, Andy called the group to the rug. He encouraged them to use bookmarks to save their places and asked them to bring their poetry books with them. The previous day, students had wanted to try to memorize some poems for homework, and as they gathered on the rug, they talked excitedly about the poems they had chosen. Two students volunteered to recite their poems for the class. The first student recited perfectly and clearly impressed her peers. They responded with applause and, as one student put it, "two thumbs up!" The second student struggled with his poem, but stuck with it and was also met with applause and encouraging words. His experience sparked a discussion of the strategies the children had used to remember and recite the poems. Andy praised the effort of the second reader and asked, "When James made a mistake, what did he do?" "He went back," replied another boy. "He went back over it," Andy said. "Is it okay to make mistakes?" to which the class replied as a group, "Yes!" On the marker board, Andy made a list of the strategies the students had described, and they all agreed that it takes hard work to remember a whole poem. Students who did not present a poem were eager to practice again and take a turn the following day.

From a discussion of the amount of time it takes to memorize a poem, Andy segued into a lesson on time, reminding students that the project they had begun the day before combined ideas and strategies from reading, writing, and math. Earlier in the week the students had talked and written about how long it takes to grow seeds into plants (seemingly forever if you are a first grader). They then considered time in the context of their own lives, mapping out a typical day in terms of clock times. On a long strip of paper, students had drawn a series of clocks and written beside each one what they normally did at the time depicted.

Consistent with Andy's belief in individualizing instruction and activities, the students had taken a variety of approaches to this project. The first student to share her day included a very detailed description ("I get up. I brush my teeth. Then I eat my breakfast . . . ") and, in fact, she had only made it to midmorning after a day's work. When she finished reading, Andy held up her strip for the class. The students agreed that Emily had a lot to say about her day. Andy used the opportunity to add, "*And* she has capitals and periods. Are some of you having trouble remembering periods at the end of the sentences?" Several students acknowledged that they were, and this led to a mini-lesson/review in which students volunteered strategies for using periods (e.g., "when I take a breath"). Throughout the discussion, Andy used positive reinforcement and summarized the sometimes winding student explanations. This "lesson" lasted approximately 3 minutes, after which a second student shared his time line. Michael took a different approach to the project, using digital clocks and highlighting different kinds of events in his day. When he finished his presentation, Andy noted, "Both people did a good job. They did it differently. Is it okay to do things differently?" Once again, he was met with a chorus of "Yes!"

Andy included whole-class sessions like this one throughout the day, with students having frequent opportunities to model strategies and approaches for one another. Students would have time to work on their time lines some more later in the morning. For now, they returned their poetry books to their desks and retrieved individual chalkboards to practice their spelling words. Their weekly spelling words came from an district-selected spelling book (Scott Foresman) and were generally grouped by word families. This week the children were working on a special set of words that begin with "wa" ("was," "want," "wasp"). As Andy dictated each word, students first wrote the word individually on their chalkboards, then checked their spelling with a partner, and finally spelled it chorally. Throughout, Andy reminded students, "The important sound here is '/wa/.' " When they had completed the single-syllable words from the spelling book, Andy added two challenge words. "These are not on your list, but I'd like you to try to spell them." The words were "wallet" and "water." Students clapped out the syllables for each word and looked for the little words in "wallet." Again, they checked their spellings with their partners, helping to correct misspelled words with a positive tone, and neither partner seemed bothered by the mistakes or the corrections. Accuracy was high. Next, Andy reviewed the "ink" spelling pattern. The last word, "stink," made everyone laugh.

When the children had cleaned their chalkboards, they returned to their seats and retrieved their chosen reading books. The expectation was that they would be reading something that was not "too easy" but that they could read by themselves. Andy reminded the class, "We have been reading lots of different kinds of materials. We've been reading about plants—some poems, some stories; we've been reading about that satellite that circles the earth. What's that? (the moon). We've also been doing some reading in the Reading Lab [an SRA box]. So this morning, you have some time when you can be *choosing* what you'd like to read. If you want to keep reading your story [begun earlier], you can do that. If you want to read about plants, you can do that." He offered a few other examples and students quickly selected their reading materials. Most chose to read picture books (both fiction and nonfiction) at their desks. Two girls read a *Henry and Mudge* (e.g., Rylant, 1996) book together; several chose short stories from the SRA box; one boy listened to a book about the solar system on tape. As students read, Andy circulated, noting what they had chosen and asking specific questions about the books. Engagement was nearly 100% and the room was quiet.

At 10:00 A.M. Andy announced that it was time to take a break, but that they were welcome to keep reading if they liked. Eight of the 21 children in the room continued to read. When the 20-minute break was over, students had time to work on their time lines until lunch. There was much quiet discussion among the children as they explained to one another what breakfast was like at their houses, or how soccer practice had gone that week. While the children worked on their time lines, Andy quietly took aside pairs of students to read with him on the rug. These pairs changed frequently and were chosen according to the reading needs of the individual children in any given week. Some groups read trade books, other read from different sets of basals that Andy had accumulated to meet the needs of particular children. No one was permanently assigned to a particular text—or even a particular kind of text. Rather, the groups and materials were dynamic, changing to meet students' individual needs.

After lunch the students assembled on the rug with their science journals. As part of their science unit, the class had planted a small vegetable garden outside the school and their excitement was palpable as they prepared to go outside to check their plants. Before they left the room, Andy reviewed the rules for behavior and safety outdoors, reminded students to bring their rulers, and asked whether they had checked the date on the blackboard so that they would know what to write in their journals when they got outside. Andy consistently used questions ("What kind of tool do you think we might use to find out how tall our plants are?") and clearly worded reminders as preventative strategies, thus preventing many behavior and learning difficulties.

Once outside, students sat in a line facing the garden, and Andy led a discussion in which students noted which plants had sprouted and which had grown since their previous observation. They referred to earlier journal entries to support their memories. Students used labeled sticks in the garden to predict which shoots were which and discussed the difference between the words "bigger" and "taller."

Following the group discussion, they had time to measure individual plants and record their observations in their journals. Most described the plant growth in simple but complete sentences: "The peas are 5 inches." "The carrots are taller than the radishes." When everyone had written at least three sentences (although this criterion was not stated), the children returned to the classroom and had some additional time to add to their observations or write other ideas about the garden. By the time they had to leave for gym, most students had completed their writing and were engaged in reading books from the bins.

The day ended with reading aloud. Andy chose a book of fiction related to gardening, and the children listened with total engagement as he read with expression. He stopped frequently to ask the children to predict what would happen next, clarify vocabulary, and laugh with his students. When the story was over, students shared their own experiences with gardening. Some stated simply that they had had gardens at their homes the previous summer. Others launched into detailed (and often hilarious) descriptions of their exploits and those of their parents as they tried to grow various vegetables and feed slugs to one poor dog. As the discussion wound down and the end of the day approached, Andy reminded the students that they had decided to practice their poems again for homework. The students gathered their belongings, including their poetry books and other books for home reading. They collected their spelling words from their desks and settled into their seats to wait for the dismissal bell.

SUMMARY

The first graders in Andy's classroom spent their days—indeed, their year—engulfed in reading and writing. Literacy permeated nearly everything they did, making it unsurprising that at the end of first grade all but one were reading at or above grade level. Andy created a context for learning in which students mastered skills in order to access more stories, and within those stories, learned and rehearsed skills. But if you asked the *kids* what they were doing, they would not talk to you about tasks and skills. They would tell you they were hatching ducks and building boats and growing vegetables. They would tell you that they were reading to their friends, writing letters, and challenging themselves to spell new words. Students in Andy's classroom spent a lot of time learning the skills of reading and writing. But they did it within the context of engaging and meaningful activities.

Andy's students were so successful in large part because of his impressive ability to monitor each student's progress and provide individuals with instruction and materials matched to their particular needs. Thus, all children could be constructively engaged in learning. Because of Andy's strong belief in the importance of oral language underlying literacy development, many lessons began with a whole-class discussion on the rug. During these lessons, students shared what they knew, modeled language and strategic explanations for one another, and learned from their peers. Then, once everyone had a foundation on which to build, students would assemble in pairs or small groups to read or write. Andy formed the smaller groups intentionally, often matching stronger readers with weaker ones. Both parties benefited from the experience. At other times Andy would meet with ability-based groups for reading. But these groups, too, were always changing. By combining a range of groupings and materials, Andy made certain that every child had opportunities to read materials at an appropriate level each day.

Despite his emphasis on the role of oral language, Andy was careful not to describe himself as a whole-language teacher. From his perspective, children needed explicit skills instruction in addition to experience with language and books. His students received plenty of instruction in spelling and decoding, comprehension and vocabulary. There was a strong emphasis on strategies in this classroom. Students were frequently asked to explain how they figured out a word or made a choice. And there was as much emphasis placed on the *processes* (the strategies) in these cases as on the actual products. Throughout the day Andy found and created opportunities to practice learned skills and to learn new ones. In addition to reading and writing skills, Andy taught students to regulate their own learning. They learned to access resources, consult with peers, work within a time frame, and plan for the next task. All of these strategies contributed to student learning and independence.

The children in Andy's classroom read and wrote across the curriculum and across the day. They read independently, in pairs and in small groups. They read books aloud to the class, they read chorally, and they listened to Andy read books aloud. Students used reading and writing skills to plan a garden, math skills to measure the plot and the vegetables they grew, and crossed into social studies when they compared their potato crop to those of the great Potato Famine. They kept science journals to describe their predictions and findings. They wrote letters to share their progress with their parents and peers. Reading and writing were not taught as separate skills in Andy's class: They were just what people *did*. And during this year, students did them a lot.

Perhaps the most memorable aspect of Andy's classroom was how much the children really wanted to be there. By matching students with materials and instruction, by helping students learn the skills they needed to read the books they chose and communicate their ideas with others, by providing plentiful opportunities for reading, writing, talking, and sharing strategies, and by maintaining a positive attitude throughout it all, Andy created an environment that was extremely motivating. Over the course of the year, Andy's students were caught in a cycle of motivation, engagement, and learning that ensured that they ended first grade as readers and writers.

REFERENCES

Adams, M. J. (1990). *Beginning to read: Thinking and learning about print*. Cambridge, MA: MIT Press.

Ames, C. (1992). Achievement goals and the classroom motivational climate. In D. H. Schunk & J. L. Meece (Eds.), *Student perceptions in the classroom* (pp. 327–348). Hillsdale, NJ: Erlbaum.

dePaola, T. (1973). *Charlie needs a cloak*. New York: Simon & Schuster.

Graves, D. (1983). *Writing: Teachers and children at work*. Portsmouth, NH: Heinemann.

Johnson, D. W., & Johnson, R. (1975). *Learning together and alone: Cooperation, competition, and individualization*. Englewood Cliffs, NJ: Prentice-Hall.

Lobel, A. (1979). *Frog and toad are friends*. New York: HarperCollins.

Pressley, M. (1998). *Reading instruction that works: The case for balanced teaching*. New York: Guilford Press.

Meece, J. L. (1991). The classroom context and student motivational goals. In M. Maehr & P. Pintrich (Eds.), *Advances in motivation and achievement* (Vol. 7, pp. 261–285). Greenwich, CT: JAI Press.

Rylant, C. (1996). *Henry and Mudge: The first book of their adventures*. New York: Aladdin Paperbacks/Simon & Schuster Children's Publishing.

Slavin, R. E. (1987). Grouping for instruction in the elementary school. *Educational Psychologist, 22*, 109–128.

Vygotsky, L. (1978). *Mind in society: The development of higher psychological processes*. Cambridge, MA: Harvard University Press.

Wharton-McDonald, R., Presley, M., & Mistretta, J. (1998). Outstanding literacy instruction in first grade: Teacher practices and student achievement. *Elementary School Journal, 99*, 101–128.

7

Georgia Leyden

KIM BAKER
RICHARD L. ALLINGTON
GREG BROOKS

Guerneville is a small resort community in northern California. The school system is a tiny K–8 independent district, with all 600 students enrolled at the single campus just a couple of blocks from the main street in this one-stoplight town. Tourism and vineyards are the primary industries in Guerneville, and employment is more seasonal than regular. Almost half of the children at Guerneville Elementary come from low-income families (46%), and family transiency is common. Some of the transiency is linked to the availability of low-cost housing in run-down cabins that once were vacation destinations but now serve, along with mobile homes, as the community's low-income housing. However, these small cabins, and the area's seasonal employment, support a mobile, low-wage work force. Nonetheless, the Guerneville campus is a relatively new and attractive facility and the elementary school exudes a warm and welcoming feeling.

A visitor to Georgia Leyden's room at Guerneville Elementary School finds the mood to be that of a community actively engaged and interested in what it is doing. Students are working in groups or

138

alone, reading and writing, sharing and exchanging ideas and information. Georgia integrates reading and writing throughout the day and across subjects. Print surrounds the students on all four walls, including students' stories, students' artwork with labels, charts of songs and poems, and a pocket board for sentences from the basal anthology used in guided reading.

In addition, Georgia has created a word wall, which began with a few words in September and has been added to weekly throughout the year. Many of the word wall words are frequently encountered words, and many are phonetically irregular, such as "know," "my," "said," and "would." (See Appendix 7.1 for a listing of words on the wall in April.) She has several activities involving the word wall, including word wall spelling, word wall as support during writing, mystery words, and use of the word wall as a reading spot during the reading-the-room activity (discussed in the next section of this chapter).

Hundreds of books are divided into (1) a hard-cover corner, displaying many books on the current social studies and science units, (2) books in baskets, which come out for independent reading time, (3) plastic crates filled with books for a daily leisure read after lunch, and (4) numerous student-published books from the Writers Workshop. These are kept in different parts of the room. The hardcover picture books are on shelves, with a pocketed free-standing bookshelf featuring books with current social studies and science themes. A rocking chair and an erasable easel are available in this area. Georgia often uses this corner for whole-class lessons and for the Author's Chair, but the students use it for individual reading time and paired-reading activities. Further down on this long wall is a rack with all the books students have written throughout the year, individually and as a class. In another corner, where Georgia holds her small-group guided reading activities and reading and writing conferences, the baskets of books for independent reading are stored. The plastic crates for leisure reading are spread throughout the room.

Georgia's language arts program involves a weekly schedule of varied reading and writing activities. At least three times a week the students have independent reading time while Georgia holds individual reading conferences. The 1989 Houghton-Mifflin basal is used twice weekly for guided reading, supplemented with appropriately leveled Storybox books at these sessions for more guided reading. The class is divided into four homogeneous reading groups for these twice-a-week sessions, but heterogeneously grouped for daily independent reading time. Georgia meets with two guided reading groups a day, and during these periods the other students have activities in the various centers located in the classroom. Friday is an independent reading day for all groups. Georgia also reads aloud daily, offering a chance for predictions, sharing of personal knowledge and experiences, and vocabulary building. She often chooses books that enhance a math, science, or social studies concept the class is working on. Each day after lunch the students have a leisure reading time. Once every other week, for one afternoon, members of a sixth-grade class join the class as reading buddies.

Writers Workshop is a vital component in the planned weekly literacy program. Twice a week, students are composing for at least 45 minutes. Georgia began the year by modeling the steps in the writing process: choosing a topic, brainstorming the self-selected topic, writing a first draft, revising with the help of peers, conferring with the teacher, editing, and illustrating when taking a piece to publication. Students choose the topics they write about, have several stories in various stages of completion, and decide which pieces they want published. Not all written pieces go through all the stages of the writing process. Only if a student decides to publish his or her work does that student proceed through all the stages and then share it from the Author's Chair. The actual Author's Chair is the aforementioned comfy rocker, where a student reads her or his polished, illustrated, published story to the rest of the class.

Writing activities are plentiful in addition to the twice weekly Writers Workshop sessions. Classroom centers that are part of the guided reading time include writing on the computer, an art center, a listening center (books on tape), and a reading center. Georgia's art center has a literacy connection that includes drawing and painting characters or doing illustrations so that the class can put together a folder or a big book. Writing assignments in response to their reading, personal journals, and whole-class–generated big books offer diverse writing opportunities. The students have cubbies and are encouraged to write notes to each other constantly. Once a week the class goes to the computer lab, where half of the students write and publish with the help of older students. Georgia believes in immersing her students in reading and writing activities: "Everything needs to tie in with reading." She strongly believes that reading and writing opportunities should be as authentic as possible and has high expectations for her students. Allowing for different achievement levels, she expects all her students to become readers and writers, becoming more competent and confident as she continually challenges them.

DAILY SCHEDULE

Students begin entering classroom at 8:20 A.M., quickly hang up their jackets, put away lunches, and then group on the rug for the beginning activity at 8:30. On Monday there is oral sharing time, when students may choose to participate in telling an experience or not. Other days students share things they "wonder about." Georgia also uses this time to specifically praise students and encourage respectful, caring behavior. "Think about how we are going to be treating each other today—how to be a good friend" started a discussion on the positive ways to act and communicate with others. Georgia quickly takes lunch count, attendance, and has two helpers writing the day of the week and the date. In the beginning of the year she modeled this activity and by January handed it over to students to do on their own. While this is going on, she engages the rest of the class in "reading the room"—reading words from the word wall, reading words from the poems and songs around the room. When the students finish their calendar information, the class reads it silently and then in unison. Then the Pledge of Allegiance is recited and a patriotic song is sung, with a student pointing to the large printed words on a chart. Again, this is an activity that Georgia did at first but has now been taken over by the students. All this usually takes 10 minutes, and by 8:40 the class is engaged in guided reading and activities at the various centers, independent reading, or Writers Workshop. As Georgia explained her approach thus:

> "More and more I want it to be that they have taken over the responsibility of these roles, but they have had modeling and support to get to that place. Everything we do, we read or write about it. It's real stuff. So they get the notion that if you want to know something, you read about it, and if you want to tell somebody something, you can write it. So when I don't remember who the messengers are, I say to Richard, who needs to have extra practice, 'Richard, can you go to the helper chart and read who the messengers are?' And if they say to me, 'Mrs. Leyden,

would you do such and such for me tomorrow?' I say, 'Oh, you better write me a note because I'm going to forget it.' Then they write this little note and plop it down in front of me."

Georgia has organized a block of 90 minutes of time for literacy activities. More than two-thirds of this period involves students daily in individual reading and writing. Writing Workshop, guided reading and working at centers, independent reading, and conferences are included throughout the week. Recess, state mandated, and a snack take about 20 minutes at 10:10 A.M., but the whole class or individual students often stay behind several minutes to finish what they are reading or writing. After recess Georgia has a math lesson, which starts as a whole-class discussion on the rug and proceeds to more individualized work at the tables. Again, literacy is stressed. For example, for the beginning of a unit on telling time, she read aloud *Bear Child's Book of Hours*, by Anne Rockwell, to tie in with the introduction of telling time on the hour and half hour. The next day students wrote their own "My Book of Hours and Half Hours," filling in clocks and sentences that matched their personal experiences.

Lunchtime is scheduled from 11:45 to 12:30, and Georgia keeps her students engaged in activities until the last possible moment. Lunches are quickly gathered, students line up, and she walks them outside to picnic benches. When students return, they can get drinks and then settle down for an independent leisure reading time. Crates of books—with different levels of complexity, including many easy books, magazines, and student-published books—are available for the children. Students share responses with each other, read with partners, or read segments to each other from the books they have chosen. There is a very low hum during this reading time. Twenty-five minutes later students either go to the computer lab for the Children's Writing/Publishing Center, or to the gym, or Georgia gathers them on the rug for reading aloud, often on a subject connected to their science or social studies units. This can lead to a writing activity done at the tables individually, or an observation and data collecting activity, such as a meadow walk connected to *Over in the Meadow*, illustrated by Ezra Jack Keats, and *Insects Are My Life*, by Megan McDonald. Other special activities, work on activities begun in the morning, and Author's Chair activities finish the day.

Reading help is provided by the reading teacher, who conducts

Reading Recovery in the morning and other sessions apart from the regular class in the afternoon. An aide in the room has been trained by the reading teacher to work with students on a one-to-one basis in the classroom. Working with a student, she says, "Don't look at me, look at the page." As the student finishes, "Good job, that's a hard page" or "I really like the way you self-corrected; what were you thinking?" Often when the reading teacher arrives at the classroom, Georgia is working with a targeted student in guided reading and asks to keep the student. The reading teacher appears to be very flexible and returns at another time. Georgia takes responsibility for all her students' achievement and progress.

TYPES OF READING

Guided reading centers on a basal anthology selection for the week, such as *Over in the Meadow*. Georgia uses the basal anthology as a source of reading material, creating an integrated reading language arts experience that expands the reading and writing opportunities well beyond that typically associated with basal reading lessons. Georgia does not use all the stories in the basal anthology, but picks those she can integrate well into the rest of the curriculum. She supplements the basal with many predictable, controlled vocabulary texts, because she believes the stories from the literature-based basal anthology are too hard for much of the class at the beginning of the year.

Typically, Georgia was all the students on the rug as she does a prereading activity. With the story *Over in the Meadow*, she had the children close their eyes and think about animals and plants in a meadow. She told them, "There is a creek, not as big as our local creek, and a tree trunk nearby with ants crawling on it. Up in the blue sky are clouds. If you are sitting back in this meadow, you would be smelling things, seeing things, and hearing things." Georgia then directed the students to the text, illustrated by Ezra Jack Keats. A discussion ensued about the fact that this is an old story, that Keats didn't write it, and that the class had read other retold stories. Georgia read it aloud from a big book edition, and the students commented this was a counting book, a rhyming book, a repeating book. "Muskrat," "snug," and "chirp" were discussed as vocabulary as she read because these words were hard to determine from the pictures.

Georgia asked questions about the muskrat, elaborated on "snug" by saying, "I like 'snug.' It reminds me of being warm and comfortable," and demonstrated "chirping" when a student asked, "What is chirp?"

With a pocket chart Georgia had the written numbers 1 through 10 in a column and blank cards across from them in another column. As the students worked on remembering which animal matched which number, they flipped the cards to reveal the correct names. Georgia also used this exercise to stress sounds and words. She used the word numbers "one" and "eight" to talk about how "one" starts with the "w" sound, not an "o" sound, and how "e" and "i" say "ay" in "eight." As students matched the animals to the numbers from the story, they silently—in their heads—read. Then, in unison they read the story again, all students appearing to be able to read. At their seats they all found the story in individual books, using the table of contents, and read chorally.

Next, Georgia had the students write in their journals about their favorite baby animal and why it was their favorite. During this time Georgia and the classroom aide circulated, helping students to sound out words. With "cheetah," Georgia directed a student to look at her mouth as she said the word, stretching it out. The student said, then wrote "ch," "e," "ta." Such sound-stretching demonstration and practice was a common feature in the classroom during writing activities. Both Georgia and her aide linked the students' sound spelling to developing phonemic segmentation by modeling stretching a word in segments and encouraging the students to do this on their own. When recess time came, several students lingered, completing their journal entries.

On subsequent days Georgia worked with smaller groups, using the pocket sentences from the story but leaving blank the animals and their activity. The students filled in these missing words by reading the sentence in their heads, talking with each other, and deciding what should fit. Afterward, they read it silently or whisper read, and then read aloud together. Finally, in individual books, Georgia directed the students to read the story loudly enough for her to hear when she moved around, but not loudly enough to disturb their neighbors. A different guided reading group had a discussion about what they heard in the story and had seen outside (the class had gone for a walk in the meadow to observe and gather data the day before). Georgia shared pages from several books about bees. Then she introduced the Storybox book *The Bee* by Joy Cowley. After reading it, they made a chart about what they knew bees could do. Students whisper-read the chart, read all the sentences together, and then each student picked a sentence to read alone. A writing assignment involved composing a sentence: "A bee can _____."

Independent reading, with books chosen from the baskets, is alternated with guided reading. The baskets are filled with teacher-selected books that the students have encountered during previous lessons. This is a quiet reading time, but students share with each other or sometimes partner read, taking turns. With the groups heterogeneously mixed and books at a variety of levels available, students model good reading strategies and fluency for each other. During this time Georgia has individual reading conferences, takes running records, jots down notes, and offers personal instruction in reading strategies to encourage self-monitoring, the use of multiple strategies, and independence. Georgia works individually or with the whole class on phonemic awareness (sound stretching) and onset and rimes (word patterns), tying them into literature with which they are familiar. However, she believes there are a number of cueing systems and that they all need to be addressed. "When my kids come to a word they don't know, I tell them to read beyond to see what happens, to come back, to reread, to think about all of the things they've used, the picture clues, what they've read beyond the words, to take what they know about letters and sounds, and to look at that word and think what would make sense or not."

By reading aloud, a teacher has an opportunity to expose students to material beyond their reading ability, develop word and vocabulary knowledge, support their making inferences and predictions, and evoke responses. Georgia uses the literature she reads aloud to point out the literary elements or phrases students can transfer to their own writing. Students read the song they sing every morning, they read poems on charts exhibited around the room, they read words on the word wall and other words displayed around the room. Silent leisure reading after lunch is a daily favorite, with students having free choice of any of the books in the room. The published books from the Writers Workshop are favorites. Georgia firmly believes that the more children read, the better readers they will become.

The Author's Chair now offers the whole class an oral literacy experience. Because students take many of their Writers Workshop compositions through the whole process to publication, there are at least two reader/authors a day. In past years Georgia had limited the questions to four after the reading. By opening the discussion to as many questions as the children want to ask, she has found that the conversation is richer and deeper, with the students making many relevant connections to their own experiences. The questions have usually encouraged the author to think about her or his book more thoughtfully. Through Georgia's relinquishing control and turning the forum over to the reader and the class, the discussions are much more open and substantial. From these discussions, Georgia says, "I learn a lot about what's going on in [the students'] books, about things going on outside of the classroom, and about what matters to them, and how I can change things in here, to help them do what they're doing."

Georgia believes that the Writers Workshop offers all students, but especially those students who are struggling with reading, an excellent opportunity to read fluently and practice good reading strategies. The low-achieving students are motivated to read their own writing—and can. She has watched as they self-correct, monitor their reading as they go back and reread when they are tracking the words and realize they are off. Their writing offers many chances for reading practice:

- When they are revising
- When they are doing the illustrations
- When reading it from the literature baskets, because they are going to sit in the Author's Chair
- When they take it home to read to their family
- When they read student-authored stories at silent reading time

TYPES OF WRITING

On Writers Workshop days, the students have reading from the literature baskets for 30–40 minutes. Then it is Author's Chair time, during which several students read their published work, answer questions, and receive constructive, positive feedback from the other students. For the last 50 minutes of the language arts period students write, rewrite, edit, illustrate, and publish. Student names are listed on the board under the stage at which they are at the time. The teacher and aide give individual attention and encouragement to the writers. There are checklist cards for editing that encourage final punctuation, capitals, and spelling. Most of the students spell phonemically, sounding out words and stretching the sounds. In January, Georgia added a priority word list of 25 high-frequency words (see Appendix 7.2). The students have a list of them on their tables and are expected to refer to it whenever they need to use these words in writing. After 3 months, students were spelling these words correctly without looking at the lists. There is much use of the word wall for spelling other words. Typical is one boy who was adding to a story on giant sea turtles. He was reading from a book about sea turtles to gather new information. He had already written two drafts, which had been revised and edited. As he wrote, he used the word wall and the information and spelling from the book he was using as a resource. Another student was working on a chapter book about animals because she had decided to combine two works in progress, one on horses and one on dogs. Other students do breakfast-to-bed stories (I woke up this morning. I ate breakfast. I went to the park. . . . I went to bed). Popular openings for many students are "One day" and "Once upon a time." Georgia attributes this to her pointing out how authors open stories with these phrases as she reads aloud. Amy, a Title 1 student (Title 1 is a major federal program), came in at the beginning of the year with little letter–sound knowledge, but Georgia states, "She got bitten by the writing bug, and is now more creative and more willing to just write whatever comes up for her." Figure 7.1 shows examples of Amy's journal and narrative writing in the spring.

During guided reading Georgia has three centers through which three groups rotate while she is working with the fourth group. At the computer center they can do regular publishing or write notes to friends. In the art center for the week the class was using *Over in the Meadow*, each student was painting a big picture of any animal of his or her choice so that the class could write a patterned big book. The following day the class worked on writing and spelling the sentences for these pictures: "This is a fox at the zoo." "This is a blackbird in the forest." "This is a bear in the meadow." That day the students wrote in response journals, wrote for their telling time book of hours, wrote their favorite word from one of the selections read aloud that was made into a poster, wrote on clipboards about their trip to the meadow—writing in their own words everything they saw, smelled, or heard. Another activity involved making murals of differ-

My teacher
read a book
to us obaut
frogs and My
favrit one
was the one
thot livb
in o léif
it wos neut

one day The Wind and the sun Were
Tocking isM The sTongiset send
The Wind i will shoWyou ThaT i
oM The sTorgiste by bloWeg ThaT
cKop off ThaT Mon so The Wind
bloW and bloW herd re and herdre bot The
Mon oldid iT on as Tiglos he could.
noW My Tern The sun soed The sun
beogon Two ThaT and holr wTl TheMon
Toock off The cope and sol doWn
andr o shady Trey and ThaT is
on The sun shoWd he Wos sTronre.

FIGURE 7.1. Writing samples from Amy, a struggling reader. At top is a journal entry, below is a narrative she composed.

ent habitats with appropriate labels: "tree," "river," "pond," and "meadow." Georgia noted that the journal writing this year was significantly better than in past years and attributed the improvement partially to the priority word list, which has allowed students to more quickly write down their thoughts.

TEACHING OF SKILLS

Georgia teaches both reading and writing skills explicitly, typically in the context of a reading or writing activity. She is opportunistic, selecting multiple occasions daily to provide explicit skill information during whole-group, small-group, and individual meetings. But Georgia is also systematic, incorporating much strategy and skill instruction into her guided reading lessons, Writers Workshop conferences, and reading conferences. All of these times offer students personalized instruction. In the small reading group using *The Bee*, Georgia prepared the students by activating their background information about bees, previewed the cover and the following pages, and set up the three readers to successfully whisper read on the first try. She then had them reread two times, stressing that the sentences should make sense. Next, she did a mini-lesson on the double "-ee" sound, starting with "bee" and making a list with "see," "meet," "beet," and "bees," all words from this story and a recently read book. The students thought of sentences about what bees can do: "Bees can sting." "Bees can collect nectar." "Bees can drink." Although they knew only the beginning letter of "collect," the students spelled everything else as Georgia wrote. As Georgia wrote "collect" she modeled stretching out the sounds of the word to be better able to hear and spell them. Georgia is very careful to set up reading and writing activities that will be successful for her students, but also challenging.

An example of a reading conference shows how Georgia encourages the use of multiple strategies: self-monitoring, decoding, and, most important, making meaning. *The Comstock Farm* was a new book for this reader, so Georgia encouraged talking about it a little, looking at the title, and discussing the opening illustration and what the student thought was going on. When the student read "country farm" instead of "Comstock Farm," Georgia praised the try, saying it was a really good word that made sense. She then clapped out the syllables in "Comstock" and directed the student to look closely at the letters, and he was able to sound it out by syllables. Early in the story the student read "greens and chickens" for "geese and chickens." Georgia drew attention to the mistake, asking, "Does that make sense?." The student quickly reread the phrase correctly. She then encouraged the use of multiple strategies—using picture cues, making sense, using letter and word patterns, and reading on to find out what happens. The student slowly, but successfully, read: "The geese and chickens and a big fat turkey walked with us on our way to the (blank) where the apples grow." The blank was "orchard." Georgia then built on the student's prior knowledge, asking, "Where do apples grow? What do we call a lot of trees?" until the student used that knowledge and the word structure to correctly pronounce "orchard." As the student read on he, became more fluent.

Another example of the focus on developing self-monitoring was observed during a quick succession of student rereadings, "for me vine/for the vine/from the vine," as Georgia asked, "Does that make sense?" Another spontaneous self-correction led Georgia to ask, "How did you figure out that it was 'carry'?" The student seemed unable to verbalize the strategies he had used, so Georgia suggested several: "Did you read on? Did you look at the letters? Did you look at the picture?" For a final misread, "fake" for "face," Georgia again stressed making sense. "Read it again and see if that makes more sense to you, from the beginning," encouraging the use of cross-checking, rereading along with making meaning. The student then successfully read, "At home we carve a jack-o'-lantern face on our big orange pumpkin."

It is clear that Georgia models and encourages the use a variety of reading strategies as students read. Although making sense and understanding what is written are of prime importance, Georgia encourages the use of letter–sound relationships, the use of word structure patterns, the use of automatic sight words from the word wall and the spelling priority list, and the students' own personal reading and knowledge base.

Georgia also encourages critical thinking and the use of strategies in whole-class activities. She has a word game that she plays with the students, first thing in the morning or before specials when they have a few minutes. She gives clues about one of the words on the word wall, allowing students to revise their guesses as they gain more information. Each group of students at a table works as a team in determining the word, yet each student writes down a guess after each clue. For example, for "girls" the clues were as follows:

1. It's a word on the word wall.
2. There are five letters.
3. It begins with the letter "g."
4. It means more than one.
5. Used in a sentence—"Mrs. Leyden, may I go to the _____ bathroom?"

Another way Georgia encourages thinking about spelling and patterns is allowing the students to help her spell. When they were composing the sentences for their big book about animals, Georgia wrote and the students spelled the words. When it came to the word "bear," she wrote several student attempts from "br-beer-bear-beerr." They discussed which were not correct and why, and settled on "bear." After deciding on "bear," Georgia brought up the other spelling of "bare" and wrote it. When "bluebird" was written, the students noticed that it was a word that has two words, a compound. In making a list to choose topics about spring things they wanted to know more about, again the students helped spell whole words, providing at least the initial sounds and patterns in words like "caterpillars," "beetles," and "butterflies."

In the beginning of the year there were a large number of students who did not recognize many letters of the alphabet and who knew even fewer letter sounds. Georgia did a great deal of scaffolding with them in their initial writing sessions. She stressed listening for the sounds, stretching the word out, and using invented spelling. She would patiently say a word over and over to them, stretching the sounds, as they worked their way through writing it down. Often they could write only the initial consonant, and that was accepted at first. John's examples, from his journal writing in September and February (Figure 7.2), demonstrate the growth he made, like so many of his fellow students.

In May, Georgia stated, "I still say to them, 'Listen for the sounds.' " Georgia used the McCracken spelling technique (McCracken & McCracken, 1986), which develops listening for sounds and writing them down. She had started syllable recognition in the fall, clapping for each syllable. She also worked with Pat Cunningham's "making words" activity (Cunningham & Allington, 1999), in which students manipulate individual letter cards or tiles to create words on

FIGURE 7.2. Two writing samples produced by John, one in September, the other in February. Note the growth in writing sounds in words.

demand. With all of these activities and lots of practice in writing their own stories, writing in their journals, and writing notes to friends, students began to incorporate more appropriate letter–sound relationships in their writing.

Throughout the year Georgia has added to the word wall, constantly doing short activities with it, directing students to it when they needed one of words for their writing, and increasing the students' sight recognition of these words. The introduction of the priority word list in January, with its 25 irregular, but high-frequency words (e.g. "are," "from," "you"), focused student attention on spelling conventions. These students, many who had started first grade without complete letter–name knowledge and with limited phonemic awareness, have progressed incredibly, writing readable prose on self-chosen topics in their journals or in the Writers Workshop, writing at home, writing to their friends, and writing notes. The one student who came to first grade already using invented spelling was working in her journal at a different level. She has incorporated many of the spelling conventions into her writing and uses few invented spellings. Another area of growth for her and the other students was in expanding their ideas and writing many sentences on a topic. Figure 7.3 shows examples of Dilenia's use of invented spelling from the beginning of the year, her progress in the use of conventional spelling, and her development as a writer who could write lengthy pieces.

Georgia encouraged such writing in the early winter by setting a timer and having the students write until the time was up. She developed effective decoding strategies through the regular presentation of mini-lessons on letter–sounds and patterns, sound stretching, modeling of sounding-out behaviors, discussion of word pronunciations, and through numerous authentic writing opportunities. In her room students are reading and writing throughout the day, actively engaged in these functions with little direct supervision. Georgia put it this way: "Even if they're doing something that's not necessarily what I've told them to do, it has to do with reading and writing that they've come up with, that they want to do with one another. I believe in that. I believe in choice." Georgia instructs them in reading and writing strategies and skills in whole-group, small-group, and side-by-side lessons. She offers individual support when necessary, but allows freedom of choice and focuses on individual growth in daily reading and writing activities.

Dear Mrs. Leyden
I like to Plant
flowrs.

The Wind and The Sun

One morning the sun and the wind
were dsideing hou was the sdrogst
They sou a man bulow. And the wind said
I can blou the cape off that man. So
the wind blou and blou but he dode not
get the cape off the man. Now it
is myTrn and the sun bgan to shin
it bgan to get worm then it bgan to get
hot then the man tok off The cape
and that is how she provd that she
was the Sdrogist.

FIGURE 7.3. Two samples of Dilenia's writing, the first composed in September, the second in April.

ACROSS-CURRICULAR CONNECTIONS

From the preceding descriptions of Georgia's instruction, it is obvious that she makes numerous connections between reading and writing, and between reading and writing and math, science, social studies, art, and music. In addition to the "meadow" episode described earlier, Georgia shared another example that demonstrates the expansion and connections that can be made.

"Last year, I was involved in the most wonderful inquiry project here. We had been studying rocks with Lawrence Hall of Science in Oakland materials. This is really science oriented, not much literature, not much writing; we're just doing science. I wanted to go with an inquiry project, but I didn't want to do something totally different from what I was already doing, so I thought I would work on the rocks. I asked my class what kinds of things they would like to know about. We did brainstorming. We ended up with a group who wanted to know something about crystals, a group who wanted to know about fossils, one about volcanoes, and one just about pure rocks. To form four groups, each headed by an adult, I first recruited a dad, who was a professor at the university. Then I went to my superintendent and said, "I need you to come in and help me and take a group for this period of time." I and another parent who used to come in once a week completed the four adults needed. Each of the four groups met with its adult every afternoon and did its inquiry. Inquiry included finding the books they needed, to find out what they needed to know. I took my students, the "pure rock" group, to my house one day, leaving the other three adults and their groups at school. We went into a creek and picked up stones. Then we had an expert from the university science department come and bring her rock collection and tell us about the various rocks. We ended up organizing a museum in the classroom, and all the rest of the primary students came through in an afternoon. My class made the signs for the museum, wrote how the classes would come in and which way they would go, made posters, and, of course, organized and wrote about the exhibits. It was one of the most exciting things. The kids were crazy about this: they were avid learners and so motivated. It was authentic—they were reading because they had a purpose for reading. They were writing because they had a purpose for writing. They were so motivated because it was what they wanted to know, what they wanted to learn."

Another lesson, a sorting activity we observed, illustrated how Georgia incorporated analysis, collaboration, and critical thinking along with categorizing and literacy development. In groups of three, students were asked to divide a supply of candies of various sizes, colors, and shapes into four groups. After they sorted the candies onto four sheets, the children in each group were expected to write what their categories were and to indicate how they decided on them. As a summing up and another literacy activity, Georgia made a chart of the various groupings and how they had been determined. Students had created a variety of categories including (1) brown, red, yellow, and rainbow; (2) light, dark, colorful, and yellow; (3) lollipops, Jolly

Ranchers, circles, and fat; (4) lollipops, rectangles, black, and light; (5) fatheads (Tootsie Pops), fat, smooth, and round; and (6) purple, yellow, rainbow, and colors "sort of the same." Students negotiated the categories, found they had a few leftover pieces that didn't fit easily, and learned to expand a category or to determine that a piece was "mostly something." One group's paper showing their categories and labels had written at the bottom, "we figrd owt to gethr."

ENGAGING CHILDREN IN LEARNING

Georgia's belief in a learning environment that encourages respect, kindness, tolerance, sharing, and growth produces a community of learners where virtually all children are engaged in productive academic work all day. Although her selection of an engaging and appropriately challenging array of curriculum materials and tasks plays a huge role here, there is more to do it than this technical expertise. Georgia has created a classroom where children rarely misbehave and where they encourage and support each other's learning. She treats her students the way she expects them to treat each other. Positive comments on behavior draw attention to the kind of behavior she wants to foster. Occasionally, Georgia uses a more direct approach, as when she took aside a boy and girl who had been verbally sparring all day. She listened to each side. Max said Ashley was bossy and always telling him what to do, and Ashley replied that she was trying to help him. Both used the example of Ashley's pointing to the word "there" on the pocket chart while Max was writing. Georgia noted Ashley's good intention, but suggested that she wait until Max asked for help. In turn, she told Max to think about his voice, asking, "How could you tell her you don't want help?" Max answered, "Please let me figure this out by myself." Georgia's encouraging reply, "Great! I love your choice of words. Okay. Now you two need to talk for a minute alone about this."

In addition, Georgia evaluates students in regard to their individual progress and effort. Individual praise of student work is typically specific, but quietly communicated to the individual student. Likewise, the specifics of student work are typically negotiated between Georgia and the student. Personal choice and authentic assignments motivate the students and allow for effective use of block time in literacy . Frequent talk among students is present and even encouraged. The talk we heard was typically supportive and task oriented. Teamwork, thinking and discussing ideas to work out answers, occurs daily. Sometimes Georgia has everyone stand up and circulate around the room to see each other's work and get ideas. When the noise level rises so that it makes conferring or teaching difficult, Georgia rings a small bell, producing silence. This happens only occasionally—once, sometimes twice, a day. Oral discussions while the teacher is reading aloud or during the Author's Chair time require taking turns and acceptance of differing opinions. Georgia wants the students "to communicate and to trust their own thinking about things . . . to know that they can be in a conversation with an adult and it can be a real conversation and exchange of ideas."

The focus of literacy activities is on real-life situations, not just busywork. Students are encouraged to help each other, puzzle through things together, support one another, and solve problems as teams. Along with this emphasis is an individual focus on self-evaluation. With reading, this means the ability to self-monitor, self-correct, and read independently. With writing, it means revising, editing, and determining what pieces are ready to be published. Establishing observable criteria so students can evaluate their performances is also part of Georgia's classroom structure. The word wall, the priority word list, and an editing checklist provide guides for students' evaluation of the surface features of their writing. Students keep personal logs of the books they have read. Writing portfolios contain work from the beginning of the year to the present.

Another important component of Georgia's classroom management is her ability and determination to release control of activities to the students as soon as they are capable of performing them on their own. Georgia told us that when she began as a first-grade teacher, she was convinced that first graders could not write. It was her attendance at a McCracken Workshop that led to the discovery that first-grade students could write using invented spelling. When she decided to implement the Writers Workshop, she struggled with the idea.

> "When I started it and being, I think, a more structured kind of person, I was thinking 'Oh, my goodness. How can I have children just moving about willy-nilly without my knowing?' One day I decided, 'Okay, this is important enough. I just want to

jump in and see what happens.' So every single year since then, there's been refinement."

Thus, Georgia has given ever more control to her students in other areas of their learning. She starts out modeling what is expected, sets up the structure, and gradually releases choice and control to her motivated learners.

SUPPLEMENTAL PERSONNEL

A remedial reading teacher offers Reading Recovery to one student from Georgia's classroom. The same teacher also provides small-group instruction to five of Georgia's students in a setting apart from the classroom. The reading teacher coordinates what she is working on with Georgia. She has trained Georgia's aide to work with another student in daily one-on-one instruction, using general Reading Recovery pedagogical practices and routines. This understanding of reading strategies and decoding is helpful when the aide works with any student in the Writer's Workshop, with students who are practicing for Author's Chair, in literacy activities at the various centers, and during independent reading time. The aide is present all morning and spends most of her time working with students individually.

First graders are not considered for referral to special education before the end of the school year. The school's philosophy is that it is important to allow students a chance to emerge as readers and writers, and other interventions should be tried first. If by the spring Georgia knows that the type of progress that is expected is just not happening, she alerts the child study team. She has made no special education referrals recently, and rarely does. The only pupils in her room considered to be disabled, typically, are those who come from another school with an Individual Education Plan (IEP) and an official label.

STRUCTURES FOR GROWTH

The principal of the school describes the traditional school procedure of lining up students as producing "enemy space." It has to do with the unrealistic expectation that five- and six-year-olds can line up without moving or bothering their neighbors. She suggests that schools sometimes create situations that make it impossible for students to behave in a natural way. If the school structure is going to create enemy space, children are going to get in trouble. Georgia is careful not to put such structures in place in her classroom. She constantly questions herself to be sure she is not making it more difficult for her students to do what they need to be doing. She describes herself as a structured person who has learned to relinquish control to her students. She wants her students to believe that they do not always need an adult there to help them.

Georgia has established this approach with a class that has had a 50% change in students during the school year. Attendance is another problem for some students. One girl has been absent 2 of every 3 days this year. Although the school is monitoring her absences, she often is absent or arrives significantly after the school day has begun. Another student has missed 36 days by the beginning of April. This is frustrating to Georgia: "If they aren't physically here with me, it's hard to teach them." Even with these constraints, Georgia is determined to provide classroom instruction that promotes academic growth for all her students.

The writing samples from Amy, John, and Dilenia demonstrate just how effective she is in working with different students. These children were representative of low-, middle-, and high-achieving students when they started first grade. Working with their different strengths and needs, Georgia individualized her attention to encourage and stimulate substantial academic development in each of them. Amy, filled with ideas she wanted to communicate, needed to learn to hear the sounds in a word, to represent them through invented spelling, and then with conventional spelling from the word wall. In the beginning, that meant she represented each word with a single letter—usually the initial consonant. John came to first grade with a basic ability to represent a word by the letters reflecting the initial and final sounds, so Georgia worked on stretching words with him and other students. He began to incorporate many consonant and vowel sounds and write longer responses. Dilenia, already a writer when she entered first grade, often wrote in her journal as Georgia worked with the rest of the class. Georgia encouraged this, but also fostered the use of more conventional spelling and more personal responses. Dilenia has shown significant growth in her ability to expand upon her ideas and write in complete paragraphs. Each of these students made tremendous progress in literacy development.

SUMMARY

It is apparent that students enjoy being members of Georgia's classroom community. It is also apparent that the students are immersed in literacy activities from the first day of school in September until they leave in June. Reading and writing are valued by Georgia, and this attitude is passed along to her students. Lessons are structured, yet allow a great deal of student choice and control. Teaching involves explicit skill instruction and recurring demonstrations of useful strategies, along with numerous and varied opportunities to practice real reading and writing so that the strategies and skills taught are consolidated into fluent reading and writing performances. Real-life integrated learning assignments motivate the students and keep them on task.

Management is no problem, because students are involved in their work. Student choice, tasks of appropriate difficulty, sharing of problems and ideas, teamwork, respecting and helping each other are features of this classroom that keep behavioral problems to a minimum. Georgia is constantly challenging her students to accelerate their progress, to become more independent readers, writers, and thinkers. She is also continually monitoring each child's progress. This is made easier, it seems, when children are routinely successful and eagerly engaged in their own literacy work.

When virtually all children are actively engaged in productive work, as is the case in Georgia's room, teachers have more time and greater attentional capacity when working with individuals or small groups. This results, we believe, in a richer and more detailed working knowledge of individuals and their instructional needs. Georgia is also continually demonstrating the use of effective literacy skills and strategies, and she has implemented a set of classroom strategies that foster student independence and growth. In the end, each student in Georgia's classroom was successful and each demonstrated enormous literacy and social development. That so many children successfully made the miraculous transition to being readers and writers is a testament to Georgia's exemplary teaching strengths.

APPENDIX 7.1. WORD WALL

A	B	C	D	E	F	G	H
and	be	can	did		for	got	he
at	big	car			from	girl	help
are	boy	came			father	girls	here
any	boys	children				go	his
	by					going	

I	J	K	L	M	N	O	P
in	just	know	like	meet	not	of	pin
is			look	Mother	now	on	please
I				me			
				Mrs.			
				my			
				Mr.			

Q	R	S	T	U	V	W	X
		see	the	up		was	
		said	to			will	
		she	this			with	
		school	that			what	
			too			would	
			think				
			take				
			they				

Y	Z
you	

APPENDIX 7.2. PRIORITY WORDS

a	I
and	in
are	is
as	it
at	
	of
be	on
from	that
for	the
	they
	this
	to
have	
he	
his	
	was
	with
	you

REFERENCES

Cunningham, P. A., & Allington, R. L. (1999). *Classrooms that work: They can all read and write*. New York: Longmans.
McCracken, R. A., & McCracken, M. J. (1986). *Stories, songs, and poetry to teach reading and writing*. Chicago: American Library Association.

Kim Baker is an Assistant Professor of Education at the Russell State College in Troy, New York, where her work focuses on the preparation of exemplary teachers of reading.

Greg Brooks is an Assistant Professor of Education at Nazareth College in Rochester, New York, where he focuses on the integration of reading, writing, and children's literature.

8

Missy Allen

I'm committed to providing whatever it takes to
meet a student's needs.   —*Missy Allen*

Missy Allen has taught first grade in Bedford, Texas, for 12 years.
She has never taught any other grade, and her bachelor of science degree was obtained in Elementary Education in 1984. She is active in
Delta Kappa Gamma, the International Reading Association, her
principal's Campus-wide Advisory Committee, and Teacher Line
(composed of 12 women in her district who perform skits as spoofs
on education for community groups, including the International
Reading Association). She has led numerous teacher-training semi-
nars in reading and math and was Texas Teacher of the Year in 1997
for her school district. From 1992 to 1995 she was a member of the
Texas division of the New Jersey Writing Project and has also been
Team Leader for the first-grade teachers at Meadow Creek Elementary for the last 5 years. All members of her team have received 36
hours of in-service training in gifted and talented education. They
build higher-order thinking skills and critical thinking projects into
their curriculum during team planning sessions. Missy values staying

current in educational research and practices and continually talks about the most recent book or research article she has read.

Her school is located in a middle-to-low socioeconomic suburban community between Dallas and Fort Worth, Texas. Although most of her students did not begin first grade with the ability to read, the majority knew the names of letters; some single-letter, sound-to-symbol associations; and what commas and periods were. Most did not understand concepts of print, including left-to-right directionality. This year's class also had greater emotional difficulties, and more children operated at the lower end of the literacy continuum than in the past. Three children were diagnosed with special education needs and were mainstreamed into her class. During the last 3 years there has been a change in the school population demographics, so that each year more children have begun first grade without having been read to at home. Missy stated that some of her less efficient readers were really gifted students, but unmotivated to read. Moreover, some of her gifted students began first grade uninspired about literacy, especially when asked to write answers to questions about books.

The prior year's kindergarten teachers heterogeneously grouped first graders at Meadow Creek Elementary. Every first grade had high-, average-, and lower-achieving students. Missy did not have a full-time professional teaching aide, but many parents volunteered in her classroom.

Our most enduring image of Missy's classroom is that every child works continuously, is highly engaged, and strives to reach the high expectations they set for themselves. As evidenced in the analysis of our observation notes, the students were highly engaged because Missy's daily schedule is well planned. Every minute is scheduled for academic tasks. These tasks rotate each 20 minutes so that the students' attention spans are never stretched beyond their developmental limits. She has also taught students to manage their own routines: who is to lead the groups, where papers are to be placed, and what is to be done when a task is completed before the 20-minute segment ends. As a result, children push themselves to the limits of their capabilities, if not with every task, with most.

Equally distinctive is that children were seeking such high levels of accomplishment for themselves, and not to obtain acclaim from their peers or Missy. For example, at 9:30 A.M. on October 17, students were involved in one of eight centers around the room. Some were working in pairs, quietly and intently discussing their own ideas about the books they had read at home the night before. Others were writing in their journals, concentrating intensely. When sharing time began, the room became *totally quiet.* Subsequently, students engaged in challenging, fulfilling work at eight centers while Missy completed one-to-one reading conferences. No extraneous, off-task behaviors or talk occurred during the entire language arts block. This atmosphere could have been mistaken for that of an adult think-tank.

This intense work, reflection, and students' self-initiation (which dominated Missy's room) did not happen by chance or because of her students' enriched out-of-school experiences. Missy built this environment through "hooking students into loving reading and writing at the very beginning of the year." She believes that a first-grade teacher's main job is to inspire students into literacy. "I foster their self-esteem, causing them to *believe* that they can read."

> "This goal, coupled with a pretty strong skills program is the key. Children of all levels of reading ability can build words, once you show them how the words are built. Then, the children at higher levels are making bigger words. I throw out in class that 'tion' says /shun/, so many children start to change 'shun' to 'tion.' Next, I modify for those children that don't get it by reteaching and restructuring my groupings. Having a very structured environment and clear, high expectations from me consistently and continually is also very important to my students. This consistency and continuity is demonstrated every time a child turns in a paper and, if he or she didn't do it right, having that student go back and check it over, and working through it with them. I also think that success depends on children doing a lot of reading and rereading of predictable and pattern books. This way students can get the confidence that 'I can read.' [They need] a lot of take-home support reading, a lot of strategies like using contextual skills and reading the illustrations. All of these strategies are really important."

In this chapter we highlight six aspects of exemplary instruction that were present in each of the highly effective teachers in our study. The elements we will illustrate in this chapter are (1) daily schedule; (2) grouping patterns; (3) linking reading and writing during writing instruction; (4) matching tasks to student competence; (5) affect and motivation; (6) connections across the curriculum; and (7) classroom management and building connections to parents. The chapter closes with an example of a typical day's activities.

Every morning, Missy's day begins with her children attending to daily duties (e.g., ordering their lunches, picking their pencils out of the class container, hanging up backpacks, and putting their journals on the desk). While students manage these tasks without her, Missy is meeting with two students about the journal entries they wrote the previous day. When students have completed their morning duties, they begin journaling about the book they read at home the night before or about topics related to their current thematic unit, which are written on a chart at the front of the room. After about 20 minutes of writing, some students share their journal writing for 15 minutes.

Math, shared reading, spelling, language arts mini-lessons, activities at various centers, "book club activities," lunch, and recess follow. In the afternoon, class begins with a 20-minute silent, sustained reading period and another hour and a half of language arts instruction integrated with content disciplines. Then students attend physical education, music, or art. They end the day with a "wrap-up," in which students create a chart of what they learned that day in math, science, social studies, health, and language arts.

Although this was Missy's "official schedule," she adjusted it frequently to include "teachable moments." Missy stated that the success of her schedule was that she was consistent and students could trust its familiarity and routine.

GROUPING SO THAT "READING BECOMES AN ADVENTURE"

B.U.G.S. BOOK CLUB SONG
(Books Uncover Great Secrets)
I'm bringing home a book for me to read,
Won't my teacher be so proud of me?
I'm bringing home a book for me to read,
I'M A BOOK BUG . . . I CAN READ!
—Missy Allen

This poem is one of the interesting and innovative devices Missy uses to empower and excite her students into reading. Missy varies her grouping and activities each day so that she can "send her students on daily literary adventures," as she calls them. She uses eight different types of reading groups each week: whole-class instruction, oral reading of books to and with students, completing mini-lessons in small homogeneous groups, learning centers, one-to-one centers, parent-led small fluency oral reading groups, pairs and peer work, and sustained silent reading or writing periods. Because she provides such high-interest groupings, her students read and write those of more than more typical first-grade teachers. Her students read as many as 10 books a week and write two multipage stories, generated by individual students weekly. She also reads animatedly to her students every day, sings chants and songs and reads poems daily, and creates continuously changing special reading centers in the classroom. Every day students have a different literacy activity to look forward to, which does not occur as regularly in more typical teachers' classroom grouping plans. To illustrate the depth and uniqueness of each of the groups every day, picture the following, which occurred during one of our classroom observations.

Missy planned to dim the lights that day, and this was her first time to do so. Students sat quietly huddled together in silence on the sharing rug, and the student author who was to share that day entered the room with a dramatic flair. Missy had helped that student make a costume fitting of a royal prince. She gave an audible drum roll, and Marcus marched into the room and regally adjusted his cloak as he reclined in the author's chair. As he readied himself to unveil his masterpiece, the audience held its breath. In tense anticipation, eyes were glued to the author as he slowly lifted the front cover away from his book and revealed its title: "The Amazing Adventure of the Gallant Prince." Students clung to every word he read and correctly answered all 10 questions he asked about his book upon recitation's end.

Posters, songs, pictures, books, magazines, and other materials that related to the week's thematic unit were displayed around the classroom and used in small-group and whole-class instruction every day. For example, on November 11, only 10 weeks into the school year, the room contained 28 books at the Word Tower Center that students had learned to read independently, 174 books that were divided into three baskets on students' desks, five sets of big book units that had already been completed and had become a paired reading center. A Word Tower Wall of slotted charts containing 95 vocabulary words that students had learned to spell hung on the left side of the classroom, a poster listing 24 different words for "said" had been constructed by students the previous day to improve their writing abilities, and eight other centers filled with print appeared around the perimeter of the room.

Missy varied her activities and group compositions every day so that she could encourage students to explore and read new books of their own. Missy also maintained a large personal library of more than 500 books that she has built with high-level, high-interest, low and high density vocabulary literature. She made sure that she covered all skills in the scope and sequence of her district's state-adopted basal series. She even used the worksheets and stories from the basal occasionally. She wanted students to be familiar with them because Meadow Creek's second-grade teachers used them for literacy instruction.

In essence, Missy planned activities that allowed students to read and write independently every day, and used the variety of her grouping methods to build motivation for her students to do so. She called these new grouping formats "reading and writing adventures." For example:

> "I think that if I put students in small groups or pairs and let them build and create sentences together, it is so much more valuable than just having students fill in blanks or circle words on worksheets. I want my students to have as much hands-on, creative activities as they can, and so I must use a lot of different types of small groups. A serendipitous benefit is that in my groups they can also do some socializing, some cooperation. I also do a lot in pairs. I think it's really important for them to do paired reading, but I also think they need to do independent work, as they do in the centers."

Further, she used large-group instruction daily. Small groups were saved for reteaching, reinforcing skills, maintaining running records, and completing learning records. Missy kept running records on students, updating them at least once every 3 weeks, to see whether the children were reading at an easy, instructional, or frustration level in their self-selected and assigned readings. Although she called small-group instructional meetings to enhance skill mastery, fluency and word attack skills were taught at every group meeting, with the use of materials of different readability levels to match each group's ability. There were no set reading groups; group memberships were changed each day and week.

To form groups, Missy identified the students who needed reteaching: "If a group of students had a hard time on a concept I had just taught, I would bring them together and work with them until they understood the concept." Moreover, she often formed ability groups, but she did not devise "Blue Bird," "Yellow Bird," and "Green Bird" groups. She read aloud more than one book each day to her students to instruct then about directionality; to teach them that words match print, that each word is a word in and of itself, that words match the illustrations and make sense; and to build interest in literacy. Her students also read silently each day for the purposes of learning self-correction, building their prediction abilities, reinforcing story grammar, enjoyment, increasing their confidence in their ability to read, and leading them into a "can-do" attitude.

Students were assigned to read with partners or in groups daily to build instant instructional opportunities and for camaraderie, socializing, having a friend, associating reading with a friend, and having fun with reading. Missy related a morning letter to the events of the day and sometimes to a morning math activity. She created math word problems that related to the thematic unit. The group edited the morning letter to improve their writing abilities, based on an error that she observed in the previous day's writing samples, or solved a math problem and found needed unnecessary data. During times at the various centers, her objectives were for students to play with language and to talk about what they were learning, but she expected them to whisper and work independently on reading and writing.

In summary, when we entered Missy's classroom, we were struck by the beauty, individualization, and functionality of every section in the room. She did not have one, but many, "fronts of the room." She had an area for grouping, another for sharing (the sharing circle), a stool in one part of the room for individuals to sit on when they shared a book, and a teacher's desk at the back of the room. All students were turned so that they could easily see everything in the classroom. Space for books was also important, as well as a reading area, so that students could have several different places to "cuddle up and read." To accomplish this, Missy brought two "kid-sized" lawn chairs to make a reading corner in the room. Students often sat on the floor in that corner. "Students especially love that little corner," Missy said during the end-of-the-year interview.

In addition to parent-volunteers listening to students read orally 3 days a week, Missy lead group reading, chart reading, poetry reading, and singing of verses that she wrote concerning the thematic units being studied. She also included shared reading and independent, silent reading in her students' daily routine.

In Missy's room, center time took about an hour. It was not scheduled every week because Missy found that such rotations did not provide enough *sustained* reading and writing time. Such uninterrupted times had proven to be necessary for her students to develop their literacy skills. When center time was scheduled, students were paired with a reading partner and only two people were allowed at any center at one time. In addition, approximately 2 weeks of each month were spent in whole-class composition activities, such as writing poetry for moms for Mother's Day or creating how-to stories based on watching a cage filled with hatching butterflies.

LINKING READING AND WRITING: WRITING INSTRUCTION

Every day Missy incorporated activities that built students' independent writing abilities. Students wrote in their journals every day. They also learned to write in numerous genres, such as "affirmation envelopes," in which students recorded positive notes about their friends and placed them in individualized envelopes. During our observations, we witnessed students' generation of lists, how-to writings, recipes, first-person stories, narratives, and descriptive paragraphs. We also saw students editing their own work. Missy did not put any red marks on students' papers, but when editing was necessary, put her changes on Post-It Notes instead. Her reason for this practice was that she wanted students to know that she honored their written voices.

Missy used another effective writing strategy. If a student thought a word in his or her writing was misspelled and did not want to stop the thinking process to ask a friend or go to a dictionary, the student could underline that word and Missy would write it correctly on a Post-It Note for the student to copy onto his or her paper before the next day's journaling period began. Most often, however, students sought to correct their misspellings independently, with help of peers, by using a dictionary, or by referencing words on the wall or room charts. It appeared that students wanted to create perfectly spelled compositions because they set high expectations for themselves, following Missy's lead.

Students wrote more than once a day. Missy also used four computers for the last step of the writing process. Final drafts were word processed most often before they were read in the author's chair (stool) or taken home. Every student published several books during the school year. Students usually took only 2 days to go through the steps in the writing process, from first draft to final product. Students could also choose to do research instead of journal writing.

Missy believed that reading and writing were intricately linked, as exemplified in her creation of the "Word Builders Club." Within this club, students were assisted with encoding and decoding written text, spelling, and building stories. A writing center provided students with an opportunity to use stationary, cards, journals, booklets, and other materials to improve their writing skills. Missy instructed the students in prewriting skills (brainstorming, outlining, organizing, etc.) and gave them considerable time to practice these techniques. When students produced finished works, she supplied them with opportunities to share with the rest of the class. Her thematic units always introduced advanced vocabulary to students, and many three-syllable words were taught each week.

When Missy reflected on how she helped her children to become writers, she said that the most important dimension was providing enough time. She found that most teachers do not structure their schedules so that students have more than 20 minutes a day to write. Missy, on the other hand, allocated as much as two 45-minute blocks of time a day to write. She said, "It is amazing what the children will come up with when given more group writing, more group writing instruction, and more group skills." She also modified her schedule each month by listening to her students. "I watch and research my students to see what I need to do as a professional and how I can modify our schedule to match their most immediate learning needs."

MATCHING TASKS TO STUDENT COMPETENCE:
THE TEACHING OF SKILLS

We observed no decontextualized teaching of skills, but we observed 10 to 19 literacy skills being taught in an hour. Skills were taught from student-generated sentences and class stories. Missy continuously referenced prior instruction and told students how to use literacy skills and why they were important. There were always charts around the room showing how to build words and sentences, as well as more than 250 words posted on the wall. These displays changed frequently to include more difficult words. Students generated words orally that matched a pattern and then wrote several of these to take home to practice reading with their parents or guardians. Moreover, all class stories focused on the teaching of a new writing skill that the students needed in order to move to the next level of ability (e.g., how to write dialogue or how to use commas in a listing).

Whenever students had difficulty reading a word, Missy retaught the concept, but in different words and with different examples in small groups. Missy taught students to decode by attending to the whole word, letter–sound correspondences, onset/rhyme, context clues, and syntactical clues. She referenced more than one of these strategies every day we observed her instruction. In every lesson, Missy taught how important a certain skill would be to increasing students' literacy as adults in real world settings. Missy told us, "Isolated phonetic teaching is *not* enough to produce strong readers."

Fluency was built by prompting students to use several decoding strategies interactively (e.g., syntax, semantics, self-correction, and reading on). Missy built time for students who were at risk to have multiple readings of the same books, patterned books, mastery of directionality, and various strategies other than sound-to-symbol knowledge to become efficient readers and writers. In summary, skills were taught contextually and presented as tools from which children could choose as they read and wrote.

AFFECT AND MOTIVATION
THROUGH OPPORTUNISTIC TEACHING

Missy used every moment for instruction and learning. She addressed the needs of every student by capturing teaching opportunities. We were struck by her ability to personalize her teaching so that students who needed more challenge received it and those who needed more support obtained it. This ability appeared to arise from *truly knowing* and *caring about every student* and using students' strengths to move to a higher level. Missy held high expectations for students and for herself. Two episodes with Brian and Josh, a physically disabled student, illustrate Missy's ability to motivate and care for her students.

Brian began first grade knowing 24 letter names and 15 letter sounds. He would listen to stories, but did not match voice to print. He never chose writing as an enjoyable activity. The only whole words he could decode were "pig," "is," and "in." His first journal entry on August 22 was scribbles; it demonstrated that he could not express himself traditionally and that he did not understand concepts of print. By November 25, Brian was reading and writing sentences. By February 12, he showed significant improvement and was particularly enamored with the Word Builders Club. (In the Word Builders Club, students generate 10 words that all begin with the same consonant, sometimes including nonsense words. Students are to write the 10 spelling patterns from 30 they have learned. These 10 words are written after Missy says a word that contains the sound of a particular spelling pattern. The purpose of the activity is to provide an enjoyable way to practice the most common English vowel patterns. Once a list has been completed, parents readminister the same list that night at home to build retention. The description parents receive comes in a newsletter [Figure 8.4, later]. An example of the Word Builder activity that Brian most enjoyed appears in Figure 8.1.) By the end of the year, Brian was generating his own narratives, which included a beginning, middle, and end, as well as location words ("belo" = "below"), possessive nouns (fish's), capital letters, and adjectives ("rand" = "round," with "striped," and "thirsty" spelled correctly). By the end of the year he was also mastering the digraph "-th," and he asked to research and present a report about snakes to his classmates.

The second example illustrates how much expertise and time Missy invested in modifying instruction to meet the needs of students with special talents, limited English, emotional disabilities, and physically disabilities. Josh had only part of an arm and wore a leg prosthesis. Missy petitioned the district for a desk she designed that could be expanded as he grew and that would allow him to write comfortably with his feet. She also purchased a desk bell so that when Josh wanted to speak, the class could "hear" his hand being raised.

We saw many similar instances in which Missy went the extra mile to provide all children with adaptive strategies so they could succeed. She did so through attending to affect. To illustrate, in April, Missy allowed Marissa to stay after school every Monday for 30

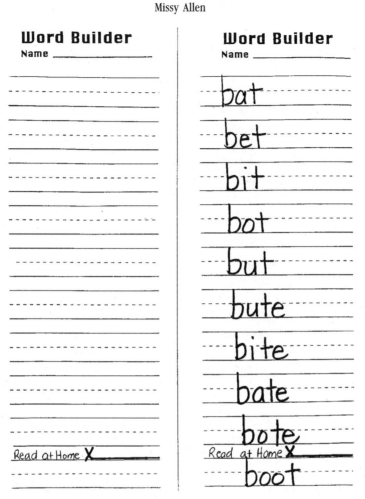

Word Builder

Name _____

Read at Home **X** _____

Word Builder

Name _____

bat
bet
bit
bot
but
bute
bite
bate
bote
Read at Home **X** _____
boot

FIGURE 8.1. Example of a Word Builders practice game to teach vowel spelling patterns and decrease students' dependency on the "sound-out-the-consonant-and-then-guess-at-the-word" decoding strategy.

minutes. She did so because Marissa needed time just to talk with her teacher. The girl was harboring anger toward school, and the time alone with Missy met her emotional needs and led her to reach a high level of success in literacy.

Missy also believed that it was important to build students' abilities to work cooperatively. For example, during one observation she told children that "tolerance grows from understanding." She defined both of these terms and then built motivation by using herself as an example. She pointed out the knee brace on her leg and explained that her weak knee needed support periodically. Then she added:

> "As a classroom, we are a 'body.' When a part of the body is weak, it needs support. Just like Roberto who struggled last week with his spelling test, but because Colleen, John, and Georgette made a special spelling group with him, and all worked together, Roberto made a 90 on his test this week! Aren't we proud of him—he kept practicing, working hard, continued to make excellent choices, and he never gave up. Let's hear it for Roberto!"

The class burst into applause. With this display of true acceptance and appreciation, Roberto's face beamed with pride.

We also saw why the children in this room did not squabble with each other as we witnessed in other first-grade rooms. Missy made her expectations clear—students were to build their affective skills and develop tolerance, patience, and collaboration through her instruction, modeling, and practice opportunities within her varied grouping systems. Children accepted and embraced each other's differences.

In summary, Missy built motivation and affect by focusing less on the "average" and more on the "individual." As she told us several times during our observations and interviews, she believed that being a teacher with goals and challenges produced a more focused and determined group of students. She viewed it her responsibility to build motivation by challenging all, especially those who had been identified as gifted and talented students. In addition, she believed that students with attention-deficit disorder (ADD) and attention-deficit/hyperactivity disorder (ADHD) needed close monitoring and her ongoing communication with parents so that each child's learning could be maximized. Missy stated:

> "An understanding heart and a truckload of training and strategies help children with ADD/ADHD. They also need extra 'wiggle' time and 'wiggle' room, as well as constant positive feedback, before they can be fully successful in the classroom. Paramount to developing students' high interest in the subject matter in my class is teaching in thematic units. Not only does it

provide motivation for me, but also for my students. Choice is essential. When I am listening to the students as they guide me into their areas of need and interest, each day, each class, is a fresh, new adventure."

CONNECTIONS ACROSS CURRICULUM

Missy integrated reading and writing through large thematic units that took place once every six weeks but contained new books and learning center/small (whole) group activities each week. She also required students to demonstrate more than one skill in compositions. As part of her integrated classroom, Missy used "book clubs" to motivate and hook children into a positive attitude about reading and provided a poetic chant (that she wrote) to help students match voice to print and use the rhythm of language to read. Three of these thematically based, integrated book clubs that we observed were the following:

- B.U.G.S. Club: Books Uncover Great Secrets Club (occurred during the science and social studies classes when the class was studying insects).
- B.A.T. Club: Books Are Terrific Club (occurred during the science and social studies classes when the class studied animals).
- S.H.A.R.K. Club: Stories Have A Real Kick Club (occurred during the science and social studies classes when the class studied fish).

Samples from the S.H.A.R.K. Club's work appear in Figure 8.2. Every class began with a book or learning experience based on the thematic unit. Most units were created anew each year, based on the interests of students in that year's class. Book clubs also included adult guest readers and students who came from grades 2 through 5 to share books about the theme with Missy's first graders. All students in Missy's class sang songs, poems, raps, or chants relative to the club's theme. Students created secret handshakes, special hats so as to have "hands-on" creations for writing prompts, and special reading events to celebrate literacy. Missy had used these clubs for 7 years.

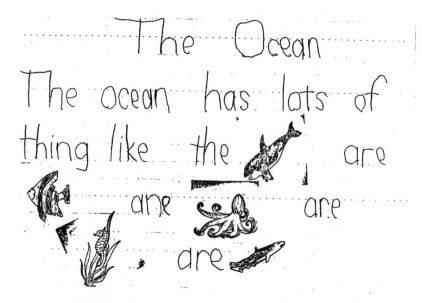

FIGURE 8.2. Use of theme-based shaped stamps in writing centers to increase students' composing abilities.

Equally important, from Missy's perspective, to connect curriculum was her Word Builders Club. She invented this club during the year we observed her class. It was designed to develop students' decoding/encoding abilities. The Word Builders Club convened daily when Missy and the children chanted: "I'm a Word Builder! I can spell! I can read! I can build words! I can build stories!" Then, using half sheets of lined paper, students spelled words, which Missy read aloud, that adhered to a frequently occurring English spelling or letter–sound pattern. By the end of the year students were generating words they had never read, by chanting and writing medial vowels, as shown in Figure 8.1. The words used in some Word Builders Clubs were used for only a few days, but most were studied for 6 weeks at a time.

All the books Missy read and all the activities in art and with parents, as well as all subject area instruction, were tied to the thematic unit. For instance, while students studied insects, she read numerous books about rain forests. Students journaled each morning about some aspect of the thematic unit. During that unit, they were also engaged in the B.U.G.S. club, and they continued to read and write words about the bees and ants in the rain forest. One day they went to visit an anthill, taking a cracker and a piece of a Snickers bar, and watched the ants come and gradually take them away. They returned in an hour to see which food scrap was gone first. Missy tied this experience to reading by asking students to sing from the printed words of "The Ants Go Marching One by One."

CLASSROOM MANAGEMENT THROUGH SETTING HIGH EXPECTATIONS AND BUILDING CONNECTIONS WITH PARENTS

Missy's high expectations were reflected in the classroom rules that were posted in the room (and expected to be followed). Never was there a discussion or teacher comment made about a discipline problem in isolation of learning. When Missy referred to any student's behavior, it was cloaked on both sides with an emphasis on learning. For example: "All you need on your desk is your journal. Why don't you also get out your pencil, a cover sheet, and your listening ears. (*Pause*) You are looking like you're ready to go and highly. . . . Where's my word?" Students respond in unison: "Motivated!"

Missy reminded students that if they were to reach their learning goals, incorrect choices must be avoided as much as possible. Like Barbara Wiesner (Chapter 5), Missy used statements of praise centered on the specific growth that a particular child's work sample demonstrated. For instance, one day as Missy was about to signal the end of center time, Andy asked her to read his story. Missy stopped and read it. It took only 45 seconds. Then she focused intently on that writing and said to Andy: "Good job. I want to tell you one thing. Look at the word 'saw.' That was one of your spelling words and you should be spelling that correctly now. Good job." Andy went immediately to his desk and picked up his pencil, looked for that word on the wall, and corrected it. Then Missy added, "What I really liked about the way you read your story was that you read just the way you talk, and that will help you read better when you become an adult." In contrast to this incident was one that occurred the same day in another first-grade classroom. A student asked his teacher a question. This teacher did not provide timely attention to this student but instead said that she would answer questions only after the reading class had ended, which would be right before lunch.

As the class left for lunch, however, the teacher had not returned to that student to answer his question, or challenge him to reach a higher level of literacy achievement.

Missy explained that self-regulation in her class was built through providing students with high-level thinking choices, embedded in challenging tasks. She created a demanding yet risk-friendly atmosphere to instill the values of personal responsibility and self-confidence. For example: "First grade is just that . . . many firsts. Patience, compassion, high expectations, organization and structure, freedom to move around and take risks, and a significant sense of humor makes a child's first year a huge success." Such instruction was complemented by parental support. It would be misleading to suggest that such qualities and strategies were established within a few short weeks. Over a period of years, Missy Allen has constantly sought and employed new and better methods to meet her students' individual needs, and she communicated with parents every week. She asked parents to perform seven different roles in their students' literacy development: (1) Read aloud to students at night; (2) listen to their students read books that she sent home; (3) sign journal entries every night after their students wrote; (4) readminister spelling tests and Word Builders Club lists at night after students had been given them during the week; (5) send books and items to be used in literacy lessons; (6) volunteer at least once to participate in some aspect of projects that she created; and (7) read the class newsletter and student report cards and send ideas to school concerning students' literacy at home, to be included in the newsletter, that validated the performances she witnessed at school.

Not incidentally, Missy never accepted half-hearted work from her students. She expected great things, and most often her students rose to the challenge. In her end-of year interview she said, "Children rise to the expectations of the classroom, given that modifications are allowed [and adaptive strategies are taught] for those students who need them." Missy's classroom was fast paced. Calling parents at night, scaffolding, and peer modeling were methods she used to help lower-level readers. Students learned from one another and were given opportunities to be leaders and helpers. Missy's students often found success in areas they originally believed were beyond their grasp.

For example, Missy often made statements to her students such as, "What do I expect?" and they would voice back to her what she expected generally and specifically for a particular lesson. Then she would ask the students, "What do you expect of yourself?" and they would voice back that they expected themselves to do a good job that day. Such high expectations increased risk taking and built students' self-esteem. They began to believe that they could read and write at high levels. Students knew that Missy would tell their parents of their successes.

Missy also asked parents to join her in accepting their responsibilities as the persons who had the power to create literacy for their children. She believed that a caring teacher without the right strategies would not produce strong readers and writers. Similarly, a trained teacher with the right strategies, but who was inflexible, uncaring, or nonreflective would not produce strong readers and writers. She also maintained close communication with all of her students' parents through "First Grade News" letters. Examples are shown in Figures 8.3 and 8.4. Missy taught parents that 10 minutes of reading every day was more valuable than an hour on the weekend.

JANUARY 12, 1997 (A Typical Day)

On January 12, 1997, students were responsible to make their own preparations for the day, such as counting lunch orders, getting pencils sharpened, buying book club tickets with the literacy bucks they had earned the prior day, and turning in library books. Next, 15 minutes at the beginning of this day (and every day) was allotted to journal writing. It was a quiet, reflective time.

Six students' names were then drawn to read their journal entries; this ensued that every student would read his or her journal entry at least once weekly, by this point in the year. Any student whose name was not drawn who wanted to share his or her writing was given the opportunity to read. At this time, the student who had had the opportunity to take Wrinkles home the previous night, read his night journal writing entitled "Adventures with Wrinkles." (Wrinkles was a brown bear, named by the students, that went home each night with a different student, along with his or her journal, and the events that Wrinkles experienced at that child's home were recorded and read to classmates the next day.)

Then a volunteer read the "morning message," which had been written on a chart by Missy prior to the students' arrival. Students

First Grade News

February 23, 1995

Dear Parent,

Next week will be B.U.G.S. Week in our class. Each day we will participate in a different activity in order to be a member of the Books Uncover
Great Secrets Club, or the B.U.G.S. Club. We have had such fun studying
plants and bugs, but this will prove to be the most motivating learning yet.

Could you please help us? Keep this reminder so your child will be prepared each day for the upcoming events.

Monday—"Potato Bug Day": Each child needs to bring a potato to deco-
rate like a bug. Please also send anything that could be used in the creation,
i.e., straight pins, pipe cleaners, feathers, pom-poms, toothpicks, buttons, con-
fetti, thumbtacks. (Go Wild)!

Tuesday—"Bug Feeler Day": We will make bug "feelers" that tell how we
feel about books.

Wednesday—"Bring a Bug to School Day": Each child can bring a real
or stuffed bug to school to share.

Thursday—"Read About a Bug Day": Your child can bring a book about
bugs, reference books, encyclopedias, or fiction and other nonfiction books.

Friday—"Be a Bug Day": Wear anything that will make you look like a
bug (Be Creative!). On that afternoon at 2:15 we will have a "Bug Sharing
Time" when we will be sharing stories about bugs, our favorite bug books,
and bug songs. PARENTS MAY JOIN US FOR THIS TIME IF YOU ARE ALSO
DRESSED UP LIKE A BUG! This has been done in the past and the children
really enjoyed the time together.

I look forward to seeing you for Public School Week next week!

Missy Allen

FIGURE 8.3. Sample of weekly newsletter sent home to parents.

edited the writing, eliminated the errors that Missy had written in the
note. The message on this day, was a song the class sang about Texas
with our names included in it so the students could thank us, the researchers (two of the authors of this book), for coming to their class
so many times. The morning message always related to new events
that would be unveiled during the day.

The next hour was spent working with math manipulatives.
Missy made individual student assessments as she passed each student's desk, and wrote additional, personalized and challenging
problems for them to solve individually. After a short rest room and

Dear Parents,

I am starting a new program at school called the "Word Builders Club."
In an effort to show the children how to phonetically build words and how to
decode words, we will be working on Word Builder sheets. We will create
the words on a sheet that is numbered to 10. After they are assessed and corrected, we will bring home the list of words. On the bottom of the list is a
place for you to sign that the list has been read at home. *Please have your
child read this list at least 3 times at home, then sign and return it to school. I
will be taking grades on these sheets.*

Some of the words will not be words in and of themselves. But we will
learn these sounds in an effort to be able to build longer words. For instance,
"bate" may not be a word by itself, but it is part of "rebate" or the proper
name "Bates."

Thanks again so much for your support! We are having a terrific year!
Your kids are great!

Missy Allen, First Grade

FIGURE 8.4. Example of how Missy sustains close communication with parents.

water break, an hour and a half was spent on shared reading, spelling with an emphasis on word parts, oral reading of thematic poems
as a whole class, and singing of thematic songs. Missy taught five
mini-lessons to the whole class concerning main ideas, context clues,
"-ate" word parts for decoding, summarizing, and writing quotation
marks. These mini-lessons were selected from the beginning section
of the school district's second-grade basal reading series.

Three word families were taught as the spelling lesson for this
day. One spelling word each week became a part of the "Word
Tower Wall" chart. These spelling words were taken from the literature read by students that week. The words on January 12 also related to the current thematic unit, sharks. Students spent at least 15
minutes every morning working with spelling words, which was a
district requirement. Then they wrote five spelling words in the air,
making up a song with each word, matching the spelling of the
words to the song (e.g., "I live in a "house-O," to the tune of
"BINGO"). Finally, the students wrote each word in shaving cream
on their desks and used letter tiles to build their spelling words, as
well as other words that had not yet been introduced but that included one of the three word patterns.

Every day that week a few chapters were read orally from a chapter book, and this day Missy read two chapters from the nonfiction book *Sharks* by Jacques Cousteau (1989). Missy reported that she did so because she wanted students to learn to listen to longer portions of text. Immediately following this shared reading, students went to lunch and had a short recess. After recess, the children automatically began DEAR (drop everything and read) time. They read books of their choice for 10 minutes. No talking was allowed during this time, and most students read at least two books independently.

For the next hour and a half, an integrated language arts, science, and social studies period occurred. On this day, this time included an hour-long rotation system whereby students moved through four centers (science experiment, computer station, reading with Missy, and social studies project in which fish murals and captions were made) and four paired reading centers in which students made words and wrote letters to peers. Today four students were also completing a research report.

The students then engaged in a 45-minute physical education period, which alternated on other days of the week with art and music classes. The last activity of the day was to reinforce the gains the students had made in the science, social studies, and language art periods and what they had learned. Students also discussed what they had enjoyed during that day's work.

SUMMARY

According to personal observations, student achievement scores, and the data obtained in this study, Missy Allen proved to increase her first-grade students' literacy more than other teachers in this study. She established a student-centered environment in which students were filled with an enthusiasm for literacy, reached high but attainable expectations, and engaged in thoughtful reflection. The aspects of her teaching that distinguished her teaching repertoire were (1) a daily schedule that included large blocks of uninterrupted time for students to create words, read, and generate their own compositions, (2) an environment that continuously displayed student-generated stories and sentences, more than 250 books, numerous new words, and many challenges every day that made learning literacy an adventure, (3) the use of student-generated stories for reading and writing instruction, (4) flexible and varied groups for instruction, (5) integrating literacy with content area instruction, (6) 45 minutes of sustained student writing every day, (7) building students' affect by instilling the belief that they could become good readers and writers, (8) contextualized skill instruction in phonics and other decoding strategies, (9) multiple mini-lessons every hour, (10) continuous, personalized teaching, (11) individualized feedback to point out specific areas in which individual students could grow, (12) high expectation for students' high levels of reflection and engagement, (13) modification of instruction to provide more challenge and/or support as individuals required it, and (14) connections with parents. Missy stated:

"In my opinion, a teacher who is organized will produce students who are organized. A teacher with enthusiasm will produce enthusiastic, motivated, and interested students. A reading and writing program that has focus will strengthen students' success in the future. A program that encompasses a variety of meaningful, hands-on strategies, teamed with a teacher who is caring, trained, flexible, and reflective, creates the perfect balance for any classroom."

REFERENCE

Cousteau, J. (1989). *Sharks*. New York: Macmillan.

9

Patricia Loden

LESLEY MANDEL MORROW
ELIZABETH BROWN ASBURY

Pat Loden has been teaching in Parkhills Public School for the 9 years that constitute her teaching career. Pat taught kindergarten for 5 years prior to teaching first grade. The administration of Parkhills School places a high priority on supporting the continued education of their teachers. Pat was financially recompensed for obtaining her master's degree from the university located near the school. In-school staff development is also a priority. A person within the district who has received the training necessary to provide the in-service work typically conducts staff development sessions. At Parkhills School, the teachers assume a great deal of the decision making about curriculum, instruction, and development and are highly supported by the administration.

Parkhills School, which includes kindergarten through second grade, is located in a suburban community on the outskirts of a major urban city in the Northeast. The school population is diverse, with 50% of the children white, 20% African American, 10% Hispanic, and 10% of various other backgrounds. The school families are typically of middle to lower-middle incomes.

The children in Pat's class are representative of the school popu-

184

lation and are diverse in their abilities as well. Of her 23 students, Pat reported that a few were reading at the second- or third-grade level and a few were emergent readers who were still unsure of the names of the letters of the alphabet. Three of her students met the requirements for basic skills instruction and worked with a reading specialist every day. The other children were at various points in between. Meeting the individual needs of such a diverse population was an important objective of Pat's.

In order to meet the wide array of individual needs represented in her students, Pat realized that her students had to become self-directed learners. Pat needed to be able to work with her students individually and in small groups to tailor her instruction to match their stages of development. Therefore, her students needed to learn how to work productively on their own. From the first day of school, Pat started teaching her students how to master the rules, routines, and procedures that forged the framework for productive independent learning.

During the first week of school Pat led the children through a series of activities that resulted in the creation of a set of rules for the classroom. Because the class created the rules, the children fully understood the reason for each rule and the consequences should a rule be broken. Pat believed that this joint effort in creating the classroom climate nurtured a sense of ownership in the children that led to a sense of responsibility for carrying out the rules.

Pat most often used literature as a basis for a discussion that would culminate in a classroom rule. According to Pat, the most important rule related to how the students treated one another. She wanted the children to feel emotionally safe and supported by her and the other students in the class. To initiate discussion around this topic, Pat read aloud the picture storybook *Lunch Bunnies* (Lasky & Hafner, 1996). The story's main character masters the challenges of the first day of school by making a friend. After reading the story, Pat asked the children to discuss their fears of new situations (like starting first grade) and how having a friend would help. She led the children to articulate the explicit behaviors of the helpful new-friend character. She then asked the children to relate the story to how they should behave toward one another. The lesson culminated with the class deciding that a classroom rule should be "I will use kind words." As Pat interacted with the students that day, she reinforced their use of supportive, friendly language.

Pat established a daily routine early in the year. Consequently, the children knew what to do in every learning context. These contexts included independent work at literacy centers, buddy reading and writing, small-group guided reading lessons, and whole-class literacy activities. Within each routine, Pat thoughtfully planned procedures that facilitated independence. For example, the literacy center housed many activities in which the children could engage. For each activity, Pat posted a chart that reminded the children about what to do. Each activity and the associated materials were slowly introduced so that the children knew exactly where they were located, how to work with them, where they were placed when not in use, and how to record the work they accomplished. The established rules, routines, and procedures did not restrict the children; rather, they provided the structure that ultimately led to the children's independence, choices, and intrinsic motivation.

DAILY SCHEDULE

The children arrive in Pat's classroom by 9:00 A.M. The first 15 minutes are spent by students recording their attendance and carrying out morning jobs. During this time Pat takes care of any necessary paperwork and writes a few quick anecdotal observations on the two children whom she will closely observe and assess throughout the day.

The morning proceeds with 25 minutes of whole-group shared reading and writing that takes place on the rug in the literacy center. Unlike most first-grade teachers, Pat does not do any calendar activities at this time. Rather, her focus is on literacy-based activities such as reading messages written by the children, composing a class morning message, or reading and dramatizing poems and stories.

The next hour and a half are devoted to Readers Workshop. During this longer segment of time, Pat meets with three small groups for guided reading and conducts at least two individual assessments. While Pat meets with the guided reading groups, the rest of the children read for approximately 20 minutes, write a response in their reading logs, and write an entry in their journals. The children then move onto learning centers, where they may work in partners, small groups, or by themselves on a variety of literacy-based activities. Readers Workshop culminates in a short whole-class gathering, which concludes by going over the daily edit.

One morning a week a 40-minute prep period is scheduled after Readers Workshop while the children go to music. Pat has five prep periods a week. The other four are scheduled after the children have left school to go home. On at least two days, the first-grade teachers meet during their prep time to collaborate on curriculum and brainstorm ideas to help specific children. Pat highly values the time spent with her first-grade colleagues as an integral part of her own professional development.

After an hour period for lunch and recess, the children return to the classroom for a read-aloud session. This too takes place on the rug in the literacy center and is a favorite time in the day for both Pat and her students. On three days of the week, reading aloud is preceded by approximately 15 minutes of "word work," in which the children manipulate letters to further develop their word skills. The children pick up the materials needed for the lesson when they come in from recess. The lesson is focused and moves at a rapid pace.

A 45-minute period for Writers Workshop comes next. Pat prizes the benefits children derive from writing and makes sure that her students write on a daily basis. Writers Workshop takes place every day, no matter what. During the Workshop, Pat meets with children for individual conferences and circulates around the room to work with students as needed.

A 55-minute Math Workshop follows. This instructional period typically begins with the whole class participating in calendar activities and moving into a math mini-lesson. The children then work independently or with partners while Pat meets with needs-based small groups.

The vast majority of Pat's teaching is theme based. Pat and her first-grade colleagues choose their themes from science and social studies curricula. Therefore, the vast majority of content area instruction takes place through shared reading and writing and learning center activities. Twice a week, Pat plans a science or social studies focus lesson that takes place at the end of the day.

Pat's schedule flows seamlessly from one activity to another. Most of her instruction is integrated so that literacy and content area instruction are masterfully woven throughout the day, as are individual and whole-class learning objectives. This process is facilitated by her consistent management techniques and her students' ability to work productively independently, in partners, or in small groups, with or without the teacher present.

PHYSICAL ENVIRONMENT

A characteristic that made Pat's teaching exemplary was evidenced in the way she organized the physical environment of her classroom. Pat believes that teaching is more than the transmission of knowledge. She believes children need to be actively engaged and interacting socially in order to learn. Consequently, the classroom was arranged to reflect and support her philosophy. Her student-friendly classroom was attractive, rich with materials that supported instruction, and well organized to facilitate student access, interaction, and independence.

Although Pat's classroom was typical in size, we were struck by her inventive use of space. The student's desks were in clusters of five to economize space and allow for group work. The perimeter of the room was divided by shelving units into well-defined learning center areas. These areas included a science and math center, a computer center, a block and building area, and an art center, which was also available for making books during Readers and Writers Workshops. Each of these areas housed materials related to content area instruction and materials that were theme related. To make the most use of the available space, writing center materials were kept on two rolling carts, which were rolled over to the students' desks during Readers and Writers Workshops.

The focal point of the classroom was the literacy center. Pat purposely arranged the room so that this area was predominant. She explained that nurturing a love of reading was her primary objective, therefore the literacy center was the most important part of her classroom. The area was made warm and inviting with carpeting, a rocking chair, large pillows, and comfortable seating areas. It was here that the class would gather for whole-group activities—shared writing on the large easel, Pat's reading aloud, or listening to students read their published works.

In the literacy center Pat had a large collection of children's literature that was sorted into baskets according to author, genre, and topic. Pat featured a different author with each theme. The featured author's works were placed on a bookshelf with the covers facing out. Books associated with the current theme under study were also placed on a special shelf with covers facing out. A separate set of shelves housed books that were organized by Reading Recovery level, which allowed for easier selection of independent reading materials. The listening center was located in one corner of the literacy center. Here children could listen to books on tape, which were often recorded by school personnel or students' family members. Materials for story retellings were also placed in this area. These included a felt board with books and accompanying felt pieces stored in plastic bags hung by the board. Children were encouraged to retell chalk-talk stories using white boards and markers. A large roll movie box and student-made mini–roll movies were available for story retellings. All the materials in this area were well organized and clearly labeled to facilitate students' independent use.

Pat had set up the literacy center beside a large bulletin board where she had placed the Word Wall. Below the board were chunk charts (which displayed lists of word families), theme-word lists, and charts used for writing (e.g., "Instead of 'said' we can write . . . "). Large copies of poems that the class chanted together were hung on a clothesline that ran along one side of the center. The poems were changed as the class learned new ones. Copies of older poems were laminated and hung on an easel with rings so they could be read again and again.

One corner of the room was set up for small-group instruction. It was in this area that guided reading lessons took place. Pat and the children sat at a half-round table. Pat purposely sat where she could have a view of the children working independently while she worked with a small group or one-on-one. All the materials needed for guided reading lessons were neatly organized on another rolling cart, which was rolled under the table when not in use. It included sets of magnetic letters, small white boards and markers, mini–pocket charts, sentence strips, record-keeping folders, and writing instruments. A large pocket chart and a white board on an easel were placed alongside the table. On the shelf behind the table, Pat had placed magazine holders designating one holder and its contents per group. In each she placed lesson plans and copies of the book she planned to use for the group's lesson. It is obvious that Pat realized that the environment is not just background scenery in her classroom, but an integral part of literacy learning, and that the environment supports instruction. Without the support of the environment, literacy-rich activities cannot take place.

READING AND WRITING—THROUGHOUT THE DAY

The students in Pat's classroom participated in a wide variety of reading and writing activities throughout the day. Reading or writing was embedded in everything that was done. During the morning gathering in the literacy center, the class participated in shared reading of a big book or poem. The text selected for shared reading was always a high-quality piece of children's literature, as well as theme-based, so that literacy and content area instruction could be integrated.

Pat believed that shared reading lessons needed to be purposeful and planned. Although Pat was quick to respond to a teachable moment, she left few learning opportunities to chance. She used her shared reading times to teach specific literacy skills and strategies, to model fluency and expressive reading, and to explicate comprehension skills. Pat always set a purpose for listening that was related to her teaching point, which was reinforced before, during, and after the shared reading.

Shared writing often took place during these morning whole-group gatherings. Pat involved the children in a variety of writing experiences. They composed language experience charts, wrote retellings of stories, wrote morning messages, composed responses, and completed story webs and maps. Pat had the children provide known information as she modeled the thinking necessary for deeper understanding. Here again, Pat aptly interwove skill instruction in an authentic, meaning-based context.

Every day the children engaged in collaborative partner reading and writing. Children were taught how to read a book with a buddy by either taking turns reading or listening and looking at the illustrations while following along in the text as another read. During Writers Workshop the children often collaborated with one another. Pat was teaching them how to edit another's work and how to ask questions that led a writer to clarify her or his ideas. Several of the children engaged in writing stories together while working at the writing center.

The children in Pat's room also engaged in independent reading and writing on a daily basis. A period of time each day was devoted to independent reading. Pat had the children keep track of their reading and encouraged them to set goals for reading more texts and texts of increasing difficulty when they were ready. Overall, Pat wanted the children to develop a love of books and nurture the habit of reading for pleasure. One homework assignment remained the same every night—read for 20 minutes. A checkout system within the well-stocked classroom library made it easy for children to take books home to read.

Independent writing occurred throughout the day. Pat made use of several journals, including a science journal, a math journal, and a daily journal in which children wrote on topics of their choice. Pat responded each day to the children's daily entry, which motivated them to write more. Pat believed that the journal dialogue gave her a way to have a special connection to each child in her class. The journals also provided a window into the children's developing literacy skills and served as valuable planning and assessment tools.

The children were engaged in an extraordinary amount of reading and writing on a daily basis, and they were engaged in literacy activities throughout the day. Literacy experiences were associated with all content area learning so that reading and writing were a natural outgrowth of all that was done. Pat's knowledge of how to offer children a wide variety of meaningful reading and writing contexts seemed to ignite a spark of enthusiasm for literacy in her students. The children never appeared to tire of participating in the literacy-based activities that were offered to them.

COMPREHENSION INSTRUCTION

Comprehension skill development was embedded in every context of reading and writing instruction. Pat told us she was aware that decoding could very easily become the focus of a first-grade reading program. Teaching children how to figure out how words work was an important part of what her students needed to learn. However, she cautioned that instruction at the word level was insufficient and must never override comprehension and making meaning. Consequently, she purposefully crafted her instruction to focus on reading and writing for understanding.

For example, Pat had assessed her students' writing and found that it lacked the detail necessary for the reader's comprehension. Even though it was relatively early in the year, Pat wanted her students to become aware of how detail adds interest and makes a story easier to visualize and, consequently, to understand. Therefore, she modeled awareness of detail by thinking aloud while reading and writing. *Stellaluna* (Cannon, 1993) was read aloud when the children were studying bats. After reading, "Down, down she went, faster and faster, into the forest below," Pat asked the children to show her by using their hands how Stellaluna fell. "Yes," she said. "If the author just wrote 'She fell down,' we would not have known that she was falling very quickly." We observed Pat to refer to detail and its ability to enhance comprehension many times throughout the day while reading and writing with the children in a variety of contexts.

Pat knew that children needed many opportunities to revisit familiar stories and to reread so as to develop comprehension. Therefore, she provided several contexts in order for her students to do so. First, the children were assigned to do some familiar reading every night as homework. Children who met with Pat for a guided reading lesson on a certain day took home a plastic bag containing four or five leveled reading books, including the new book they had read that day. Pat also taught the children how to self-select books that were within their ability to read. On Back to School Night, she taught parents the "rule of thumb"[1] so that they could help their children select books to read, and showed how illustrations and repetitive text support early readers. In addition, the children had opportunities to reread and to retell stories in the literacy center, using books with accompanying retelling materials. Buddy reading and picture reading of challenging texts was encouraged. The children read their own writing during Writers Workshop. The class was full of environmental prints and charts that provided contexts for functional reading.

SKILLS INSTRUCTION

Pat's knowledge about the teaching of skills and her ability to integrate skills instruction into authentic contexts throughout the day were impressive. She was well acquainted with the developmental processes of reading and writing. She knew what her students had to learn in order to become better readers and writers, and she purposefully created many opportunities for discovery and explicit teaching of those necessary skills and strategies.

Most often skills were taught within the context of theme-based literature and poetry. At times, for reinforcement, she would use commercially prepared programs or worksheets. For example, Pat wanted her children to begin to build a bank of sight words so that

---

[1]The "rule of thumb" is as follows: (1) Choose a book. (2) Open to the middle of the book. (3) Start reading. (4) If you come to a word you don't know, put one finger down (pinky first). (5) If you have to put your thumb down (5 missed fingers) the book is too hard. Choose another book.

their reading would become more fluent. She chose five sight words per week on which to focus her instruction. The words she chose were identified by assessing the children's reading and writing. First, Pat found a poem that related to the theme under study that contained the words on which she wanted to focus the children's attention. The poem was introduced through a shared reading. After a discussion based on making meaning, Pat asked the children to find and circle the words. These were spelled aloud and added to the large bulletin board designated as the Word Wall.

Pat had the children chant and move while spelling the words several times throughout the day. Rather than designate a certain time for this activity, Pat spontaneously integrated it throughout the day. For example, while they were lining up to go to music, she asked the students to march and chant the "a" words on the Word Wall. Pat knew that her children not only learned from this activity but really enjoyed it, because they asked frequently to "do the Word Wall." This type of skills instruction was focused and short. The emphasis was on spelling the words conventionally in authentic reading and writing contexts, rather than learning to spell the words as an end in itself.

GUIDED READING AND WRITING INSTRUCTION BASED ON INDIVIDUALLY ASSESSED NEEDS

Pat believed that instruction was most effective when it was based on the children's individual needs as developing readers and writers. She realized that some whole-class instruction was beneficial to all her students, but she relied mainly on smaller instructional contexts to facilitate individual student progress. Interactions with her students in small groups and one-on-one were considered to be critical instructional contexts. They provided the primary means for instruction that was on the cutting edge of the children's learning. Pat planned small-group instructional periods such as guided reading groups. She continually circulated around the room and spontaneously interacted one-on-one with the children at the point of their need. Pat interacted with her students throughout the day, directing her comments toward specific skills, strategies, and ways of thinking that would lead to further development in reading and writing.

Pat relied on frequent, authentic assessment to provide insight for formulating teaching goals and objectives for small-group and one-on-one interactions. Pat had devised a systematic way to regularly assess her students. Each day she chose two children, whom she called her "focus students," whom she watched closely throughout the day and formally assessed. She directed specific questions to those children during whole-group instructional periods and observed them as they worked independently. She kept running records, assessing their story retellings and noting specific reading strategies and behaviors. She kept a file on each child and referred to the files when planning instruction, making grouping decisions, or preparing for conferences.

Writers Workshop provided another opportunity for further assessment. Before dismissing the children to get their materials for writing, she called their names and asked them to report where they were in their writing process. She made note of their responses on a checklist she had devised to keep track of her students' progress. She met with students daily to discuss their works in progress. During these conferences, Pat discussed their work by masterfully questioning the students so that they articulated their thought processes and procedures. This powerful interaction guided the student toward the realization of what he or she needed to improve. More anecdotal records were made and added to the child's file. Because of this data collection, Pat knew each of her students intimately as readers and writers. She used the information as a basis for interacting with students individually and in small-group contexts to further their development. She purposefully directed the students to connect what they knew to what they were learning. She carefully guided their thinking so that they saw how skills and strategies were used in authentic contexts. Thus, instruction in this classroom was based on Pat's knowledge of her students rather than a preplanned curriculum. Pat's purposeful observation and assessment practices were the foundation of all instructional practices.

FOLLOWING PAT LODEN IN HER CLASSROOM THROUGHOUT A TYPICAL SCHOOL DAY

On a typical day of observation, Pat Loden's first graders engaged in literacy activities as soon as they arrived in the classroom. Each child located his or her name and photograph on the "I'm Here!" section of the bulletin board and turned the photo face up to indicate that he or she had arrived at school. Two children were responsible for tallying the number of children present and the number of children absent on the daily attendance slip. Lunch choices were listed on the board, and each child was responsible for signing in under his or her choice for the day. Pat had been modeling how to tally the lunch totals during math and planned on adding "lunch tally" to the morning jobs list next month.

Pat included a wide variety of activities in the list of morning jobs, all of which required the children to read, write, or do math. The children's names rotated on a daily basis, so that the job list had to be read by the students every morning. Two children wrote the date on the calendar. One student completed the days-of-the-week chart while another placed Unifix cubes on the weather graph. One child measured pellets and water for Squiggy, the hamster. Two boys measured water for the plants. The "Reporters" wrote one or two sentences of daily news. Because it was early in the year, Pat made available structured sentences that the Reporters could choose to use. These simple sentences included "Today is _____," "We will _____," and "My news is _____."

The theme being studied was good food and nutrition, and Pat integrated this theme throughout the literacy activities during the day. For example, the children who were not assigned morning jobs could choose to read, independently or with a buddy, books about good food. They got started writing in their journals and were encouraged to write what they ate for breakfast. They solved the daily word problem, which had to do with counting, adding, and subtracting, using lima beans.

Every morning Pat has a sentence or two written on the board that contains spelling and grammatical errors that require editing or omitted letters to be filled in. The children can work independently or in pairs to note the errors and correctly rewrite the sentence on strips of brightly colored paper kept near the sentence. Today the sentence said: "This mornin__, I ate to pieces of toast and a c__p of melk for mi breakfist. It is important to et breakfist in the mornin__ to sta__ heal__y."

Pat clapped a four-beat rhythm pattern, which the class echoed. This signaled to the students that they had 5 minutes to complete their tasks and gather on the rug. Gathering time began with the Reporters reading their daily news. Pat complimented the boys' use of punctuation, hearing sounds in words, and letter–sound correspondence. She interactively rewrote some words in their text, explaining, "If the words were written in a book, it would look like this." She then composed her own morning message about a visitor who would be coming to the class later in the week. As she wrote, she "thought out loud," highlighting composition strategies, concepts about words, and concepts about print. Pat modeled how to say words slowly in order to hear letter sounds, using the Word Wall as a source for spelling sight vocabulary, leaving spaces between words. She used the word "nutritionist," which was new vocabulary for the students, that went along with the theme they were studying.

Because she was teaching the children how to write questions, she wrote a morning message as a riddle, in which she gave the children three clues about a surprise guest. Using the clues, the children would solve the riddle and know the visitor's occupation. Pat explicitly taught the use of the question mark and how to differentiate a question from an declarative statement.

After the students had solved the riddle and deduced that the visitor was a nurse who specialized in good eating habits, Pat told the children that while they were working in the writing center they were to compose two questions they would like to ask the nurse nutritionist. Pat planned on having the children compose interview guides during the following two days, which they would use to interview the guest nurse on the day of the visit. A question planner worksheet was modeled for the children and placed in the writing center for later use.

Pat next directed the class's attention to the poem about pasta called *A Matter of Taste* (Merriam, 1992) that was written on chart paper. Pat chose this poem because it related to the current theme of food and contained questions as well. Pat pointed to the text as the children enthusiastically read along. After they had chanted the poem, Pat asked the children to suggest movements they could do to dramatize the poem while they chanted chorally. The discussion about the selection of movements created a rich context for comprehension development and using meaning as a source of information while reading and writing.

After dramatizing, Pat asked whether anyone noticed something in the text of the poem they would like to show to the rest of the class. One child quickly raised her hand and pointed out the question in the poem. Other children noticed punctuation marks and sight words that were on the Word Wall.

Typically, Pat used a theme-based poem as a contextual means of introducing high-frequency words, which were added to the Word

Wall each week. Pat had several word sources throughout her class-room that were added to almost daily. One was the alphabetized Word Wall that displayed high-frequency vocabulary. Attached to the chalk rail beneath the Word Wall were chunk charts displaying lists of word families. A theme-related vocabulary chart hung next to the Word Wall. The words on this chart related to the monthly theme. This month's chart included the words "nutritionist," "healthy," "meat," "vegetables," "dairy products," and others. The words were written on laminated oak tag and attached to the large chart with Velcro. The children could remove the words if they needed to look at them more closely while writing stories or journal entries. At the conclusion of each theme, the charts were put on rings and hung on a chart stand that stood by the Word Wall.

After whole-group shared reading and writing, a 90-minute Readers Workshop began. During this time, the children worked in-dependently of the teacher on literacy-based activities while Pat met with groups of children for guided reading instruction. At this time Pat typically assigns the children "Do Now" work, and the children move into learning centers. This morning's Do Now began with ap-proximately 20 minutes of independent silent reading. The children may choose to read books from their book baskets, which contain books that were read during guided reading lessons, or they may choose new books from the classroom library. Pat has a large selec-tion of books that are organized into bins according to their Reading Recovery level. During silent reading the children may select books from the bin that correlates with their reading level. The students keep track of what they read in their personal reading logs. Here they record their reading goals for the week, authors, book titles, and number of pages or number of books read. Once a week the children write their opinions about something they read and support their opinions with information from the text. They may, for example, choose to write about the most exciting part of a story and why they found it to be so. Do Now assignments conclude with journal writ-ing. Books related to the current theme were available, such as the poetry book of food poems, *What's on the Menu* (Goldstein, 1992), *Growing Vegetable Soup* (Ehlert, 1987), and *What Food Is This?* (Hausher, 1994).

After writing in their journals, the children referred to the choice board to move into learning center activities. Some children chose to work with a partner to do the daily edit and math word problem before moving into learning centers. The children were divided into five groups of four to five children, representing varying levels of ability. Each group had three centers in which they could work that day. They followed the order that was listed on the choice board and moved from center to center when they determined they had completed their task of choice. The centers were the literacy center, which included a Listening Post and Read-the-Room materials, the Poetry Corner, the letter and word work center, the writing center, the Story-telling Corner, a center for writing Internet pen pals on computers, and a science center. In the science center the children were to examine the characteristics of apples and pumpkins. The materials included two pumpkins and two apples, one of each cut in half and one of each whole. There were magnifying glasses, Venn diagrams, crayons, and markers. In small groups children were to examine the similarities and differences between apples and pumpkins, using their senses of smell, touch, and sight. They used the Venn diagram to record how pumpkins and apples are different (written in the outer sides of the Venn diagram circles) and how they are the same (using the overlapping middle portion of the diagram). Each center area was well organized, had reminder charts of what to do and how to behave. The different activities in the center had a component that provided the reader with information about what the child had completed.

As the children worked independently, Pat met with small groups of students who were reading on similar levels, and had like reading behaviors, for guided reading. Pat regularly used running records and story retelling assessments to determine how the children would be grouped and what they needed to learn through guided reading lessons. The class was currently divided into five groups, ranging from students who were emergent readers to those who were reading fluently above grade level.

Pat typically begins her guided reading groups with a mini-lesson appropriate to the needs of the children. For example, one of today's lessons began with instruction on how to decode by looking for small known words and chunks within a larger unknown word. She used the word "vegetable" as an example because there are several words within, such as "table," "able," "get," and "tab," and it is a word related to the theme being studied. The mini-lesson is followed by a book introduction. Each book is introduced differently, according to the needs of the children in the group. The children are then directed to read the text on their own. While the children read silently, Pat circulated around the table, having each of the children quietly read aloud to her. She reinforced the skill presented in the mini-lesson when a student was struggling to decode. At the conclusion of the story the group discussed how the story had ended. Pat then wrote specific words from the text on the white board and asked the children to tell her how they could look for little words and chunks in these words to help them read the text. She encouraged reading for meaning by asking the children whether the words made sense in the story and whether they reflected the way we speak.

Between guided reading groups, Pat met one-on-one with two children whom she referred to as her "focus children" for the day. These were the two children who would be closely observed and assessed. During her conferences with the focus children, Pat discussed their reading log entries, offering specific suggestions as to how to improve written responses and spell conventionally, and to encourage realistic goal setting. After meeting with each child, Pat recorded her observations on a recording sheet that she had made and placed it in the student's file folder. Pat also added to a running record on the focus children, then listened to a story retelling and asked some probing comprehension questions.

Pat used the clapping signal once again to indicate that Readers Workshop would be over in 5 minutes. The children began to put their materials away and gathered on the rug in the literacy center. Pat reinforced the good behaviors she had observed during the independent work period. "I heard quiet voices," she said. "What good self-control you have!" She then quickly went over the daily edit, asking the children to provide her with the corrections that needed to be made. The children then lined up to go to music. After music there was lunch and recess.

While the children were at music, Pat laid out containers of letters and letter holders in preparation for a word-building lesson that would follow lunch and recess. She used several theme-related words for this exercise. Pat commented on how the children enjoyed these lessons. This was evident as the children came in from recess, when they cheered to see the letters laid out. The word-building lesson moved at a rapid pace and lasted for about 15 minutes.

Word work was followed by reading aloud, which took place on the rug in the literacy center. The children obviously enjoyed hearing *I Wonder How Bread Is Made* (Curtis & Greenland, 1992); every child was engaged in the story reading and participated enthusiastically in discussing what was read.

Pat smoothly transitioned into a Writers Workshop mini-lesson by asking the children to comment on how the authors used words other than "said" when writing dialogue. She directed the children's attention to an overhead projection of a page on which she had written several sentences from the story *I Wonder How Bread Is Made*. The children circled the words that were used in place of "said" as Pat wrote them on a large chart. She encouraged the children to consider using these words in their writing to make it more interesting to their readers. As the children independently worked on their writing projects, Pat met one-on-one with children who were ready to confer prior to publishing and sharing their stories.

The remainder of the afternoon was taken up by an integrated math/science lesson wherein the children were estimating and then measuring different types of pasta of varying lengths. The lesson began with a whole-group time in which the class did calendar activities typically associated with a morning routine. Pat explained that calendar activities are primarily math oriented, and thus she uses them to begin her math period by activating students' mathematical thought processes, rather than include them in the morning whole-group time, which is literacy based. The day had flown by, and, much to everyone's surprise, it was time to leave. After singing the good-bye song, the children lined up to head home.

SUMMARY

Investigations into exemplary practices in early literacy attempt to capture as many dimensions as possible of expert performances to describe teaching excellence. With this type of research, investigators examine real-life situations in which many variables are successfully integrated. The results of the studies on effective and exemplary teaching have many similarities. A list combining some findings about effective and exemplary teachers and their classroom practices includes the following characteristics:

- Varied teaching strategies are used to motivate literacy learning.
- Teachers create excitement about what is being taught.

- There are high expectations for student accomplishment.
- Instruction is adjusted to meet the individual needs of students.
- Guidance is provided in structured lessons for the acquisition of skills.
- Extensive feedback is provided for students.
- Children are treated with respect.
- Opportunities are provided for children to practice skills learned.
- Classrooms are rich literacy environments with accessible materials.
- Varied structures for instruction are utilized, including whole-group, small-group, and one-on one-settings with the teacher.
- Opportunities exist for children to work independently of the teacher, either alone or in social cooperative groups.
- Emphasis is placed on careful organization and management of strategies and structures for optimal literacy development to occur (Morrow, Tracey, Woo, & Pressley, 1999; Pressley, Rankin, & Yoki, 1996; Ruddell & Ruddell, 1995).

Pat's classroom definitely has the characteristics identified in studies of effective and exemplary instruction. Her school supported and facilitated exemplary practice. Professional growth related to student success was recognized. The atmosphere in the building was professional and collaborative. Pat willingly put forth great effort, hard work, and dedication to ensure her students' success. Differentiating her instructional contexts and activities in order to meet students at their various points of learning was both time-consuming and challenging. Yet Pat saw it as the essence of good teaching and would do no less. In addition, Pat had a natural talent for teaching. She thoroughly loved her work and her students. The affect in her classroom was warm and rich. Moreover, she brought to her classroom a rich experiential knowledge base. Pat saw herself as a lifelong learner, one who was continuously learning more about how children learned and how best to teach them. She had a sound, balanced, research-based philosophy of education, which was the basis of her classroom instruction.

It is not by chance that the children have come to enjoy learning in Pat's classroom. The affective quality of her room is indeed exemplary. She has worked hard to create a caring community of learners filled with cooperation and respect based on high expectations and achievement. Throughout the day she was quick to praise and reinforce her students' developing academic abilities and personal qualities such as tenacity and perseverance.

We would be remiss not to tell of the obvious enjoyment of Pat and her students as they participate in learning activities throughout the day. Her students are busily engaged from the time that they enter the room until they prepare to go home. They are continually challenged to work to the best of their abilities and to stretch further. Yet they appear to be having fun and express delight in reading and writing. Pat, too, is quick to tell of her love of teaching. It obviously shines through all she does.

REFERENCES

Cannon, J. (1993). *Stellaluna*. New York: Scholastic.

Curtis, N., & Greenland, P. (1992). *I wonder how bread is made*. Ann Arbor, MI: Lerner.

Ehlert, L. (1987). *Growing vegetable soup*. Singapore: Tien Press.

Goldstein, B. S. (Ed.). (1992). *What's on the menu*. New York: Viking.

Hausher, R. (1994). *What food is this?* New York: Scholastic.

Lasky, K., & Hafner, M. (1996). *Lunch bunnies*. New York: Little, Brown.

Merriam, E. (1992). A matter of taste. In B. Goldstein (Ed.), *What's on the menu* (p. 10). New York: Viking.

Morrow, L. M., Tracey, D., Woo, D., & Pressley, M. (1999). Characteristics of exemplary first-grade instruction. *The Reading Teacher, 52,* 462–476.

Pressley, M., Rankin, J., & Yokoi, L. (1996). A survey of the instructional practices of outstanding primary-level literacy teachers. *Elementary School Journal, 96,* 363–384.

Ruddell, R., & Ruddell, M. R. (1995). *Teaching children to read and write: Becoming an influential teacher.* Boston: Allyn & Bacon.

Elizabeth Brown Asbury is a doctoral student at Rutgers University. She will complete her degree in May of 2001. Ms. Asbury has been teaching for Rutgers as a Graduate Assistant in the area of early childhood literacy development. She received an award from the New Jersey Reading Association for her research for her dissertation and has presented at the National Reading Conference and at the International Reading Association numerous times.

Part III

Thoughts about Teacher Development

Based on the studies of the past few years, we feel confident in our understanding about the nature of grade-1 teaching that is effective in promoting literacy achievement. Developing this envisionment of excellent first-grade instruction was no small accomplishment. In the end, we came up with a viewpoint on grade-1 instruction that was very different from any of the perspectives in the marketplace of ideas about grade-1 teaching, with our envisionment neither whole-language nor skills instruction. What we discovered was that effective grade-1 teachers go well beyond whole-language instruction in respect to skills instruction, and well beyond skills instruction in respect to the incorporation of literature into instruction and the development of young writers.

But how did these teachers become so good? If we understood that, we might be in a position to develop more excellent grade-1 teachers. In the final two chapters of this book, we take up that question. Chapter 10 is a study of effective grade-1 teachers' perspectives on their own professional development. Chapter 11 includes the insights of the authors of this volume, based on their experiences in this research and their greater experience as teacher educators.

10

How I Became an Exemplary Teacher
(Although I'm Really Still Learning
Just Like Anyone Else)

Jeni Pollack Day

There is a great deal to be gained from reading about exemplary classrooms. These case studies, however, are only snapshots of the individual teachers' career-long development. After studying these teachers, we became concerned with another question. How is it that these teachers developed this expertise? What influences led to their development? It is especially important to ask this question now, as policymakers and the public have an increasing hand in influencing how teaching is understood and improved. For example, this comment was made to me by a physician whom I sat beside at a conference last fall: "While I find your work on exemplary teachers interesting, I have serious doubts of its usefulness to the general population of teachers, because, quite frankly, I don't think that most teachers are capable of becoming exemplary themselves." Although I was discouraged by her statement, I was not surprised, as she seemed to reflect the general lack of faith in teachers evidenced across the country in the past decade (Berliner & Biddle, 1995). Her statement, however, captured important questions in the study of exemplary teachers and methods. Are exemplary teachers somehow different from other teachers? Or is it possible for any teacher to become exemplary? And, again, how did these exemplary teachers develop their expertise?

Policymakers have long debated these questions as they work to improve teaching and teachers. Should policies aim to develop exemplary teachers or exemplary programs? Should we nurture teachers with the hope that they will become expert at their craft, for example, through professionalization or increased certification standards, or ought we standardize teaching so that there is little opportunity for teachers to expose children to poor teaching?

Although many educators continue to cite the need to invest in teachers as skilled professionals (Darling-Hammond, 1997; Duffy, 1997; Leiberman, 1988; Shannon, 1989), the public still seems unconvinced, preferring to trust accountability and curricular mandates in order to guarantee effective teaching (Goldhaber & Brewer, 1999; Raspberry, 1999; Riley, 1999). Children who receive poor teaching are often substantially behind their peers, even despite optimum parental involvement (Snow, Barnes, Chandler, Goodman, & Hemphill, 1991, Bembry, Jordan, Gomez, Anderson, & Mendro, 1998) Because children's futures are at stake, parents and policymakers put the highest priority on providing children with the soundest educational environment possible. Mandating practices, and ensuring them with accountability testing, seems the safest way to ensure effective teaching.

Other researchers, however, have questioned whether any program that does not draw upon teacher expertise and critical decision making is doomed to be poorly implemented (Duffy & Hoffman, 1999). Further, teaching that is heavily influenced by standardized test accountability measures is often stifled and uncreative, resulting in less-than-optimal learning (Johnston, 1998). If accountability testing and curriculum mandates are poor means for developing teacher expertise, how does that expertise develop? What might be the most helpful way to encourage exemplary teaching?

This chapter attempts to answer some of these questions by drawing on a larger research study (Day, 1999), designed to determine what changes these teachers had made and what they believe influenced their development of exemplary practices. More particularly, it looks at the thoughts of first-grade teachers as they reflect on the experiences that helped them gain their expertise. To complete this study, I interviewed 30 exemplary teachers in first and fourth grades as to why they teach the way they do and why they are the teachers they are. What experiences did these teachers have that might help other teachers interested in improving their practices? What methods did they find most useful? How might school districts encourage and facilitate this type of teaching? I was particularly interested in whether these were things that any teacher or district might do. Were they reasonable for a majority of teachers, or were they things that would require more time and resources than most teachers had available? Might any teacher become exemplary?

The rest of this chapter is divided into two sections. The first section frames the chapter by identifying changes teachers made. What were the common threads in exemplary teachers' experiences? The second section then discusses what first-grade teachers considered most important to their growth as teachers.

HOW TEACHERS CHANGED

Finding commonalties among teachers' changes was difficult. The changes that the exemplary teachers made were in apparently random and conflicting directions. Some teachers discussed using more whole-class instruction, whereas others noted using more small groups. Some teachers mentioned drawing on more whole-language methods (reading workshop, process writing), and others mentioned drawing on them less but increasing structure and explicit lessons in their classrooms. Several teachers continued to use the basal, although they reported utilizing it in different ways over the years. All teachers mentioned constantly adding new ideas to their curricula, but those methods were varied. Examples included reciprocal questioning, encouraging student response to literature, and the use of word sorts and word activities.

What I finally found to be the common thread was that the exemplary teachers used the various methods more strategically, pulling pieces from here and there to match their programs with the needs of their students. Rather than promote a method or pedagogy for its own sake, these teachers began looking at the specific needs of their students. The teachers noted that their most important changes were due to their own learning, which increased their expertise in how children learn and how different methods might support that learning. Rather than adapt children to a particular method, teachers adapted the methods they used to the children with whom they were working at a particular time.

The teachers also noted a change in their conception of the role of teacher. Although they had begun their careers as lecturers or presenters of information, they moved toward seeing themselves as resources, coaches, and mentors. As they became more sensitive to how children learn, they moved away from simply giving children information and toward facilitating children's exploration of children's own theories and interests.

WHAT INFLUENCED TEACHERS
TO TEACH THE WAY THEY DO?

The teachers mentioned many influential experiences that helped them choose and develop the program and practices they currently used. I was particularly interested in the advice of exemplary first-grade teachers for other teachers, insights based on what they found most influential in their own learning and growth as teachers. Here, then, are exemplary teachers' own words, summarizing what they considered to be most important to their development.

1. *Work with children every chance you get.* It is especially valuable to have one-on-one time with children when learning new things about children's learning.

> "Really, I feel my philosophy was developed once I actually got into a classroom and started working with children. And then there were opportunities to try out the different parts of knowledge that different instructors shared with me. . . . Number one is getting in there and working with the children. And that had a tremendous effect on me."

> "[For a class I took] we worked in a program in a school that was in decline. And we'd have students one or two at a time, and we'd make plans for them and make games for them. And it was a lot of hands-on. It was one of the best classes I took."

"He was so specific in his focus, and I thought, 'Oh, okay, now I see what we're doing.' It seemed as though the other teaching courses were kind of 'Do this,' and it didn't really make sense. But his really made sense because we went and worked [with children]."

2. *Work with other teachers every chance you get.* If the school organization does not set up opportunities for teachers to work together, make your own opportunities by finding existing support groups within the larger district or community, by looking to graduate classes, or by gathering support from teachers within your school.

"There was another person, the gal who was the language arts coordinator in our district at the time. She put together a support group for people who were trying to get into integrated language and whole-language [instruction] when it first came out. And she used a group that basically had gone through the New Jersey Writing Project. We met once a month to share ideas and things. She was very influential."

"I have wonderful colleagues who are interested in keeping up with what's going on. Working together with other people is really one of the most important things that you can do."

"We have grade-level meetings. We talk about [our classes]. If you are lucky enough to be in a good grade level where there are teachers who are all on the same level, it's great, because you really just go through it together."

"When you see somebody else's enthusiasm, it's usually very contagious."

"I find that I'm the kind of person who needs some affirmation. If I don't feel that somebody is affirming my work, not me particularly, but my work, it's difficult for me to know that I'm doing the right thing. I need that."

3. *Reflect on what you are doing. Look for ways to do it better.* Talk to other teachers for ideas. Ask teachers what they are doing

and share ideas. Even if your school is not conducive to sharing ideas, try to find at least one colleague, within or outside the school, with whom you can share.

> "We meet in our vertical [cross-grade-level] teams. And I love those days, because we get to hear feedback from other teachers about what they're doing in their rooms and how it spirals from one grade to another. We were supposed to end at two, and we were still talking at quarter of three . . . it was so interesting."

> "I was writing [activities] up and using them with young children, then going back and dialoguing with people about what we were doing. What was important was talking with other people and hearing other people's ideas and what's working or not working for them with the kids they are working with."

> "I would say the most influential thing in my teaching is not working in isolation. Having colleagues to bounce ideas off, who listen to you when you are dissatisfied with the way things are going in your room, and who are open to trying new things."

4. *Observe children. Never stop learning.* Learning how to look at children and understand how they learn and develop is the most important thing you can do to improve your teaching. Sometimes learning involves challenging your own beliefs about what children can do, and expecting more of students than you have before.

> "My first year I absolutely did not believe that first graders could write. Period. And anytime, in any teacher's manual or in some kind of activity where they said, 'Have your student write such and such.' I'd say, 'They have got to be kidding. Obviously, they don't know anything about first graders, because first graders can't write.' Then that summer I went to the McCracken workshop, and they talked a lot about invented spelling and the fact that the kids could write in journals and listen for their own sounds. I now have the belief that the more they write, the better readers they become."

> "When I was just working with [first graders], it was really evident to me that children have their own way of learning and that

there are activities and ways of delivering instruction that are definitely going to be more effective for them. And that made me want to . . . once I took one class, then I just wanted to keep taking more and more and more."

"They're writing because they have a purpose for writing. And they are so motivated because it's what they want to know and what they want to learn. So I want to do more of that."

"The second most significant change is that I am able to do more forms of assessment. What I feel are authentic forms of assessment. And to do them more frequently and on a consistent basis. And the way that ends up affecting my instruction is that, of course, the information I'm getting from my assessment helps drive my instruction."

"I wanted to do it, and then I saw the change in my students and the change in my attitude to be there, and how much more exciting it was. And how much more progress they made and their enthusiasm for reading. That really pushed me toward integrated language, big time."

5. *Find an opportunity to share your expertise.* Even if you do not feel qualified to be an expert, find an area in which you are particularly interested and build on that interest by learning more and sharing what you know with others. We know how much we learn as we teach children. There is also a lot to learn by teaching other teachers.

"Our district created a training program to meet the in-service hours that the entire primary staff throughout the district had to put in. And as part of that training program, they chose people from each site whom they felt would be good literacy coaches to provide training. So instead of bringing in outside people, they picked people whom they felt were 'experts' at individual sites. I was one of those literacy coaches. We had some training, and then we provided a year-long series of trainings for maybe 300 K–2 teachers. I learned so much doing it."

"They called me up and asked, 'How would you like to write a curriculum for the first grade?' It was a killer, it felt as though I was never at home. But we had a good time. I mean, it was such a learning experience."

"I attend a lot of workshops and I give workshops. And I think that also influences me, because I find that when I give workshops I learn a lot—from people and interactions—and the others have done something similar, but a little different. I think teachers are really creative people."

6. *Find staff development and experiences that focus on understanding the reasons behind methods, and understanding the big picture of children's educational experiences, rather than just learning how to do a method or strategy.*

"I think, just having things kind of pointed out to you. For instance, are you doing a shared reading or are you doing a read aloud? And I always knew that you should do both, but nobody ever said that and pointed out the benefits of each. I kind of knew it, but I guess [the staff developers] made it more formal."

"Another major factor was the training I received as a Reading Recovery teacher. Just understanding reading strategies, helping me organize my own hierarchy of how a child learns to read, what the strategies look like, how to support those strategies and push them to the next level, how to keep doing that constant stretching that helps a child become an independent problem-solving type of a reader. It also helped in leveling the books that we were using. I guess the knowledge that I got using so many books helped me in selecting books at the appropriate level for the kids."

"I think most of the change in how I've taught really has had to do with . . . I've taught everything from first to eighth. And most of the change came when I actually dropped down. I started in the upper grades, and the biggest change in how I taught really was dropping to first grade. I could see how school all worked together, and I knew what I wanted them to learn from having taught students at different ages."

7. *Take change slowly. Make small changes.*

"I would say definitely that my philosophy hasn't changed drastically, but it may have become more solidified. And, certainly, with every child, something new gets added to it . . . in minor ways. Probably over a period of time [I've made] a mountain of changes."

"I moved slowly away from the traditional stuff [when I returned to teaching]. I really had never done it before, but was doing [three basal reading groups] just because that was the good thing to do. Cause, you know, after being out 13 years, you just kind of learn and watch a lot the first couple years."

8. *Look to your own experiences for ideas, understanding.*

"I developed a process writing program very early, before it became a big deal in the literature. [It came about because] I was not very good at writing. You know, I was always scared about writing. When I went to high school, I had to write my first term paper. And it was as if somebody told me to jump out of an airplane. I don't think they had made me do enough writing all along. And then all of a sudden somebody decides, oh yeah, write a paper. Nobody really trained you to do that."

9. *Learn most from the students who aren't succeeding.*

"My groupings also used to be, when I first started, homogeneous. And my top readers got stronger and stronger and stronger; my struggling readers . . . they grew, but I could see their self-esteem, at about midyear, just keep getting lower and lower, because the gap between those who could and those who couldn't was so huge and the material was so focused on those who could."

"I had a teacher that I admired a great deal as I was going through my early teaching, and she never seemed satisfied with her teaching, even though she was a great teacher. And I think I continue to feel that way about my own children and my own teaching. Not that I'm not happy with what I'm doing, but I keep looking for a way to hook that one child who's still struggling or to find a more efficient way to do it."

"But it's constant reflection about everything. I mean, that's gotta be. Some days when I am just so impatient with [my lowest student], or anybody else, I have to step back. I have to step back and say, 'Okay, what's going on here with him? How much of this is me? Is this appropriate that I'm giving him? Do I need to take that away?' And, you know, oftentimes, it's really not them. Oftentimes, it's that we've set it up inappropriately."

10. *Love what you do.*

"One thing that is very influential to my teaching is that I really love what I do. I'm very motivated. I'm not saying it doesn't get to me every now and again. There are certain days, now especially in first grade, I don't have an aide in the room, and it's very tiring. But I really do . . . I enjoy trying to find a better way."

"I just really enjoy it. I enjoy teaching. I enjoy seeing kids learn. I enjoy taking a child who is struggling or a reluctant reader and seeing him get all excited about it. I just find it to be very rewarding and very challenging. My father's been telling me, 'You just need to go do something that pays you.' I was thinking about that this week; I thought, I guess I could quit and go sell medical supplies and I'd make more money, certainly. But, then, it's just people selling medical supplies. I mean, there are no intangibles there in my opinion. I like the intrinsic values that I have in getting up and going to school. Kids are so much fun."

11. *Relax and don't take your authority so seriously.*

"My mom was just a fun person to be around. And that's the kind of mom I was, and that's the kind of teacher I wanted to be."

"I've had a lot of young teachers on our team, and the ones that I see that get into power struggles with the kids are the ones who get really serious about it and start taking control and trying to control the kid. And, basically, you can't control any kids, in my opinion. Now, there are things I can do to help them be more co-operative. But, you can't control them. And I think my sense of humor . . . I can look at [most misbehavior] and think, 'Oh, you're so funny,' and just move right along. And it takes all the joy out of being the troublemaker. I usually like those little guys that push the envelope. But then I was raised with four brothers. You know, four big brothers, so what can I say? I was used to that."

12. *Get administration on your side.* Having a principal who supports and encourages you is crucially important. If your administrator is doubtful or less willing to allow teachers to experiment, work together to make a case for the program you want.

"I went to the principal and said, 'I think one of the main things that's contributing to the fact that our students aren't reading well is that they aren't reading things at their level. We don't have books at their level, so they can't get more fluent and they can't gain more vocabulary if all we've got are these basal books. They really need fluency.' So she took that message to the site council, and they've been quite receptive and generous in giving the primary staff more money, and, actually, this year, I think they gave $200 to K–8 teachers to buy books."

"And then we got a new principal, and she absolutely sparked interest in everybody to do different things, and she's just . . . it's incredible. It really shows you that change can be great if you allow it to happen. She has really influenced me, and I've felt that I could just do anything. So she's been a big influence on my teaching."

"[I appreciate] the district that I work in because they are so, I think, progressive, and so easy as far as letting you try things and treating you like a professional. I never felt like . . . there's just never that kind of fear. You know, like the feeling 'Oh, my gosh, am I doing this right? Is my superintendent going to walk in and see them doing what she doesn't want them to do?' I've never felt like that. As I'm talking to other people, I know that I'm really, really lucky that way."

"I was very fortunate; there's a lot of leeway in my school district as long as you can show your children achieving at the end of the year. You know the child needs to meet certain outcomes, but how you get there was pretty much . . . there was more freedom in selecting what we were using. We had a supportive principal who wanted research and materials, and understanding our enthusiasm for it, allowed us to use workbook money to purchase literature materials. Our district is very good at making you buy into any new program by requesting your input, and it's a process. It's never, 'Here it is, this is what you are going to do.' "

"I guess the thing that has always been nice in our district is, 'try it. It doesn't have to be perfect. And let's talk about it.' Let's talk about what went wrong, let's talk about what went right And it was just as much fun and helpful to talk about what went wrong as about what went right. So there was never a principal walking around saying, 'It's a little loud in here.' or 'Why aren't these books . . . ?' You know, you never felt as if you were being policed about anything. You could kind of go at your own pace, and I think when you let adults do that, better things will happen."

CONCLUSION

Exemplary teaching ability is not a magical, mystical thing that people either have or don't have. It develops as teachers become expert observers of students and learning, as they seek continually to learn and grow, and as they reflect on their own teaching and experiences in learning.

These teachers described their development as a continuous process of refining their teaching, based on their own reflection and observations of students and talking about these observations with other educators. We find that teachers who are the most successful are those who see themselves as constantly wanting to grow more, not those who believe they have everything figured out. Exemplary teachers tend to ask more questions than other teachers, not because they don't know what they are doing, but because they want to learn more.

These teachers have a good sense of their own abilities. Rather than paint a rosy picture of their classrooms, or lament all of the things that they were not able to do or might have done better, exemplary teachers are very sensitive to both the stronger and weaker practices in their classrooms. Dissatisfaction with their own teaching was the starting point for future learning. This happened particularly as teachers studied the students who were struggling most in their classrooms, and used those struggles as a means to understand where their own teaching was lacking for those children.

Exemplary teachers believe that excellent teaching consists of observing and understanding student perspectives on what they are learning, and examining materials in light of how well they fit with a particular child's needs. Rather than promote a method or program for its own sake, they look at it in light of the specific children in front of them and whether it would be better or worse in meeting a need. One teacher explained, "In regard to programs or anything else, I'm never motivated by them, because I'm thinking, oh well, how long will this last?"

Finally, although exemplary teachers welcome high standards for their teaching as a means to verify their success in meeting student needs, not one of them mentioned those standards as influencing their teaching. Accountability measures and mandated practices may create anxiety, but they do not address how teachers go about improving the work they are already doing. While policymakers continue to debate the issues and ponder ways to bully, entice, or compel teachers to improve, the best teachers are already going about the most important business there is, improving educational experiences for each of their students one day, one year, one child at a time.

REFERENCES

Bembry, K., Jordan, H., Gomez, E., Anderson, M., & Mendro, R. (1998, April). *Policy implications of long-term teacher effects on student achievement.* Paper presented at the annual meeting of the American Educational Research Association, San Diego, CA.

Berliner D., & Biddle, B. (1995). *The manufactured crises: Myths, fraud and the attack on America's public schools.* Reading, MA: Addison-Wesley Longman.

Darling-Hammond, L. (1997). *Doing what matters most: Investing in quality teaching*. New York: National Commission on Teaching and America's Future.

Day, J. P. (1999). *The acquisition of exemplary teaching capacity*. Paper presented at the annual conference of the American Educational Research Association, Montreal, Canada.

Duffy, G. (1997). Powerful models or powerful teachers: An argument for teacher-as-entrepreneur. In S. Stahl & D. Hayes (Eds.), *Instructional models and processes of reading*. Mahwah, NJ: Erlbaum.

Duffy, G., & Hoffman, J. (1999). In pursuit of an illusion: The flawed search for a perfect method. *The Reading Teacher, 53*, 10–16.

Goldhaber, D., & Brewer, D. (1999). Teacher licensing and student achievement. In M. Kanstoroom & C. Finn (Eds.), *Better teachers, better schools*. Washington, DC: Thomas Fordham Foundation.

Johnston, P. (1998). The consequences of the use of standardized tests. In S. Murphy, *Fragile evidence*. Mahwah, NJ: Erlbaum.

Leiberman, A. (1988). *Building a professional culture in schools*. New York: Teachers College Press.

Raspberry, W. (1999). Classroom riffs. *The Washington Post*. 25 June 1999, p. A29.

Riley, R. W. (1999). *New challenges, a new resolve: Moving American education into the 21st century*. Paper presented at the sixth annual State of American Education Speech, Long Beach, CA.

Shannon, P. (1989). *Broken promises: Reading instruction in twentieth-century America*. New York: Bergin & Garvey.

Snow, C., Barnes, W., Chandler, J., Goodman, I. F., & Hemphill, L. (1991). *Unfulfilled expectations: Home and school influences on literacy instruction*. Cambridge, MA: Harvard University Press.

Jeni Pollack Day is a doctoral candidate at the University at Albany, State Universitiy of New York, and a research assistant at the center for English learning and achievement. She has conducted research on classroom talk, the needs of struggling readers, and the effect of policy on teachers and teaching. Her most recent research is concerned with teacher education and the role of professional development in shaping exemplary teachers.

11

Concluding Reflections

Without a doubt, the most frequent question we have been asked since initiating this program of research is, "How can really excellent grade-1 teachers be developed?" It is a good question. It is also a very difficult question, one we have been reluctant to address, because all of us are careful scientists who do not feel comfortable going beyond our data. Thus, when we wear our "careful, conservative, scientist" hats, the answer is that we do not know how to develop excellent grade-1 teachers at this point. That was not a question we addressed in the investigations reported here, except in the interview data reported in Chapter 10.

Most who have heard us beg off about how to develop excellent teachers have not found our cautiousness to be very satisfactory, often contending that our immersion in the culture of grade 1 for much of the past decade must have led to some intuitions about how to develop excellent grade-1 teachers. Thus, rather than decline to answer the question, in this concluding chapter we begin with some of our best intuitions about the development of expertise in teaching grade 1. In offering these insights, however, we advise that there is much scientific work to be done before anything like a definitive set of conclusions on this topic can be offered.

OUR INTUITIONS ABOUT THE DEVELOPMENT
OF EXCELLENT GRADE-1 TEACHERS

In the development of excellence in grade-1 teachers, experience matters. We will not say that there are no "naturals" who teach grade 1 well—teachers who somehow have all the right intuitions and arrive at the first-grade teaching assignment with more than enough knowledge of phonics, children's literature, and the need to be sensitive to children's individual differences—but we are certain there are relatively few of them. We do not dismiss the possibility of naturally gifted grade-1 teachers entirely because we did encounter at least one in the course of these investigations, a young woman who, by all accounts, was a dynamite grade-1 teacher from the first day she stepped out of teachers college and into the classroom. Certainly, as we watched her during her second year of teaching, there was much that impressed us, a competence that seemed well beyond her years. Our wonderful memories of that beginning teacher, however, are in the context of the memories of a great many first-year teachers whom we have encountered in our various roles, who really struggled as they taught grade 1. Teaching first grade does not come easily to most young people emerging from an elementary education major.

Although we are pessimistic that a 4-year degree (or even a master's degree) in elementary education is all that is required to be an excellent grade-1 teacher, we do not believe, as some do, that this signals criminal neglect by the teachers colleges and schools of education. Our view, consistent with much of the best thinking about the development of professional expertise (Lesgold et al., 1988), is that the development of such expertise takes a great deal of time and actual immersion in the practice of the profession. Granted, experiencing an elementary education major can provide much background information to launch a career, but it is just a starting point. Much learning will also occur as a function of teaching grade 1. This is such a fundamental point that we elaborate on it as our first intuition about the development of excellent grade-1 teachers.

Teachers Become Excellent by Learning from Experience

What cannot be missed in observing an excellent grade-1 classroom is that everything the teacher does seems to work. What cannot be missed in visiting many other grade-1 classrooms is that there are often stories that dull the grade-1 listener, tasks that many children cannot do, and teacher expectations that are not aligned with the realities of their students' competence. An important difference between the excellent grade-1 teacher and the not-so-excellent grade-1 teacher is that the excellent grade-1 teacher has learned from experience what works with grade-1 students and what does not work with them, and she or he continues to use only what works.

Throughout this book we have related how excellent grade-1 teachers monitor their students carefully. Such monitoring provides plenty of information about individual students' achievements and challenges, but it also provides a great deal of information about the effectiveness, appropriateness, and appeal of various pieces of the curriculum. The individual aspiring to be a great grade-1 teacher needs to hone her or his monitoring skills, making instructional decisions for individual students on the basis of what is monitored but also making long-term decisions about the curriculum on the basis of such monitoring. When the students are bored stiff with a story, that's a good sign that perhaps another story should be used next year. When the approach being tried this year to develop decoding proficiency does not work, the excellent teacher does not use it a second year. When it works for only some students this year, the excellent teacher tries another approach with students who did not benefit.

Teachers Become Excellent by Learning to Match Students to Tasks

An exceptionally important motivational principle is that the most motivating tasks are those that are a little challenging to the student—neither too easy nor overwhelming. Consistent with this principle, excellent grade-1 teachers generally do not give everyone in the class the same task to do; rather, they individualize assignments. Sometimes this means students are doing very different things at the same time, sometimes it means they are doing the same thing with adjustments on a student-by-student basis (e.g., some students are required to compose just a one-sentence story, others a story with several sentences, and still others a story that is several pages in length). Guided reading is common in grade-1 classrooms headed by excellent teachers, with each child reading a book that is just a bit harder than those the child can read with ease. An important competency for a grade-1 teacher to develop is the ability to match students to tasks and to adjust the same task so that it is challenging for both the weakest and the best students in a class, as well as all the students in between. The good teacher has learned how to make appropriate demands on all students in the class. Excellent teachers acknowledge that a one-size-fits-all approach does not work, and they develop lessons that fit the sizes in their rooms. The excellent teachers observed seemed especially concerned to attend to the development of children who came to grade 1 already far behind, using a variety of methods to reach these children.

In addition, the excellent grade-1 teachers we observed did not promote competition between students. Rather, consistent with contemporary educational motivation theory (e.g., Ames, 1984; Nicholls, 1989), they stroked students for improving relative to where they were previously. Excellent grade-1 teachers both monitor student improvement and praise it.

The individual aspiring to be an excellent grade-1 teacher will think hard about motivating her or his students, with the motivational plan including appropriately accelerating task demands for every student and a great deal of acknowledgment of individual student achievements. A plan of this type includes encouraging reasonable risks—asking students to try books a little harder than those they are now reading, and stimulating students who can write a page to try writing a little more than a page. Excellent teachers develop a can-do attitude in their students: They develop the understanding that with a bit of effort, students can do a little better today than they did yesterday and that tomorrow they will be doing better still. They assist students to correct reading and writing errors so that students do not fall into the habit of thinking that less than their best is acceptable. The excellent teachers observed definitely did not permit less-than-best efforts to become habits.

In summary, we think the most important core motivational understanding to develop in grade-1 teachers is that it is a good thing for there to be different tasks and different standards for different students. We recall that the excellent teachers we have studied, all of whom adjusted instruction and assignments to the abilities of students, had very engaged classes and produced high-achieving students. In contrast are memories of classes in which many students struggled with the same assignment that bored classmates who found it too easy.

Teachers Become Excellent by Learning How to Teach Skills

Excellent grade-1 teachers teach phonics skills, but the higher-order literacy competencies, such as comprehension and composing, also are central to their efforts. Thus, the aspiring grade-1 teacher needs to learn the essential phonics skills, the comprehension strategies used by good first-grade readers, and how writing can be accomplished through planning, drafting, and revising.

How can such learning to teach skills occur? We do not think that most teachers emerge from teachers college with a sufficiently complete understanding of word recognition, comprehension, and composition strategies to teach them well. An understanding of the teaching of phonics, comprehension, and composing can be deepened through reading a number of sources; there are many articles and books on these topics (see Pressley, 1998, for suggestions). Sometimes, however, there is a fast-track shortcut. A teacher who is in a district that has adopted a particular reading program may find the reading program manuals to be excellent sources of information about essential phonics, comprehension, and composing. Program manuals often contain much information about the phonics children need to know, as well as information about how to teach comprehension and composing strategies. Excellent grade-1 teachers told us that they had learned from these manuals. Among the insights we gained by spending time in grade 1 is that basal manuals often offer a lot of very good information about teaching reading, information that has been helpful to past generations of teachers as they struggled to become teachers of beginning reading.

In endorsing teachers' reading of program manuals as possible sources of information about the teaching of reading, we do not want to imply that buying a program and following the manual is all that is required to be an excellent grade-1 teacher. In fact, what was striking in the excellent classrooms was that the teachers generally were not following programs but, rather, devising their own curricula, curricula reflecting what is known about development of word recognition, comprehension, and writing skills. Moreover, even though there were some stand-alone lessons on particular phonics, comprehension, and composition skills, there was a much greater emphasis on the use of these skills while doing actual reading and writing. Hence, although phonics workbooks are common in many grade-1 classrooms, we did not see them much in use in excellent grade-1 classrooms. We did see some use of reading programs, but we did not see slavish adherence to any one program in excellent classrooms. Rather, the basal reader—and sometimes several basal readers—was only one of a number of sources of material, with the basal manuals providing only some ideas that drove the lessons in the classroom.

Excellent grade-1 teachers have learned that published materials can often play a role in their classrooms, and that the teacher supplements are often very helpful to the teacher in developing a complete understanding of the teaching of reading. Even so, the excellent grade-1 teacher does not simply do as the materials specify, but uses the materials reflectively in ways that make sense in her or his curriculum and with her or his students.

No matter how much background reading a teacher does, however, much learning about phonics, comprehension, and composing occurs as the teacher attempts to teach these competencies. Again, how much learning is achieved probably depends on how well the teacher is monitoring the students' learning and reactions to curriculum materials. When things do not go well, the excellent teacher recognizes that the healthiest response is to change teaching tactics, rather than persist with an approach that is not working, blaming the kids for not "getting it" (e.g., believing that the reading program is just too hard for her or his students), or hoping that someone else (e.g., the remedial reading teacher, district consultant, teacher aide, or parent) will solve the problem.

In short, we saw a great deal of skills instruction in excellent grade-1 classrooms, but no rigid adherence to a particular program. Rather, we saw the intelligent orchestration of skills teaching that seemed to work well with the students taught, skills teaching that often included tactics borrowed from a number of programs and traditions. Thus, it was common to see teachers encouraging students to sound out words, as prescribed by phonics programs, but also encouraging students to check to determine whether the word sounded out made sense in the context being read, an approach emphasized in whole-language classrooms. The excellent grade-1 teacher does not simply follow a program or a particular approach, but rather intelligently selects from the materials available to her or him. Moreover, much of the skills instruction is ad hoc, given as needed to students struggling with something (e.g., a mini-lesson on the "-ing" ending when a student has sounded it out with a great deal of effort rather than just recognizing it). Such instruction is always active (e.g., requiring the child to make up lots of words ending with "-ing"), rather than passive (e.g., doing a worksheet on "-ing" words).

Teachers Become Excellent by Learning How to Immerse Children in Fine Literature

The excellent teachers we have studied immersed their students in fine literature. The students read lots of wonderful stories—to the teacher, classmates, and their parents. The teacher also read terrific literature to the students. This immersion in outstanding literature contrasts with more haphazard readings in many of the more typical classrooms, and, in some cases, very little reading at all as compared with what went on in the excellent classrooms. The excellent teachers needed to learn much in order to do this. They needed to learn which stories and books the children liked, which ones could be read by grade-1 students and at what points in grade 1, and which stories were real interest grabbers when the teacher read them. Excellent teachers also have a deep knowledge of which books connect to important curriculum content in science and social studies, as well as an understanding of which pieces of literature just seem to go together.

The excellent teacher also figures out how to marshal others to surround children with literature. These teachers know how to connect with parents so that they want to read with their children in the evenings. They work with the librarian and the resource teacher to ensure that grade-1 students get the most out of library and resource opportunities (e.g., negotiating with the librarian for certain library readings, encouraging resource teachers to read to students whenever there is a chance to do so in the resource room). They know how to get more books for their classrooms (e.g., through taking advantage of book club premiums, persuading parents to donate books when children at home have outgrown them). The excellent teacher has built up an extensive knowledge base about how to manage her or his students' world so that there is no escaping books and no escaping adults who want to interact with the children through books.

Teachers Become Excellent by Learning to Encourage Student Self-Regulation

A hallmark of many approaches to classroom management is an emphasis on the teacher's being in charge of the classroom. Although all of the excellent teachers in our studies have had well-managed classrooms, what was striking was that this order was, in large part, a result of student self-regulation rather than the teacher's saliently exercising control. Excellent teachers develop students who control themselves, and all of the excellent grade-1 teachers we observed encouraged their students to self-regulate. From early in the year, students were taught not to rely on the teacher to direct their every movement but, rather, to make intelligent choices about how they spend their time (e.g., students were taught that if they had nothing else to do, that was a sign that they should be reading a book; students were taught that when they were finished with a first draft, they could reread it themselves or have a classmate read it and offer suggestions). Students were encouraged and expected to use each other as resources as well, further reducing their dependence on the teacher. Making intelligent choices during reading and writing was especially encouraged. Thus, students were taught that when they encountered a difficult word, there were a number of tactics they could choose. Attempting to sound out the word was often taught as the preferred strategy, but students were also taught that they could look at the pictures for clues, reread the text leading up to the word, or skip the word for the moment and return to it after reading on for a few lines. Similarly, when they wanted to write a word they did not know, students were taught that they had choices: Try to sound it out and write the word as it sounds, use the first sounds of the word and look it up in a dictionary, use key words on the word wall, or ask another student for help with the spelling. Students taught by excellent teachers learned early in the year that they needed to check their writing by reading over their stories to see whether they made sense; they were also taught to check their writing for capitalization, punctuation, and spelling. In contrast, of course, are the many grade-1 classrooms we have visited in which the teacher was constantly lording over the students, issuing orders all morning and afternoon, with students constantly asking the teacher to read difficult words encountered in text or to spell words as they attempted to write. Those aspiring to be excellent grade-1 teachers must think hard about how they can develop their classrooms so that students are self-managing much of the time rather than relying on the teacher to control their movements and activities.

Teachers Become Excellent by Learning What Students Need to Know

There was much teaching of content in the excellent grade-1 classrooms, ranging from key vocabulary to elementary science concepts to literature. The excellent grade-1 teacher has a good understanding of the content that grade-1 students need to learn, including the content specified in district and state mandates. This knowledge is built through experience, although we believe that some teachers are better attuned than others to identifying important content for students to learn. There is no doubt, however, that good grade-1 teachers develop a thorough understanding of the grade-1 curriculum. This includes knowing what stories can be used when, to complement certain ideas in social studies and science (e.g., which book is a real interest grabber for Martin Luther King Day, which stories connect well to the unit on ecology), as well as which of these stories can be read by the students and which are better read by the teacher and discussed by the whole class.

Thus, the beginning grade-1 teacher is well advised to be thinking hard about which vocabulary words students need to know and making certain that those words are taught, which social studies and science concepts are essential and finding ways to teach them that include literature and writing, and which writing mechanics and grammatical conventions are musts for the successful grade-1 student and how students can be taught these essentials.

Just as important as figuring out what grade-1 students need to know is figuring out what they do not need to know. We have definitely noticed a depth approach in excellent grade-1 classrooms, with this depth approach largely reflecting that excellent grade-1 teachers separate the grade-1 curriculum wheat from the chaff. Important vocabulary, important concepts, and important skills get repeated coverage and emphasis across the school day and year. Less important terms, ideas, and competencies get less coverage and in some cases do not appear at all. The selectivity obvious in excellent classrooms contrasts dramatically with the decided nonselectivity in nonexcellent classrooms. There were many times when we sat in typical classrooms asking ourselves, "Now, why is the teacher covering this, reading this story, teaching this vocabulary word?" In excellent classrooms, that thought never crossed our minds, for what was covered was always transparently important information for the grade-1 student to know or a clearly important skill for the grade-1 student to acquire.

In summary, the role of prior knowledge in student learning is well established. Excellent teachers have an understanding of what students need to know in a particular domain in order to understand the materials or tasks coming up next. They also find ways of figuring out what their students know already (and what they don't) so that they can fill in the gaps and make new topics meaningful for their students.

Summary

In short, we think that excellent teachers become excellent teachers largely through their own efforts. It is they who learn from their experiences and recognize the importance of doing so. It is they who decide that their classrooms are going to be sensitive to students' differences—adjusting tasks, lessons, and demands according to the abilities and needs of individual students. They learn about essential skills instruction, going well beyond what was taught in teachers college about phonics, comprehension strategies, and composition skills; they become teachers who teach such skills systematically and provide students many opportunities to apply these skills and strategies as they read good literature and write. As part of learning how to teach skills, good teachers also figure out how to teach skills so that students use them in a self-regulated fashion. The excellent teachers we have studied are determined that their students will be in charge of themselves more than the teacher in charge of them. They recognize that education at its best is education that develops self-regulated learners, readers, and writers. They take a personal, professional responsibility for all students in their classes becoming readers and writers. Excellent teachers have honed their curricula, filling them with important content and emphasizing essential skills and competencies.

Certainly, an important insight derived from this research project is that excellent teachers have largely developed themselves as excellent teachers. We hope this book provides an envisionment of just how good grade-1 instruction can be, and in doing so, stimulates many more grade-1 teachers to begin to do as excellent teachers have done, to begin to change their school days to resemble the school days we have observed in excellent grade-1 classrooms.

Why do we think that providing such an envisionment is so important? We were struck repeatedly that the more typical teachers we observed, including some who were anything but excellent as teachers, often had no idea that there were other ways of teaching grade 1, even though many had been grade-1 teachers for years. Mediocre teachers often have no idea that there exist elsewhere classrooms in which all students are engaged, in which students are making greater progress than their own students in becoming readers, and in which students are writing much longer and more sophisticated compositions than their own students. One of the reasons that more typical grade-1 teachers do not become excellent grade-1 teachers is that they seem not even to realize that they could do better, that there is much more engaging instruction going on in other teachers' classrooms. Teaching really is a lonely profession, with too few opportunities to watch others teach and too little emphasis on learning from other professionals.

We think that it would be very good for beginning grade-1 teachers, in particular, to have an opportunity to spend time with really excellent grade-1 teachers. Throughout this venture, we have had an opportunity to see quite a few student teachers, with the striking observation that student teachers really do learn a lot from their host teachers. For example, when we have observed student teachers in more typical classrooms, they internalize many approaches that do *not* seem promising from our perspective. More positively, when student teachers spend time with excellent grade-1 teachers, they get a great start on becoming excellent grade-1 teachers themselves. As teacher educators, we are convinced that much effort should be put into identifying really excellent grade-1 teachers and making certain that our student teachers be placed with them. We cannot think of anything more effective we could do for a young grade-1 teacher than to place her or him in the company of the kinds of teachers featured in this book.

In offering the hypothesis that many grade-1 teachers may become better grade-1 teachers through their own efforts, we are doubtful that all teachers can do so. A cartoon from *The New Yorker* captures our thinking on this issue: A lifeguard is relaxing in his chair, talking to some people on the beach, while a swimmer in the ocean is obviously struggling to stay afloat. The caption reads, "We're encouraging people to become involved in their own rescue." For many, the first year of teaching first grade is analogous to the efforts of bathers struggling to keep their heads above water, and some beginning first-grade teachers do not succeed. Some of those who are failing, however, we think may be able to become successful grade-1 teachers with more organizational support (Allington & Cunningham, 1996), and that is an idea we intend to explore further in the work that lies ahead. We also hope that readers who are grade-1 teachers will come away from this text determined to be more like the excellent teachers covered here than like typical grade-1 teachers.

TOWARD A THEORY OF EFFECTIVE GRADE-1 INSTRUCTION

There have been two prominent theories of effective grade-1 instruction in the marketplace of ideas for the past quarter century. One was the whole-language approach, inspired somewhat by the Chomskeyan notion that if language competence develops by immersion in language tasks—which it does—then reading and writing should develop through immersion in reading and writing tasks. In the case of the whole-language approach, a theory of literacy development was created by analogy to a theory of language development, with whole-language being a fairly elaborate theory offered well in advance of much relevant research. That is, whole-language was a theory created by whole-language theorists with too little experience in grade-1 classrooms.

In contrast, the skills approach, which was the main alternative to whole-language instruction, was too often informed by experiments involving only weak readers, whose word recognition skills were positively affected by explicit teaching of phonemic awareness and/or phonics instruction relative to a control group of weak readers who did not receive such instruction. That is, the skills approach was largely a creation of experimental psychologists.

Benton Underwood (1975) offered an important set of insights about theory development. He argued that far too many theories were created from the armchair with little attention to the generation of validating research. It might have been expected that Underwood, as an experimental psychologist, would have favored theory development through experimentation, but, in fact, he concluded that relying on experimentation alone could never result in an adequate theory. Rather, the first step in theory generation should be correlational work. Underwood (1975) reasoned that if no correlational connection could be found between processes expected to affect performance and performance outcomes, a relationship between the target processes and outcomes was unlikely, offering no motivation to do experiments aimed at demonstrating a causal relationship between the processes and outcome. That is, although correlation does not imply causation, causation certainly implies correlation, and in the absence of correlation, there is no reason to expect that there could be a causal effect.

Researchers interested in effective education have now generated an impressive body of correlational data about the processes prominent in effective schools and classrooms. Prior to our efforts, researchers such as Chall (1967) documented well the correlation between word recognition skills instruction and achievement in early reading. Ruddell (1997) reported the association between teacher monitoring and teacher feedback and the impact on students, as well as the association between the depth of teacher knowledge about reading, writing, and elementary content and its impact on pupils. Ruddell (1997), Au (1998), Moll (1998), and Ladson-Billings (1994) all provided much evidence that elementary instruction sensitive to student culture and informed by student experiences was associated with greater student learning than less-connected instruction.

The new contribution of our work was an intensive focus on grade 1, with the many factors and practices distinguishing more effective grade-1 literacy instruction from more typical instruction, as detailed in the chapters of this volume. Having done such work, we are in a position to propose a causal theory, following Underwood's (1975) logic. That theory, of course, is that if teachers can be developed to behave more like the effective teachers we studied, achievement in grade 1 will increase because of the change in teaching. We think that getting to a test of this causal theory is important.

Some will look at what is offered here, and their reaction will be that we have generated a list of characteristics of excellent grade-1 classrooms but not a theory. In their eyes, a theory would relate the components of an excellent first-grade classroom and, in particular, specify interactions between the components. We believe, however, that such specification is not warranted based on what we observed. Although there were common components in the excellent classrooms that were not present in more typical classrooms, these classrooms were not exact duplicates of one another. For example, there were different balances of skills and literature in the excellent classrooms we observed. Although self-regulation was encouraged in all of the excellent classrooms, there were different mechanisms for doing so in the various classes. By offering only a list of components, we were able not to go beyond our data. Of course, specifying in more detail the interactions and relationships between components could have been accomplished by specifying the many teacher-specific interactions between components that we observed, but we think it better simply to point out that excellent teachers work on all the components at once (i.e., skills, literature, self-regulation, etc.). They find relationships between the components and balancing of components that make sense in their classrooms. In doing so, they seem to be extremely child centered (i.e., rather than curriculum centered or focused on the state achievement test). They are also exceptionally responsible, believing that is it up to them to teach the students in their class to read and write, rather than believing that the responsibility can be farmed out when the going gets rough or being willing to accept that some students will not learn how to read. They also do a lot of talking *with* students about what they are reading, how they are figuring out words, and what students believe should be in their compositions. As compared with other teachers, they do much less talking *to* students. There are lots of instructional conversations between excellent teachers and their students, filled with suggestions for the students and complete with explanations about how language works and why it works that way. The excellent teacher persuades and informs rather than issues teacher-to-student directives.

The changes we are asking grade-1 teachers to undertake are not easy ones. They are changes that probably take place over a number of years. When change can take place only over a number of years, that increases the difficulties in getting to a causal test. At best, even if a causal test can be devised, it will be years before the outcomes of such a study will be known. More positively, perhaps, we are very much aware that previous work on effective education has had an important impact on educational practice in the absence of a causal experimental test. A number of researchers have documented that effective elementary schools have strong administrative leadership, maintain high expectations of students, are safe and orderly, emphasize basic skills, and frequently monitor student progress (Firestone, 1991). Many elementary schools across the country, perhaps as many as 41% of schools, were affected by these findings, and there was a general sense that this effect was positive (General Accounting Office, 1989).

Given that we leave this study of effective grade-1 classrooms very much impressed by the attractive classroom worlds we encountered, we would voice no objections if grade-1 teachers across the country try to transform their classrooms to be *something like* the classrooms we studied, even in the absence of causal data. We emphasize *something like* because we do not intend the message that these classrooms could or should be copied exactly by first-grade teachers who want to improve their teaching. Despite the many similarities across the excellent first grades we have visited, they are each unique, largely because a very intelligent teacher has made very intelligent choices that make sense with the kids in her classroom, given the expectations and resources of the community. There is no script for an excellent grade-1 classroom, although there are general directions (which are identified in this volume) that have the potential to be part of an excellent classroom. When we get to our causal test, we expect to work with teachers to persuade them of the power of the general directions highlighted in this book. Even so, if we work with five classrooms, we are certain that the result will be five unique classrooms, each with its own personality. It would be fine with us, however, that if by the time this causal test of our thinking is completed, many more teachers are honestly able to say, "But my class is something like that already!" than can make that claim in 2001.

In all the work we have carried out in grade-1 classrooms, we have observed nothing to support some of the quick fixes now being suggested in the marketplace of ideas about reform of primary-level education. There is nothing in our data to support solutions like the mandating of scripted lesson texts in phonics, particular curricular pacing rates in grade 1 (e.g., coverage of short vowels by November and long vowels by February), or particular published materials. We have also seen nothing that provides a defense for "blame-the-kid" explanations of poorly performing grade-1 classrooms, for some of the best teachers we have seen teach in schools serving students who are very economically disadvantaged. In contrast, what we present here is a great deal of data converging on the conclusion that effective grade-1 teaching involves a number of elements of instruction, which can be thoughtfully organized and orchestrated in classrooms that turn on and promote the literacy development of diverse students. When that happens, first grade is attractive and exciting.

Finally, a striking feature of all the very effective grade-1 classrooms observed was that the classes were so peaceful. As experienced classroom watchers, we are accustomed to encountering disputes between students and witnessing disciplinary events. We rarely observed fighting, quarreling, or aversive teacher–student interactions during our visits to these excellent grade-1 classrooms, however. The exemplary teachers and their students truly live in peaceable kingdoms. One student in Andy Schultheis's (see Chapter 6) class put it this way: "I wish I lived here!" Our wish is that every 6-year-old could attend first grade in such a class, with our most fervent hope being that this volume will stimulate many teachers to transform their classrooms into educational worlds that develop students' minds and hearts.

REFERENCES

Allington, R. L., & Cunningham, P. M. (1996). *Schools that work: Where all children read and write.* New York: Addison-Wesley Longman.

Ames, C. (1984). Competitive, cooperative, and individualistic goal structures: A motivational analysis. In R. Ames & C. Ames (Eds.), *Research on motivation in education* (Vol. 1, pp. 117–207). New York: Academic Press.

Au, K. H. (1998). Constructivist approaches, phonics, and the literacy learning of students of diverse backgrounds. In T. Shanahan & F. V. Rodriguez-Brown (Eds.), *Forty-seventh yearbook of the National Reading Conference* (pp. 1–21). Chicago: National Reading Conference.

Chall, J. (1967). *Learning to read: The great debate.* New York: McGraw-Hill.

Firestone, W. A. (1991). Educators, researchers, and the effective school movement. In J. R. Bliss, W. A. Firestone, & C. E. Richards (Eds.), *Rethinking effective schools research and practice* (pp. 12–27). Englewood Cliffs, NJ: Prentice-Hall.

General Accounting Office. (1989). *Effective schools programs: Their extent and characteristics.* Washington, DC: General Accounting Office.

Ladson-Billings, G. (1994). *The dreamkeepers: Successful teachers of African-American children.* San Francisco: Jossey-Bass.

Lesgold, A., Glaser, R., Rubinson, H., Klopfer, D., Feltovich, P., & Wang, Y. (1988). Expertise in a complex skill: Diagnosing x-ray pictures. In M. T. H. Chi, R. Glaser, & M. J. Farr (Eds.), *The nature of expertise* (pp. 311–342). Hillsdale, NJ: Erlbaum.

Moll, L. C. (1998). Turning to the world: Bilingual schooling, literacy, and the cultural mediation of thinking. In T. Shanahan & F. V. Rodriguez-Brown (Eds.), *Forty-seventh yearbook of the National Reading Conference* (pp. 59–75). Chicago: National Reading Conference.

Nicholls, J. G. (1989). *The competitive ethos and democratic education*. Cambridge, MA: Harvard University Press.

Pressley, M. (1998). *Reading instruction that works: The case for balanced teaching*. New York: Guilford Press.

Ruddell, R. B. (1997). Researching the influential literacy teacher: Characteristics, beliefs, strategies, and new research directions. In C. K. Kinzer, K. A. Hinchman, & D. J. Leu (Eds.), Inquiries in literacy theory and practice: *Forty-sixth yearbook of the National Reading Conference* (pp. 37–53). Chicago: National Reading Conference.

Underwood, B. J. (1975). Individual differences as a crucible in theory construction. *American Psychologist, 30*, 128–134.

Index